Logic-Based Therapy and Everyday Emotions

Logic-Based Therapy and Everyday Emotions

A Case-Based Approach

Elliot D. Cohen

LEXINGTON BOOKS
Lanham • Boulder • New York • London

Published by Lexington Books
An imprint of The Rowman & Littlefield Publishing Group, Inc.
4501 Forbes Boulevard, Suite 200, Lanham, Maryland 20706
www.rowman.com

Unit A, Whitacre Mews, 26-34 Stannary Street, London SE11 4AB, United Kingdom

British Library Cataloguing in Publication Information Available

Library of Congress Cataloging-in-Publication Data
Names: Cohen, Elliot D., author.
Title: Logic-based therapy and everyday emotions : a case-based approach /
   Elliot D. Cohen.
Description: Lanham : Lexington Books, 2016. | Includes bibliographical
   references and index.
Identifiers: LCCN 2015046057 (print) | LCCN 2015049185 (ebook) | ISBN
   9781498510462 (cloth : alk. paper) | ISBN 9781498510479 (Electronic)
Subjects: LCSH: Rational emotive behavior therapy. | Psychotherapy.
Classification: LCC RC489.R3 C64 2016 (print) | LCC RC489.R3 (ebook) | DDC
   616.89/14—dc23
LC record available at http://lccn.loc.gov/2015046057
   978-1-4985-1048-6 (pbk : alk. paper)

∞™ The paper used in this publication meets the minimum requirements of
American National Standard for Information Sciences—Permanence of Paper
for Printed Library Materials, ANSI/NISO Z39.48-1992.

Printed in the United States of America

Contents

Contents

Preface

How Logic-Based Therapy Came to Be

The theory of Logic-Based Therapy (LBT) emerged as a result of a complex set of personal circumstances. This history is illuminating inasmuch as it shows the rootedness of the theory in the vicissitudes of human existence, in this case, my own. The seeds of the theory were planted in the academic year 1978–1979, when I was awarded a grant from what was then the Department of Behavioral Studies at the University of Florida to develop a primer on the application of the theory of value to practical decision-making. In the same year, my father suffered a fatal heart attack at the age of 60. At the moment of his heart attack, the telephone was not working due to a downed telephone line. Consequently, my mother had to go next door to a neighbor to call 911. By the time the paramedics arrived my father had passed away. As a young philosopher, who was engrossed in the application of reason to practical life, it seemed to me that I should remain resolute and "rational" in dealing with the tragic death of my father. As a result, I did not give myself time to mourn his death, but instead continued to conduct my research and writing without interruption. Unfortunately, this decision took its toll on my emotional life. For the next eight years, until sometime in 1987, I was functional and prolific outwardly but hollow inside, simply going through the motions. In 1985, I published my first book on practical decision making entitled, *Making Value Judgments: Principles of Sound Reasoning*. This book, which grew out of the grant work I had done at the University of Florida, showed how to construct practical reasoning utilizing the mechanism of the practical syllogism, a deductive form of argument having two premises and a prescriptive conclusion; and it showed how to find fallacies in its premises. At the time, my wife, Dr. Gale Cohen, was a graduate student working on her master's degree in counseling and had noticed a resemblance between a counseling theory she had been studying and my work. The theory she pointed out was Albert Ellis's Rational-Emotive Behavior Therapy (REBT), then called Rational Emotive

Therapy (RET). I took an immediate interest in the theory and began comparing and contrasting it to the theory of practical decision making developed in my new book. While my model used the practical syllogism, Ellis's used a causal model he called "The ABC Theory," which postulated three "psychological points": an Activating event (point A) and a Belief system (point B), which jointly caused a behavioral and emotional Consequence (point C). Coming from the perspective of a philosopher and logician, I was inclined to translate Ellis' psychological points into premises and conclusions of the practical syllogism. In 1986, I had a version of my theory ready to try out in a clinical context. I hypothesized that many problems of living were exacerbated by "bad logic," that is, practical syllogisms with fallacious premises. In particular, I decided to look into whether at least some of the problems that couples encountered could be helpfully addressed by identifying the fallacies in their practical syllogisms. Accordingly, I enlisted the help of a local mental health agency, Alpha Health Services, in Fort Pierce, Florida. The psychologist for this agency, Dr. Paul Eddy, had gone to graduate school with Albert Ellis and looked favorably upon my psychotherapeutic approach inasmuch it was based on RET. As such, he was receptive to supervising my project. My services were offered free to clients whom Dr. Eddy thought might benefit from a philosophical approach such as mine. These were clients who were educated and possessed an aptitude for abstract thinking. Given that my clients were so screened, I was not in a position to draw any conclusions about the utility of my approach for broader populations. Still, what I discovered was that many of my clients suffered from relationship problems that were fueled by faulty thinking errors inherent in the premises of their practical reasoning. In 1987, my first article titled "Use of Syllogism in Rational Emotive Therapy," which discussed this new interdisciplinary approach, appeared in the *Journal of Counseling and Development*. Around this time, I began to come out of the shell that encapsulated my emotions after the death of my father. I began to work through the anger that was inwardly brewing for eight years. Two weeks before my father's death, I had an opportunity to visit him. It was about a five hour drive from Gainesville to Hollywood, where he resided, and I chose not to take the trip because "I had too much work to do." As such, I built a wall around my self-condemnatory guilt. Had I taken the opportunity, I would have seen him before his untimely death. I had not seen him for a few months, and a visit was already overdue. These thoughts grew louder as the walls around my emotions began to crack. "Why didn't I visit him when I had the opportunity! Damn!" "How could the phone not have worked at that crucial moment!" "Shit like this mustn't happen!" "Damn those bastards [at AT&T]!" "Had the phone worked, my father would still be alive." These thoughts were grist for philosophical analysis, yet I, the philosopher, never took the time—at least not until eight years later.

Instead, I demanded perfection in an imperfect universe where, unfortunately, shit does happen. I damned the phone company, myself, and the universe because they failed to meet up to my absolutistic demand. I made a contrary-to-fact claim about what would have happened—even though I really didn't know that my father would have survived his heart attack even if the phone did work at that moment my mother first tried to call 911.

Depression:

Shit must never happen

If shit must never happen, then if my father died due to a phone not working, then the world is not what it must be.

Therefore, if my father died due to a phone not working, then the world is not what it must be.

My father died due to a phone not working.

Therefore the world is not what it must be.

Guilt:

If I preferred my work over visiting my father, which turned out to be the last opportunity I'd ever have to see him, then I must disturb myself about it for the rest of my life.

I preferred my work over visiting my father, which turned out to be the last opportunity I'd ever have to see him.

Therefore, I must disturb myself about it for the rest of my life.

Anger:

If AT&T's failure to keep the phone lines operational contributed to my father's death then those rotten bastards should not be allowed to exist.

AT&T's failure to keep the phone lines operational contributed to my father's death.

Therefore, those rotten bastards should not be allowed to exist.

Here were pieces of the reasoning that I had harbored for eight years without formulating and inspecting them, and which fueled depression, guilt, and anger. I had harbored contempt for the world and the things in it because they failed to meet up to my perfectionistic demand that things happen the way I wanted them to happen. My numbness began to subside because I started to see that the premises of my reasoning were unrealistic. But it didn't happen just by virtue of coming to this realization. While I began to refute each of these premises, I still felt their emotional force. I still had an emotional journey to take; for I had to attain greater security about an imperfect reality that doesn't always happen as one prefers and I had to attain greater respect for this imperfect universe. These were my Guiding Virtues, and I am still working on them—philosophically and behaviorally. Philosophically, I have come to have greater respect for this imperfect world, for with Plato, I see that the earthy existence is impermanent and lacking in certitude. But, with Leibniz, I also realize that the world is greater than the sum of its parts. I have no illusions that the death of my father was unfortunate. Life is not without regrets. But I am also aware that the world was better for having had him in it, and that many good things have happened in my life after his death. In this I have attained greater peace of mind as a result of having attained greater metaphysical security, that is, security about reality itself. This is a philosophy that I try to apply in living my life. I look for the good even though I know there are bad things. The latter do not consume my world view. I have suffered many unpleasant things but I have also tried, as Nietzsche suggested, to grow stronger, and to learn from such experiences.

Paradoxically, the work that I wrapped myself around in order to protect myself from confronting my irrational ideas ultimately helped me to deal rationally with them. It was this work that has helped me to see my own twisted logic. But it was also my own twisted logic that helped me to work out my theory, and the theory continues to evolve, and, therewith, I also continue to evolve as both philosopher and human being. Such is the birth and life of the theory and practice of Logic-Based Therapy.

In 2007, Albert Ellis passed away at the age of 93. He was, in many ways, my surrogate father. He encouraged and inspired the development of LBT, and I am forever grateful to him for his guidance. He was always there to lend support, and, while incredibly productive, always seemed to find the time to read and comment on my work. Shortly before his death, I visited him in the hospital. There I promised him that I would devote my life to the development of LBT, and he seemed very pleased. Al was a psychologist who saw the virtues of philosophy; I, a philosopher who sees the virtues of psychology. As discussed in the introduction to this book, LBT is philosophical at its core; and Al's insights are indelibly embedded in it.

In contrast to earlier books on LBT, I believe this book makes important adjustments to the theory and practice of LBT. Its method has been further fine tuned with greater emphasis on the Guiding Virtues, and more attention to the logic of different emotions such as anxiety and depression. Its distinctive approach is to glean insights from case examples, rather than the converse. These case examples, which have had client names and identifying details removed or changed, have been derived from the large, diverse pool of cases in which I have assisted. This highly accessible, case-based approach contains an extensive treatment of LBT's Cardinal Fallacies and examination of emotional reasoning. It also discusses, in detail, LBT's Theory of Emotion, and the relationship between reason and emotion. Additionally, the introduction addresses the types of clients likely (and unlikely) to benefit from LBT, the training of LBT practitioners, and the scope of ethically responsible practice.

I think Al would have liked this book!

EDC

Introduction

The Nuts and Bolts of LBT

Philosophers are known for their calm, rational approach to living, at least in the academic arena, if not in their own personal lives. So, can they help others approach everyday living in such a manner without losing the distinctly emotive character that makes us human beings? This is a question I have taken seriously since the mid-1980s, when I began to develop Logic-Based Therapy (LBT), now one of the world's leading modalities of "philosophical practice." In my three decades of research, development, and clinical applications, the theory and practice of LBT has borne out the incredible potential of philosophy and logic, tempered by empathetic regard and authentic caring, to promote cognitive, emotional, and behavioral adjustment in confronting the problems of living.

Time and time again, I have seen individuals make constructive changes in their lives as a result of reframing their life perspectives with the aid of the LBT framework. These results have been repeated across oceans, from East to West, with renewed hope for the future by individuals wrestling with problems of ordinary life, from writer's block to problems getting along with family, to confronting cancer, to the death of a loved one. I have seen individuals, with varying philosophical perspectives—from communitarian to rugged individualistic outlooks, from Buddhistic universal compassion to Hobbesian self-interest—find creative ways to confront their behavioral and emotional problems. Such problems of living are not, as such, the domain of abnormal psychology. They are the challenges and vicissitudes that all or most of us confront in the course of everyday living. Indeed, there is definitely great utility in having a modus operandi for confronting, overcoming, and moving beyond such problems, especially one that congenially works across diverse cultural perspectives and philosophies of life; and, which has the potential to be learned and applied by many with a high measure of success. LBT aims to provide such a useful set of logical and philosophical tools for confronting a myriad of problems of living.

LBT IN PRACTICE: A CASE EXAMPLE

Clearly, one sphere of human existence rife with problems of living is that of interpersonal relationships, for example, finding "the right one." When such a quest appears insurmountable, forlornness is a common emotional response. To give you a general idea of how LBT would approach such a problem, consider the case of Sarah, a thirty-six-year-old, heterosexual female who has not been able to find the man she wants to "spend the rest of her life with." Recently, she tried internet dating, but to no avail.

"Meeting someone online was never my idea of meeting the right guy; but not even that worked. Some of them were fat; some were bald; and others, well, I just don't want to go there." She explained to Dr. Roderick Hart, her philosophical practitioner, "The last thing I ever wanted was to meet someone online, but not even that worked. I'm thirty-six; I will be alone the rest of my life. What kind of life is that anyway!?" Here were pieces of Sarah's reasoning, elliptical and incomplete, what logicians call an enthymeme. It was Dr. Hart's job to help Sarah fill in the missing premises of her "emotional reasoning," inspect it for irrational premises, refute any such premises, and then use the power of Guiding Virtues and the prudential wisdom of antiquity enshrined in philosophical theories, to rescue her from her depressive thinking.

Putting the pieces of reasoning together, resonating empathetically with Sarah's loneliness and sense of futility, Hart reflects back Sarah's emotional reasoning, filling in the gaps, checking to see if they are on the same page. "So, you are saying that, if you haven't found the right guy by now then you are destined to live a lonely, unfulfilled life. So, since you haven't found this guy, you are resigned to such a life."

"Yes, that's exactly it," responds Sarah.

Once exposed, Dr. Hart can now challenge the premises of the client's emotional reasoning. "You say that you haven't met the right guy; but have you ever met anyone who was serious about you?" asks Hart.

"Yes," retorts Sarah. "But there was something wrong with each of them."

"So, they weren't perfect?"

"Not even near perfect!"

"So they have to be at least near perfect?"

"Yes, otherwise I'm just settling!"

"So you think that you must meet this perfect or near perfect guy, and if you don't then you will just be settling, and live *un*happily ever after?"

"That's right."

"But no one is perfect or even near perfect, so your demand that you meet such a guy all but guarantees that you won't find 'the right guy.'"

As such, Dr. Hart unravels the emotional reasoning that drives Sarah's forlornness, showing her that it rests on an irrational, self-defeating demand for perfection. But can one still find meaning, happiness, and purpose in an imperfect world? Is the determination of who is the right guy a subjective one, not at all part of the fabric of the universe? Do we ourselves define such meanings? The latter would be what existential philosopher Jean-Paul Sartre would maintain.

In relaying the story of a young man he once met while in prison, Sartre recounts how the man experienced a number of setbacks such as the death of his father, poverty, a botched romance, and a failed military exam. This man, says Sartre, could have interpreted these unfortunate turns of events as signs that he was a "total failure;" he could have become embittered and filled with despair. Instead, he interpreted them as a message from God that he was not meant for the secular life but instead to serve God. So he joined the Jesuit Order. "Who can doubt but that this decision as to the meaning of the sign was his and his alone?" Sartre admonishes. "One could have drawn quite different conclusions from such a series of reverses—as, for example, that he had better become a carpenter or a revolutionary. For the decipherment of the sign, however, he bears the entire responsibility."[1]

Indeed, against the backdrop of Sartre's admonition, Sarah's presumption that the "right guy" has never and will never come along is seen as a self-limiting decision for which she bears the ultimate responsibility; not at all an indelible state of the universe beyond her will. And, from the same perspective, the perfectionistic demand that the world *must* confer such meaning for her, rather than she for the world, is exposed as Sarah's own refusal to take responsibility for what she herself takes to be this perfect, or near perfect guy.

Set within the context of such illustrative case examples as that of Sarah, this book is about human interpretation of life events and the human emotions arising out of them. It is about how logical analysis and philosophical theorizing can help to overcome self-defeating, irrational thinking and help people to think and feel better. In particular, it shows how LBT, one of the first systematically developed modalities for philosophical practice, can be used to help people attain happiness amid the vicissitudes of life. It is about how this philosophical and logical approach to dealing with life challenges can help to relieve the stress of strong negative emotions such as intense guilt, rage, depression, and debilitating anxiety. And it is about striving for excellence in living, not just avoiding unnecessarily emotional stress.

LBT AT A GLANCE

As the case of Sarah illustrates, people can make themselves upset by deducing irrational conclusions from "emotional reasoning" containing fallacious premises. LBT helps people to construct such reasoning; identify and refute its fallacious premises; and replace them with rational premises. This approach uses the prudential wisdom of antiquity enshrined in philosophical theories to construct these rational replacements. It also features eleven Guiding Virtues, paired with eleven Cardinal Fallacies; and it uses the latter virtues to guide construction of philosophical antidotes to these faulty thinking errors. In addition, it shows how to apply such philosophies by constructing a behavioral plan ("plan of action") to put these philosophical directions into practice. Subscribing to the Aristotelian principle that good habits arise as a result of practice,[2] it connects with some of the behavioral techniques and methods of cognitive behavior therapy to help clients build strong rational habits.[3] It also incorporates ideas from humanistic approaches such Carl Roger's Person-Centered approach.[4] As you will see, LBT is itself both humanistic and cognitive-behavioral in character, and accommodates philosophical constructs from a diverse body of other approaches including existential and phenomenological ones.

LBT'S CARDINAL FALLACIES
AND THEIR GUIDING VIRTUES

LBT's eleven Cardinal Fallacies are faulty thinking errors that undermine rational behavioral and emotional reasoning.[5] These fallacies are: Demanding Perfection, Awfulizing, Damnation (of self, others, or the cosmos), Can'tstipation, Bandwagon Reasoning, Dutiful Worrying, Manipulation, The-World-Revolves-Around-Me Thinking, Oversimplifying, Distorting Probabilities, and Blind Conjecture. Each Cardinal Fallacy, in turn, has its own Guiding Virtue that offsets it and provides a new positive direction. Thus, in finding the fallacy, one also finds the virtue toward which to strive. For example, Sarah is engaging in Demanding Perfection when she refuses to consider a man who is not "perfect or near perfect" according to her conception of such. The Guiding Virtue of Demanding Perfection is, in turn, Metaphysical Security, which involves accepting the imperfect nature of reality itself, including human reality; so that, according to LBT, Sarah's stated goal should be to aspire to a deeper appreciation, acceptance, and level of comfort with the idea that people are not perfect or near perfect, and that such a view summarily leads to rejecting all of mankind as unsuitable.

Table I.1 illustrates each Cardinal Fallacy and its corresponding Guiding Virtue.

Table 1.1

Cardinal Fallacy	Fallacy Type	Guiding Virtue
1. Dutiful Worrying	Emotional	Prudence (in confronting and resolving moral problems)
2. Demanding Perfection	Emotional	Metaphysical Security (security about reality)
3. Damnation (of self, others, life, or the universe)	Emotional	Respect (for self, others, life, or the universe)
4. Awfulizing	Emotional	Courage (in the face of evil)
5. The-World-Revolves-Around-Me Thinking	Emotional	Empathy (connecting with others)
6. Oversimplifying Reality	Reporting	Objectivity (in making objective, unbiased judgments)
7. Distorting Probabilities	Reporting	Foresightedness (in assessing probabilities)
8. Blind Conjecture	Reporting	Scientificity (in providing explanations)
9. Can'tstipation	Behavioral	Temperance (self-control)
10. Bandwagon Thinking	Behavioral	Authenticity (being your own person)
11. Manipulation	Behavioral	Empowerment (of others)

As you can see, each Cardinal Fallacy has a "Fallacy Type" designation. These designations define the fallacy's location and function within an individual's emotional reasoning. Generally speaking, the designation "Emotional" signifies a fallacy that generates a destructive or self-defeating emotion; "Reporting" signifies a fallacy involving a factual (inductive) error in one's emotional reasoning; and "Behavioral," signifies a fallacy leading to self-defeating action. Each of these fallacy types is addressed in detail in chapters 2, 3, and 4, respectively.

The Guiding Virtue for each Cardinal Fallacy, as listed in the above table, provides an ideal that challenges one to strive for excellence in living. This is different than simply helping one to relieve stress brought about as a result of faulty thinking. For example, on the one hand, there is a difference between being able to control one's tendency to become intensely angry while still feeling the urge to explode into a fiery rage; and, on the other hand, being temperate. The temperate person does not have such an urge and tends toward emotionally responding in level-headed ways. LBT accordingly helps clients with an anger management problem to set as her goal that of becoming temperate. The idea of having such an aspiration can be extremely useful. When people perceive themselves as striving to become virtuous, they are more likely to stay focused and accept the challenge. Like becoming a fine virtuoso or a great athlete, the virtue becomes an ideal to work toward. Realizing that ideals are never completely actualized in this imperfect world, one realizes that such a pursuit is a life challenge and that one is never fully actualized. Thus there is always the opportunity to continue to practice and to make improvements.

These Guiding Virtues also provide the standards for selecting philosophical theories, that is, philosophies that promote the given virtue and provide antidotes to the respective fallacy. Thus, in Sarah's case, Sartre's self-defining theory—namely, that people, not the universe, bear full responsibility for interpreting the meaning of a sign—can be used to help her overcome her Demand for Perfection in her search for the ideal man. As such, each fundamental concept of LBT sets the stage for the next:

CARDINAL FALLACY → GUIDING VIRTUE → PHILOSOPHY

LBT's primary goal is, therefore, not only to help individuals overcome debilitating or destructive emotions, but also to aspire toward virtuous living. The method of LBT for accomplishing this double-edged goal consists of a six-step framework for dealing constructively with one's behavioral and emotional problems:

1. Identify the emotional reasoning
2. Check for Cardinal Fallacies in the premises
3. Refute any Cardinal Fallacy
4. Identify the Guiding Virtue for each fallacy
5. Find an uplifting philosophy that promotes the Guiding Virtue
6. Apply the philosophy by implementing a plan of action

These six steps provide a rational framework for confronting problems of living. This framework is congenial and is intended to work across diverse belief systems. That is, LBT does not tell individuals what philosophical perspectives to take, but instead allows them to choose, from a wide range of contrasting perspectives, a philosophy that is, for them, "uplifting" or inspiring. For example, an atheistic client might be inspired by Jean Paul Sartre's aforementioned self-defining philosophy in addressing a problem of living because it places the power to decide in the hands of human beings rather than in God;[6] whereas a devout theist might find Aquinas' essentialist view about striving to be like God, through one's activities, to be more inspiring.[7] As such, LBT is pragmatic. In the words of William James, it tends to perceive the truth of a philosophical belief or conviction in terms of its "cash value"[8]—how well it works to help the client overcome her self-defeating or destructive emotions and to aspire to the higher human callings set by the Guiding Virtues.

This book develops and shows how to implement each of the above six steps through the analysis of cases involving problems of living. The first part of the book examines each of the Cardinal Fallacies and their respective Guiding Virtues. The second part applies the six-step method in dealing with particular emotions.

ELIGIBILITY OF CLIENTS

The six-step method of LBT is a highly accessible approach to dealing with everyday emotions in the context of managing problems of living. Still, because it employs philosophy and critical thinking, it cannot be presumed to be suitable for all people, especially those who are not inclined toward abstract, conceptual approaches. The LBT practitioner should therefore conduct a brief, preliminary interview, prior to beginning the actual assistance, which may occur at the beginning of the first session. The following dialog illustrates such an interview:

"Hello, Jerry, my name is John Lambert."

"Nice to meet you, Doc. You are a doctor, right?"

"Yes, I am; but not a medical doctor. I am also not a psychologist or other mental health specialist. I have a doctorate in philosophy."

"Philosophy! Wow! So you are going to psychoanalyze me?"

"No, psychoanalysis is a psychological approach. I am a philosopher."

"So what do you do then?"

"I help people to use critical thinking to address their problems of living. For example, suppose someone, let's call him John, is having a problem getting along with a coworker. Suppose the coworker is spreading lies about him behind his back; and John is seriously thinking about quitting his job, even though he needs the money and doesn't have any other job prospects at the time."

"So you would tell John what he should do about it?"

"No, I wouldn't tell him what to do. That would be for John to decide. Instead I would assist him in getting clearer about his feelings and the reasoning that has led him to feel as he does; and I would help him to think more rationally about his situation if his thinking were unrealistic or self-defeating."

"I'm confused. The guy is talking shit about John. What he's doing is bad, right?"

"That is one way to look at it. But there are other possible perspectives. For example, according to the Dali Lama, a very learned Buddhist spiritual leader, our enemies can be our best teachers. Do you think this philosophy could help John feel differently about his coworker?"

"Just that John needs to teach that guy a lesson for talking shit about him!"

"Do you see any other interpretation?"

"No, not really."

Evidently, Jerry does not have an enlightened understanding of what philosophy is; but this does not render him ineligible to undertake LBT; for some of my very successful clients have, at the outset, fit this description. It is also not necessarily problematic that Jerry wants to know if Dr. Lambert tells people what to do about their problems of living. In fact, in my experience, one of the biggest challenges many clients (and sometimes even some new practitioners) face is realizing that the LBT practitioner is not there to give advice about what to do.

However, a much more serious concern is that Jerry does not seem to grasp the connection between philosophical concepts, such as the Dali Lama's idea about learning from one's enemies, and the problem at hand. For example, the situation might offer John an opportunity to gain greater tolerance and patience in dealing with others, a lesson that could be invaluable in attaining peace and happiness in life.[9] Rather than exploring the idea further with Lambert, Jerry confusedly adapts it to suit his owe preconception about a (perceived) "need to teach that guy a lesson." His thinking is fixed on the concrete situation, and he is closed to alternative perspectives. As such, he is not likely to benefit appreciably from LBT. In contrast, clients most suitable for LBT tend to be inquisitive; open to alternative perspectives; comfortable with thinking on an abstract, philosophical level; and are able to cogently apply philosophical concepts to particular situations.

In my experience, many of those who seek out philosophical counseling do have such a penchant for philosophical thinking; but this is not always the case. As such, it is the LBT practitioner's responsibility to make a determination, prior to lending assistance, as to whether the prospective client is suitable for this kind of approach to dealing with problems of living. Otherwise, there is significant potential for wasting time and resources of both practitioner and client. Generally, a practitioner can make such a determination by conversing briefly with the individual in question about the nature of philosophical counseling and/or LBT. Presenting the prospective client with an example to consider, such as the one provided in the above scenario, can be a useful way to see if a philosophical approach to addressing practical problems is a good fit.

Of course, some prospective clients, who have the aptitude for LBT, may nevertheless be extremely resistant to the process, belligerent, or otherwise unwilling to cooperate. There are also ethical reasons for not assisting a client or for terminating assistance, for example, a mutual sexual attraction, conflict of interest, or other circumstance portending loss of objectivity.[10] LBT practitioners may therefore need to exercise discretion in deciding whether to take on or terminate assisting a client.

LBT AND PSYCHOTHERAPY

As discussed below (section on Making Referrals to Mental Health Practitioners) some individuals seeking LBT may not be eligible because they suffer from mental disorders, which are exclusively the domain of clinical psychologists, mental health counselors, clinical social workers, and other psychotherapists. *However, from this fact, it does not follow that psychological and philosophical approaches are not complementary practices.* In fact, LBT is a synergistic amalgamation of the philosophical and psychological, and therefore profits from both worlds. Unlike some of its rival approaches,[11] LBT does not attempt to separate these practices. Consequently, its approach is and should be of interest to psychotherapists who seek a philosophical approach, as well as philosophical practitioners who seek some of the insights and tools of contemporary cognitive behavior psychotherapy. Moreover, like REBT, its approach is accessible to the masses who are more often interested in how to feel and do better than about whether philosophy and psychology are intertwined.

Nevertheless, what is true of the part is not necessarily true of the whole. This is an important principle to keep in mind with respect to the relationship between psychological approaches and LBT regarding doing and feeling better. While LBT includes techniques used in cognitive behavior therapy and other psychotherapies, it is itself not a psychological approach. This is because psychological approaches look for causal explanations for mental processes whereas LBT examines logical arguments for their soundness.[12] Thus, psychologists and other mental health practitioners have assembled an ever-increasing body of knowledge that attempts to provide the antecedent conditions that elicit psychological change, including the underlying causal etiology of dysfunctional behavior and emotions. Thus, cognitive behavior approaches, including REBT, perceive the relationship between the events in people's lives and their interpretations of these events as conditions that cause certain maladaptive behavioral and emotional responses or mental disorders. Person-Centered approaches emphasize environmental conditions, such as the relationship between a parent and a child, as causative of a failure to thrive. Behavioral therapies attempt to discover the causal laws that establish conditioned responses (operant as well as classical variants) to environmental changes. Psychoanalytic approaches look for the causes of present maladaptive behavior and emotions in childhood events that have been repressed. In contrast, LBT looks for fallacious premises in people's here and now practical reasoning to help them change their reasoning. It applies critical thinking strategies toward improving practical reasoning skills. It is thus a humanities discipline whereas psychological approaches are social science approaches. Broadly speaking, the humanities are interested in *epistemic justification*, that is, the justification of knowledge and value claims. The social sciences seek to find the causal laws that determine mental processes.

Any attempt to reduce LBT to a form of psychotherapy is therefore misguided. Such reductionism itself engenders a fallacious inference from what is true of the parts (the elements of LBT including those used by psychological approaches) to what is true of the whole (LBT as an integrated system for helping people confront their problems of living). This is not to deny that some psychological approaches also sometimes challenge clients to justify their knowledge and value claims. However, to the extent that such approaches do so, they are engaging in philosophical practices.

TRAINING FOR LBT PRACTICE

The latter point is cogent because philosophical practice does not have to deny its substantive connection with psychology in order to justify those with credentials in philosophy, rather than psychology, engaging in this form of practice. Thus, the fact that LBT involves the use of logic and philosophy, for helping clients to reason more soundly, renders training in philosophy (for example, an M.A. or Ph.D. in philosophy) pertinent and appropriate for purposes of practicing LBT within the scope of such training.[13] The fact that LBT utilizes some techniques also used in psychotherapy (for example, communication and relationship-building skills, homework assignments, and bibliotherapy) does not detract from this point. It simply shows that philosophical practice, as a form of "applied philosophy," can benefit from using some techniques or tools that have been constructively introduced into certain modalities of applied psychology (that is, psychotherapy). For example, as you will see, Person-Centered Therapy and many other forms of psychotherapy utilize such skills as active listening and empathetic understanding as aspects of viable counseling. LBT also cultivates and uses such skills. However, these skills have been shown to be efficacious in other helping professions (for example, in the teacher-student relationship) as well as in improving personal relationships.[14] Thus, the incorporation of these skills by philosophical practitioners does not render them practitioners of psychotherapy. Yet, in doing so, philosophical practitioners, in particular LBT practitioners, can gain considerably from psychotherapeutic theory and practice. This does not mean that some psychotherapeutic tools are not "off-limits" to philosophical practitioners. For example, LBT practitioners, who are not otherwise qualified to administer hypnosis, are rightly prohibited from utilizing such a possible means for helping clients confront their irrational premises.[15]

However, training in philosophy does not make an individual a philosophical practitioner any more than it makes her an instructor of philosophy. There is, in both, need for learning how to harness such training to allow it to work therapeutically in the one case and pedagogically in the other. Thus, many instructors of philosophy spend considerable time observing their own instructors, working as teaching assistants, attending workshops and conferences, taking education courses, as well as spending considerable time in the classroom, before they can claim to be competent instructors of philosophy. Not uncommonly, newly minted Ph.D.s in philosophy find themselves thrown into the deep waters of instruction without having had ample preparation in graduate school for teaching philosophy. While some in this situation take to the classroom like a duck to water, others may be at a considerable loss of how to teach effectively. The case of philosophical practice is analogous in some respects. Training for philosophical practice requires attention to considerations that are not ordinarily a part of the teaching environment. Thus training programs in philosophical practice such as the National Philosophical Counseling Association's (NPCA) Primary Certificate Program in

Logic-Based Therapy, as well as its advanced programs and mentorships, include a practicum and require trainees, themselves, to serve as clients in the LBT process.[16]

PHILOSOPHICAL COUNSELORS AND CONSULTANTS

The NPCA also recognizes that graduate training in philosophy together with its certification in philosophical practice does not suffice to address cases for which psychological training and licensure are indicated. Accordingly, the NPCA recognizes two kinds of philosophical practitioners: (1) philosophical counselors and (2) philosophical consultants. Philosophical counselors may use the six-step approach of LBT to treat psychological problems that fall into psychiatric categories such as Major Depression and Generalized Anxiety Disorder (GAD) inasmuch as, in addition to certification in LBT, they also hold a recognized master's or doctorate in a mental health field, and are licensed to practice within this field in their practice states. For example, they may be licensed mental health counselors, clinical social workers, clinical psychologists, or psychological counselors. Such additional training is necessary, at least in part, because the client may require some alternative therapy or combination of therapies to successfully work with the diagnosed problem, for which only the psychotherapist is appropriately trained.

In contrast, LBT consultants hold a recognized master's degree or doctorate in philosophy in addition to certification in LBT. The philosophical consultant does not treat mental health problems diagnosed in the *Diagnostic and Statistical Manual of Mental Disorders* of the American Psychiatric Association.[17] Instead, such a practitioner restricts her practice to working with specific, non-psychiatric problems of living.[18] The NPCA publishes a list of problems of living that can be the province of philosophical consulting as well as philosophical counseling. Such problems include but are not limited to the sample problems provided in Table I.2.[19]

The philosophical consultant addresses the particular presenting problem.[20] When this problem is satisfactorily addressed, the consulting ends. As such, philosophical consulting tends to be brief, often no longer than one to three one-hour sessions. This approach is appropriately called "consulting" because the client "consults" with the practitioner on how to think more rationally and philosophically about the particular problem at hand; and how to use the new perspective in devising a fresh plan of action for addressing the problem. For example, a client may be upset about the loss of a job and come to the LBT consultant for help in addressing this specific problem. The philosophical consultant in turn uses LBT to help the client come to terms with the

Table I.2

Sample Problems Addressed by Philosophical Consultants

Moral issues
Values disagreements
Political issues and disagreements
Writer's block
Time management issues
Procrastination
Career issues
Job loss
Problems with coworkers
Disability issues
Financial issues
Retirement
Aging
End of life issues
Midlife issues
Adult children of aging parents
Problems with family
Family planning issues
In-law issues
Breakups and divorce
Parenting issues
Becoming a parent
Sibling rivalry
Finding out one is adopted
Falling in and out of love
Loss of a family member
Loss of a pet
Friendship issues
Peer pressure
Academic or school-related issues
Rejection
Discrimination
Religion and race-related issues
Entertainment-related issues
Technology-related issues

job loss. She does not, however, continue to work with the client to help him overcome a more general psychological problem like GAD, for example. For this, the philosophical consultant makes a referral to an appropriately trained psychotherapist or philosophical counselor. As you will see, in subsequent chapters, LBT can provide a powerful resource for helping clients confront their problems of living.

The term "problem of living" in this context is non-psychiatric. For example, the loss of a job is not, per se, a psychological problem. Whereas the philosophical consultant addresses this particular problem, the psychotherapist, as such, is primarily interested in treating any underlying psychiatric problem that generates the client's response to the problem at hand. The LBT consultant does not treat the underlying problem. Rather, she looks at the reasoning that is generating the specific problem. This does not mean that the consultant does not impart valuable critical thinking skills that can be used by the client to address other problems that may arise. However, it is problems of living, not psychological disorders, which are addressed by philosophical consultants.

MAKING REFERRALS TO
MENTAL HEALTH PRACTITIONERS

The problems of living addressed by philosophical consultants are also not ones that portend serious and imminent harm to self or others, for example, a client who is contemplating suicide if he does not solve his problem. Nor are such problems ones that relate to perceptual problems, such as, psychoses; nor are they related to personality disorders, for example, Paranoid Personality Disorder or Borderline Personality Disorder. Again, these problems are the province of trained psychotherapists. Table I.3 provides a list of indications adopted by the National Philosophical Counseling Association, based on the *Diagnostic and Statistical Manual of Mental Disorders* (DSM-5)[21] for which referral should be made.[22]

Any bulleted entry on the set of indications in Table I.3 would be grounds for a philosophical consultant to refer a client to a mental health practitioner. For example, in the case of a client who is contemplating killing himself because he sees his situation as hopeless, the LBT consultant would make a referral to a mental health practitioner. This means that consultants should have prior arrangements with mental health practitioners for such purposes. If there is imminent danger to the client, an intervention may need to be arranged to prevent the harm.[23] If a consultant has questions as to whether a referral is indicated, based on the criteria adopted by the NPCA, then the consultant should consult the mental health practitioner. Accordingly, the working relationship between philosophical consultants and mental health practitioners is very important to ethically responsible philosophical practice. It is also one that can have reciprocal benefits to both consultants and mental health practitioners. For example, while mental health professionals do see clients who do not suffer from underlying mental disorders, such treatment is not typically covered by clients' insurance. As such, cases of this nature may be reasonably referred (by the psychotherapist) to the philosophical practitioner.

Table I.3

Referral Indications for Philosophical Consultants

Neurodevelopmental Disorders
- Enduring pattern of inattention and/or hyperactivity-impulsivity that is inconsistent with developmental level, which significantly impairs a major area of functioning such as social, academic, or occupational
- Developmental deficits in capacity for social-emotional communication/interaction including nonverbal communication/interaction, and in forming and maintaining interpersonal relationships

Psychotic Disorders
- Hallucinations
- Delusions
- Disorganized thinking or speech (loose associations, tangents, incoherence)
- Catatonic behavior and other abnormal motor behavior

Bipolar and Depressive Disorders
- Manic episodes
- Suicidal ideation (contemplating committing suicide) along with one or more of the following:
  - Specific plan
  - Expression of intention
  - Past history of suicide attempts or threats
  - Family history of suicide
  - History of psychiatric diagnosis or commitment to inpatient facility
  - Other serious health problems—perceived or actual
  - Hopelessness
  - Self-damning
  - Alcohol / substance abuse
  - History of trauma / abuse
  - Cultural / religious/ personal acceptance of suicide
  - Recent loss—relationship, financial
  - Access to lethal means
  - Impulsivity/aggressiveness
  - Knowing others who have committed or attempted suicide
  - Lack of support system, single or living alone
  - Elderly or young adult male
- Sadness, emptiness, or irritable mood most of the day, on most days, which significantly impairs day-to-day activities ongoing for at least one year
- Sadness, emptiness, hopelessness, or irritable mood, most of the day, on most days; and/or loss of interest or pleasure in all or most activities, most of the day, on most days; causing significant distress or impairment in social, occupational or other major areas of functioning; including at least five of the following changes:
  - Sadness, emptiness, hopelessness, or irritable mood, most of the day, on most days
  - Loss of interest or pleasure in all or most activities, most of the day, on most days
  - Significant otherwise unexplained weight loss/gain or decrease/increase in appetite
  - Insomnia, excessive daytime sleepiness

(continued)

Table I.3 *(Continued)*

Referral Indications for Philosophical Consultants

- ○ Psychomotor agitation (e.g., fidgeting, purposeless leg movements, or pacing) or psychomotor retardation (e.g., slowed speech or walking)
- ○ Chronic fatigue or energy loss
- ○ Persistent feelings of worthlessness or inappropriate guilt
- ○ Diminished ability to think clearly, concentrate, or make decisions
- ○ Recurring suicidal ideation without a specific plan; with a suicide attempt; or with a specific plan
- Chronic, severe, persistent irritability, including frequent temper outbursts and a tendency to be angry
- Mood swings tending to occur during menstrual cycle

Anxiety Disorders

- Phobias—persistent, ongoing, exaggerated, intense fear or anxiety about a specific sort of object (e.g., snakes) or situation (e.g., heights)
- Panic attacks—sudden intense fear peaking in minutes characterized by changes such as pounding heart and feeling unable to breathe
- Ongoing, day-to-day, excessive anxiety or worry about a number of different activities or events, which causes significant distress in social, occupational or other major areas of functioning

Obsessive-Compulsive Disorders

- Obsessions—repetitive, persistent, intrusive, unwanted thoughts, which interfere with or cause significant distress in social, occupational, or other major areas of functioning
- Compulsions—repetitive behaviors or mental activities one feels driven to engage in, having no real connection to what it is intended to guard against, which interferes with or causes significant distress in social, occupational, or other major areas of functioning
- Preoccupation with perceived bodily defects, which interferes with daily functioning
- Hoarding—ongoing difficulty getting rid of things regardless of their actual worth, such that the clutter prevents room use, and causes distress in day-to-day living

Trauma and Stress Disorders

- Flashbacks; nightmares; or intrusive, unwanted, distressing memories or thoughts about an event involving death, destruction, injury, or sexual violence

Dissociative Disorders

- Dissociative Identity—taking on two or more identities
- Dissociative Amnesia—inability to recall specific events during a specified period of time, including periods of travel or wandering (so-called dissociative fugue); or general inability to recall personal identity or life history
- Depersonalization—sense of being an outside observer of oneself
- Derealization—sense of unreality of one's surrounding environment

Somatic Symptom Disorders

- Distress about perceived or possible somatic (bodily) pains or health problems

Feeding and Eating Disorders

- Purging, overeating, bingeing, self-starvation, poor appetite, or persistent eating of nonfood substances

Table I.3 *(Continued)*

Referral Indications for Philosophical Consultants

Elimination Disorders
- Elimination problems—bedwetting or clothes wetting, defecating in clothes or on floor

Sleep-Wake Disorders
- Insomnia, excessive sleepiness or sleeping, breathing problems, sleepwalking, nightmares, sleep-talking, leg discomfort, or other sleep-related problems
- Fatigue or loss of energy

Sexual Dysfunctions
- Sexual problems—ejaculation, erections, arousal, penetration, low sex drive, or related problems
- Distress about one's gender

Disruptive, Impulse-Control, and Conduct Disorders
- Persistent pattern of:
  ○ Verbal aggression or outbursts
  ○ Physically violent behavior, including threats or destruction of property
  ○ Fire setting
  ○ Torturing animals
  ○ Lack of conscience or remorse, i.e., seeing people as objects/pawns

Substance–Related and Addictive Disorders
- Alcohol, caffeine, cannabis, hallucinogens, opioids, sedatives, hypnotics, anti-anxiolytics, stimulants, tobacco, gambling

Neurocognitive Disorders
- Neurocognitive decline—Delirium, Alzheimers, Dementia, and other brain diseases

Personality Disorders
- Enduring, deeply ingrained pattern of maladaptive and inflexible behavior and thinking across a broad spectrum of areas of living, which interferes with or causes significant distress in social, occupational, or other major areas of functioning, including:
  ○ Paranoid ideation
  ○ Social detachment
  ○ Instability of interpersonal relationships, self image, and affect
  ○ Grandiosity
  ○ Inability to empathize
  ○ Social inhibition
  ○ Submissiveness
  ○ Fear of separation
  ○ Preoccupation with orderliness

Paraphilias
- Voyeurism, exhibitionism, frotteurism, sexual sadism or masochism, pedophilia, fetishism, transvestism

The classes of mental disorders presented in Table I.3 tend to be broad classifications and therefore do not require philosophical consultants to have expertise in identifying and distinguishing between particular mental disorders. For example, a consultant may believe that a client has an anxiety disorder, but is not expected to specify which one. Indeed, as stated in the DSM-5, "scientific evidence now places many, if not most disorders on a spectrum with closely related disorders that have shared symptoms."[24] Therefore, this makes diagnosis of mental disorders challenging even for mental health practitioners highly trained in recognizing and classifying the myriad of nuanced mental disorders distinguished in the DSM-5. Accordingly, philosophical consultants avoid assigning psychiatric labels to their clients or potential clients. For example, a client who suffers from delusions may share some features with many mental disorders such as delusional disorder, obsessive compulsive disorder, delirium, major neurocognitive disorder, schizophrenia, schizophreniform disorder, depressive and bipolar disorders, and schizoaffective disorder.[25] A philosophical consultant would not venture to distinguish between such differential diagnoses. While this is necessary for diagnostic and treatment purposes, it is not necessary for purposes of referral. It would instead be sufficient for her to conclude that the individual in question *appears* to be delusional and that this is grounds for referral. And, even here, the ascription of "delusional" is not considered to be confirmed, which is left to the mental health professional to determine along with any possible diagnostic labels. The consultant makes a determination as to whether there are grounds for referral, not as to whether the client has a specific diagnosis. For purposes of referral, such broad classifications as included in Table I.3 suffice.

The case of philosophical consultants may be compared to other professionals such as teachers, guidance counselors, human resource officers, and attorneys, who sometimes refer students, employees, and clients to mental health professionals for evaluation. In making such referrals, it is not assumed that a psychiatric diagnosis has been made. Rather, the situation has been flagged and referred to those who are in a position to make such an evaluation as appropriate.

Of course, a teacher is concerned with instructing a student in a particular content area, for example, mathematics; and an attorney is concerned with helping a client to attain a legal end, for example, getting a divorce. In the process, the student or client may have behavioral and emotional issues that arise in the course of instruction or representation. For example, the student may experience math anxiety and the client may become depressed in going through the legal wrangling of the divorce. But helping the student or client address these emotional issues is not squarely part of the primary purpose of the profession. In contrast, the emotion experienced by the client going through a divorce may be more directly a concern of the philosophical consultant. This is why there is need for more careful articulation of referral guidelines in the case of philosophical consultancy than in the case of professions such as teaching and legal practice.

The criteria given in Table I.3 therefore elicit guidelines for referral purposes only. They set the parameters for professionally responsible practice. The following dialog provides an example of how a referral might proceed according to these standards:

"Good afternoon, Dr. Kirby."

"Good afternoon, Valery. How are you doing?"

"Pretty much status quo."

"Can you tell me about what you mean?"

"I'm a bundle of nerves. I think I was born this way."

"Is there anything, in particular, that you are nervous about?"

"Well yes. I was just promoted and now I am expected to fly a lot."

"So you are nervous about flying?"

"Yes, I am coping by drinking a lot when I fly. It gets me through the flight but then I am wasted by the time I get to the meeting. So I really worry about screwing up. I'm really screwed no matter what I do. I am starting to think that 'worry' is my middle name."

"Do you want to tell me about that?"

"Yeah. I worry about *everything*. I have always been this way but it's getting worse and I just feel like things are out of control."

"By worrying about 'everything,' what do you mean?"

"I worry about the kids getting to school on time; I worry about my husband's health (he's got a heart condition); I worry about driving in the rain; I worry about getting fired; I worry about anything that comes to mind. When my son tells me he got an A on a math test, I think that maybe he might fail the next test, and he won't keep up his average. Instead of being happy when good things happen, I worry about something happening to screw it up. I am a mess. I don't know what to do. Can you help me?"

"It appears that your issues are beyond my expertise. Philosophical consultants can address anxiety about a particular life challenge, but, as you say, you worry about 'everything.' This appears to be something that would fall within the expertise of a psychological practitioner."

"Well, I do have an issue going on right now that I could really use some philosophical insight. Can you help me with *that*?"

"Tell me about it."

"Like I said, I just got a promotion; but I also had another offer at a much larger firm. This may be a once in a lifetime offer but I have cold feet, and it's keeping me up nights worrying, not knowing what to do."

"We could address that, but you would need to be working with a psychological practitioner too. I would like to recommend you to Dr. Carla Anderson. Here is her card. She is very good with chronic worrying. If you still want to talk about your job situation after you meet with her, then I would be happy to do so."

"That would be great! Thanks for your help. I will definitely set up an appointment with Dr. Anderson, and hope to be back in touch with you soon."

"Very good! Thanks so much for coming in to see me. Take care."

"You too!"

In this case, Dr. Kirby sees that Valery has "Ongoing, day-to-day, excessive anxiety or worry about a number of different activities or events" as well as "Persistent, ongoing, exaggerated, intense fear or anxiety," and, therefore, concludes that Valerie satisfies at least two of the standards in Table I.3 for having an anxiety disorder.[26] However, notice that Dr. Kirby is careful not to offer a diagnosis of Valery's condition. Instead, she provides enough information to suggest that her case falls outside the purview of her expertise. "Philosophical consultants," she explains, "can address anxiety about a particular life challenge, but, as you say, you worry about 'everything.'" The language reflects Valery's language, and does not contain any diagnostic terms, such as "Generalized Anxiety Disorder" or other psychiatric labels. Indeed, it also avoids the use of broader psychiatric categories such as "anxiety disorder" and even the broadest of psychiatric terms, "disorder." Such classifications would still be to provide (or to begin to provide) the client with a diagnosis. However, the purpose here is to refer, not to diagnoses. As such, Dr. Kirby refers Valery to a psychological practitioner in her network, Dr. Anderson. It is then Valery's responsibility to follow up on the referral. This is true unless she presents an imminent, substantial risk of harm to self or other. In the latter case "disclosure may be made provided that it is made to the appropriate party or authority and no more information than necessary is disclosed."[27]

If Valery does pursue therapy with Dr. Anderson, Dr. Kirby is willing to consider helping her to deal with her apparent anxiety about the prospect of changing jobs. This is because she has then acted in an ethically responsible manner in seeing that Valery is receiving appropriate psychological care. In this manner, philosophical consultants can work cooperatively with psychological practitioners to help clients confront their behavioral and emotional problems in a manner that recognizes the qualifications and expertise of both philosophical and psychological practitioners.

In the above manner, the NPCA has, for the first time in the history of philosophical practice in the United States, established a clear procedure for making referrals based on a comprehensive set of standards. Within these established professional boundaries, philosophical consultants conduct ethically responsible practice in addressing a myriad of problems of living such as those enumerated in Table I.2.

Indeed, many of the behavioral and emotional problems addressed in this book fall within the stated professional boundaries. In chapter 1, I begin with an everyday life situation that exemplifies the interplay of reason and emotion in the context of interpersonal relations. Through which, LBT's theory of emotion is presented.

NOTES

1. Jean-Paul Sartre, "Existentialism is a Humanism," in *Existentialism from Dostoyevsky to Sartre*, ed. Walter Kaufman, Meridian Publishing Company, 1989. https://www.marxists.org/reference/archive/sartre/works/exist/sartre.htm.

2. Aristotle, *Nicomachean Ethics*. In McKeon, R. (Ed.), *The Basic Works of Aristotle* (New York: Random House, 1941).

3. Elliot D. Cohen, The Theory and Practice of Logic-Based Therapy (Newcastle upon Tyne, UK: Cambridge Scholars Publishers, 2013).

4. Ibid.

5. Ibid. For empirical data regarding the prevalence of these fallacies in selected student populations, see Elliot D. Cohen, "Philosophical Counseling: A Computer-Assisted, Logic-Based Approach," *Inquiry: Critical Thinking Across the Disciplines*, Vol.15, No.2, Winter 1995; "Is Perfectionism a Mental Disorder?," *International Journal of Applied Philosophy*, Vol. 26.2, Fall 2012.

6. Elliot D. Cohen, *The New Rational Therapy: Thinking Your Way to Serenity, Success, and Profound Happiness* (Lanham, MD: Rowman and Littlefield, 2007).

7. Ibid.

8. William James, *The Meaning of Truth*, Preface. http://www.authorama.com/meaning-of-truth-1.html.

9. James D. Patteson, "Rational Buddhism: Antidotes to the Eleven Cardinal Fallacies Presented in Elliot D. Cohen's *The New Rational Therapy* From Buddha and Some of His Greatest Disciples," International Journal of Philosophical Practice, Vol. 3.3, Spring 2015.

10. See Elliot D. Cohen and Gale S. Cohen, *The Virtuous Therapist: Ethical Practice of Counseling and Psychotherapy* (Belmont CA: Brooks/Cole, 1999).

11. See, for example, Gerd B. Achenbach, "Philosophy, Philosophical Practice, and Psychotherapy," in *Essays on Philosophical Counseling, ed.* Ran Lahav and Maria da

Venza Tillmanns (Lanham, MD: University Press of America, 1995); Elliot D. Cohen and Samuel Zinaich, *Philosophy, Counseling, and Psychotherapy* (Newcastle upon Tyne, UK: Cambridge Scholars Publishing, 2013).

12. National Philosophical Counseling Association, "Philosophical Practice," NPCA website. http://npcassoc.org/philosophical-practice/.

13. As discussed later in this chapter, philosophical practitioners trained in philosophy but not also in a mental health area practice outside the scope of their training if they attempt to address cases involving mental disorders.

14. Carl Rogers, *On Becoming A Person: A Therapist's View of Psychotherapy* (New York: Mariner Books, 1995).

15. National Philosophical Counseling Association, "NPCA Standards of Ethical Practice," Standard 9. http://npcassoc.org/wp-content/uploads/2014/08/NCPA_-Standards-of-Ethical-Practice-_-2014.pdf.

16. National Philosophical Counseling Association, Training and Workshops. http://npcassoc.org/training/primary-certificate-in-lbt/.

17. American Psychiatric Association, DSM 5.

18. National Philosophical Counseling Association, Standards of Ethical Practice. http://npcassoc.org/wp-content/uploads/2014/08/NCPA_-Standards-of-Ethical-Practice-_-2014.pdf.

19. National Philosophical Counseling Association website.

20. In LBT terms (to be discussed in Chapter 1), the philosophical consultant restricts her practice to specific intentional objects.

21. American Psychiatric Association, *Diagnostic and Statistical Manual of Mental Disorders*, 5th Edition (Arlington, VA: American Psychiatric Publishing, 2013).

22. National Philosophical Counseling Association, "Philosophical Counselors versus Philosophical Consultants," NPCA website. http://npcassoc.org/practice-areas-boundaries/

23. Elliot D. Cohen and Gale S. Cohen, *The Virtuous Therapist: Ethical Practice of Counseling and Psychotherapy* (Belmont, CA: Wadsworth, 1999).

24. American Psychiatric Association, *Diagnostic and Statistical Manual of Mental Disorders*, p. 6.

25. Ibid., p. 93.

26. See Table I.3, "Anxiety Disorders."

27. National Philosophical Counseling Association, "Standards of Ethical Practice," Standard 14. http://npcassoc.org/wp-content/uploads/2014/08/NCPA_-Standards-of-Ethical-Practice-_-2014.pdf.

Part I

THE SYSTEM OF
LOGIC-BASED THERAPY

Chapter One

Minding Your Emotions

Reason and Emotion in LBT

It was Halloween and Willy Witherspoon came back to his dorm room from a costume party at the University Student Commons only to find in the trash the empty box of the carrot cake he had purchased for a late-night Halloween snack. Willy went immediately to the refrigerator peering inside hoping to find the cake, but instead found remnants of the same old pizza from the week before and some cold ones lined up on the door shelf. No sign of the cake!

"That selfish pig!" he exclaimed, referring to his roommate, Johnny, who, like the cake, was nowhere to be seen. "He ate the whole cake I bought, leaving nothing for me," he snarled.

Just then, the dorm room door opened, and in walked Johnny, smiling from ear to ear, sporting a clown costume and a brightly painted clown face. "Hey Willy," said the cheerful clown.

"What are you gloating about, you selfish pig!" exclaimed Willy. Don't you have any manners or consideration for anyone but yourself?"

"What the f#$% are you talkin' about, man? What's wrong with you!?" shouted Johnny.

"You know damn well what's wrong with me, so stop making like you don't know! What gall eating the entire carrot cake, not leaving even a sliver for me! How can you be such a selfish pig!"

"What are you talkin' about, man! Your friend, Jimmy, came by earlier to see you. He had his dog, Marv, with him. We were talkin' in the common room and heard a noise in the kitchen. When we got to the kitchen, Marv was lickin' his chops, the cake box was lying on the floor, and Marv had some of the cream on his snout. So why don't you yell at Marv. I didn't eat your f#@%&# cake, not even a piece.

Anyway, I don't even like carrot cake! Maybe next time you can get a cake I like too! What about pumpkin!? Ya think maybe!? It's Halloween, man!"

"Sorry, about that man. When I saw the empty cake box, I just thought…"

The incident of the missing carrot cake illustrates a practical context in which there can be strong emotions, and high levels of stress generated quite unnecessarily. In such everyday experiences it is easy to miss the complexity of what is actually going on inside one's mind and to assume that some environmental stimulus (the empty cake box) simply caused an emotional response. However, the language that we use to frame such events, and the way this language underlies a chain of reasoning is not usually apparent to us, especially when we are in the throes of the emotional experience. Being able to "look inside" the emotional experience, dissect it into its various components, and to understand precisely what is going is a skill that is often not cultivated, exercised, or even recognized. Nevertheless, this so-called meta-affective skill (the ability to think about your emotion and not merely experience it) can save us from the abyss of much needless emotional turmoil that can take its toll on our happiness over the course of a lifetime. Herein lies the keynote of Logic-Based Therapy (LBT), that we own and operate our own emotional self-torture chambers by virtue of deducing self-defeating, emotionally-destabilizing conclusions from irrational premises. Thus, in the case of the missing cake, Willy Witherspoon needlessly upsets himself about his roommate Johnny having eaten the entire cake, in concluding that he was a "selfish pig." But did Johnny really eat the entire cake? And what if he really did? Could Willy have avoided such emotional stress by attending to his *emotional reasoning* and the manner in which it interfaced with other aspects of his emotional experience?

Emotional reasoning is the reasoning that can originate or sustain an emotion. However, in order to understand the structure of such reasoning and how it relates to emotion, it is necessary to understand LBT's theory of emotion. So, appropriately, this chapter discusses LBT's concepts of emotion and emotional reasoning, and shows how they are related. As you will see, emotional reasoning is, in a sense, embedded in its respective emotion, so that LBT rejects the popular (and ancient) view that reason and emotion are separate and distinct aspects of the human psyche.

LBT'S THEORY OF EMOTION

This view of the connectedness of reason and emotion aligns with the neuropsychological approach taken by Antonio Damasio in his landmark book,

Descartes' Error.[1] In the latter book, Damasio distinguishes between "primary" and "secondary" emotions. The former emotions, he maintains, are prewired responses to environmental stimuli. For example, you hear a loud noise and become frightened; you are being attacked by a wild animal, say a bear, and immediately take flight; you have your toe stepped on in a crowded room and you become angry. Such stimuli cause biochemical changes in your body. In the case of being attacked by a bear, the amygdala in the temporal lobe of the brain is activated and automatically engages the hypothalamus, which pumps adrenaline into the bloodstream, preparing the person for "fight or flight." These emotional processes do not necessarily involve "higher brain" functioning such as reasoning. Instead, they also occur in other animals that do not have a highly developed set of cerebral cortical functions as do humans. So, Damasio rejects the naïve perspective that reason is involved in *all* emotions.

However, Damasio distinguishes primary emotions from secondary emotions, the latter involving a "mental evaluative process" performed on the neocortex of the human brain.[2] For example, unlike a primary emotion, a secondary emotion—such as sadness about losing a loved one—is infused with cognitions, indeed, ones involving negative evaluations.

According to LBT, this Damasian evaluative process of "secondary emotions" can be analyzed in terms of practical reasoning. Further, it holds that a primary emotion can be sustained by such reasoning, even if it does not originate from it. For example, if someone walking behind you screams in your ear, you may temporarily become angered. If you continue to be angry after the initiating stimulus is removed, you are likely sustaining the emotional response through a reasoning process. "You crazy SOB! What the hell are you doing playing such a sick joke on me. You ought to be tarred and feathered!" In such a case, a primary emotion turns into a secondary emotion, which involves an additional "mental evaluative process." As will become evident, the evaluative process of such secondary emotions can be understood in terms of practical reasoning, which plays a decisive role in sustaining and/ or originating emotional responses.

The bodily changes that occur during an emotional episode also figure in the cognitive processing that goes on in emotions. According to Damasio, the *perception or awareness* of the visceral changes occurring in your body during an emotional episode—changes in blood pressure, muscle contractions, endocrine activity, etc.—constitute "feelings,"[3] which can be stored in the brain and provide "feedback" when making decisions about matters related to ones that originally generated the feelings. For example, according to Damasio's "somatic marker"[4] theory, in trying to decide whether you should make a reservation at a certain restaurant, the feelings you experienced when you last dined at that restaurant (the physical discomfort you felt when you had to wait two hours to get served) may replay in your mind, thereby helping you to decide not to make the reservation. Damasio maintains that such a feedback mechanism can be instrumental in helping to guide practical decisions.

According to LBT, awareness of such bodily changes (or "feelings") is a component of an emotional experience, which can interact with practical reasoning either by way of the reasoning generating such feelings, or, conversely, by way of the feelings influencing the reasoning itself. For example, concluding that a person is a dangerous psychopath can produce bodily feelings (such as a lump in the throat), which, in turn, can influence one's decision of whether to meet and greet him. In this regard, LBT also recognizes "emotional loops," according to which irrational emotional reasoning can generate bodily feelings; which, in turn, can influence further irrational changes; which, in turn, can produce more intense feelings; which, in turn, can continue to loop back. Such vicious cycles are associated with intense stress such as steadily increasing anger, often resulting in self-defeating, regrettable behavior.[5]

THE DOCTRINE OF INTENTIONALITY

LBT also subscribes to the view that all states of consciousness have *intentional objects*. This means that such states refer to events or states of affairs outside themselves. "The essence of consciousness, in which I live as my own self is their so-called intentionality," stated Edmund Husserl, the founder of contemporary phenomenology, a school of thought that introspectively studies the nature of consciousness. "Consciousness is always conscious of something."[6] This includes all emotions, whose intentional objects can appropriately also be called *emotional objects*. Thus, in the case of secondary emotions, one is angry, depressed, sad, anxious, or guilty *about* something. While it is true that people also experience "free floating" or "generalized" anxiety, such anxiety involves a general tendency or disposition to be anxious about a number of different things.[7] Feelings also appear to have intentional objects inasmuch as they involve awareness of visceral changes. Such mental states, however, *always* refer to states of the body or parts of the body. For example, a person may feel a lump *in the throat*; or may feel a non-localizable jitteriness *inside*. In contrast, emotions can be about *events external to the body*. This seems to be true of both primary and secondary emotions. For example, fear may be of the bear quickly approaching (primary emotion). Sadness may be about the loss of a loved one (secondary emotion).

However, whereas the intentional (emotional) objects of primary emotions are always sensible objects in the immediate environment—they can be seen, felt, heard, tasted, smelled, etc., the objects of secondary emotions can be non-tangible, non-sensible or abstract. For example, one can be depressed about not being perfect. Such objects can also be *possible* rather than actual. For example, one can be anxious about the *possibility* of losing one's job. Also, the emotional objects of secondary emotions may not exist. Thus, one can feel guilty about having harmed someone, even if no one was actually harmed. As such, emotional problems can sometimes (quite often) be about nonexistent things.

Indeed, LBT holds that secondary emotions can (in part) be defined by the kinds of emotional objects to which they refer. Thus, as Robert Solomon asserted, "the specific object is what defines the emotion."[8] For example, some emotions, such as moral indignation and romantic love, he said, are focused primarily on human beings, whereas fear and sadness are not necessarily about human beings. Similarly, LBT maintains that the objects of anxiety are future contingencies about what will or might happen *if* something else happens, for example, what will or might happen if I fail a test or don't get a job. The objects of anger are human actions, for example, someone keying your car. The objects of guilt are moral principles one perceives oneself to have violated, for example, experiencing guilt about not having told the truth.

Further, secondary emotions are also (partly) defined and distinguished by the *ratings* of their emotional objects. Indeed, emotions such as joy and love rate their objects, or aspects of their objects, positively; while emotions, such as sadness and anger rate their objects negatively. "The heart of every emotion," stated Solomon, "is its value judgments, its appraisals of gain and loss, its indictments of offenses, and its praise of virtue, its often Manichean judgments of 'good' and 'evil,' 'right' and 'wrong.'"[9]

Evaluative terms, or terms that rate, are terms that function linguistically to do more than simply describe or report facts. Instead, they are conventionally used to do things such as condemn, condone, reject, accept, commend, discommend, admonish, recommend, proscribe, prescribe, demand, request, and so forth.[10] Thus, calling someone a "selfish pig" is pejorative and said to have negative "emotive meaning" or "force."[11] This is because such a rating *condemns* the (entire) person and is associated with a negative emotion such as anger. In contrast, a rating of "wonderful person" approves and lauds the person and is associated with favorable emotions such as love and admiration.

LBT accordingly holds that different emotions (E) can be identified and distinguished in terms of *both* their objects (O) and their ratings (R). LBT expresses this way of identifying distinct emotions in terms of the formula, E = (O + R). Table 1.1 characterizes some of the common, negative emotions that LBT addresses in terms of the latter formula:

Table 1.1

Emotion (E)	Intentional Object (O)	Rating (R)
Anger	An action	Strong negative rating of the action or the person who performed it.
Guilt	A moral principle one perceives oneself to have violated	Strong condemnation of the perceived violation or oneself.
Sadness	An event or state of affairs	Serious negative rating of this event or state of affairs on the basis of its perceived negative effect on one's own life, on the lives of others, on the world, or on some part of it.
Depression	An event or state of affairs	Strong, negative rating of this event or state of affairs on the basis of which one persistently, over a period of time, bleakly perceives one's own existence as worthless or hopeless.
Grief	The loss of a loved one	Strong, negative rating of this loss on the basis of which one intermittently bleakly perceives one's own existence.
Anxiety	A possible, future state of affairs.	Strong negative rating of this possibility such that one perceives a need to ruminate about it.

ANXIETY

The intentional object (O) of anxiety has three attributes: (1) it is future-oriented; (2) it is possible, not certain; (3) it is predictive. As such, the intentional object of anxiety is always a conditional state of affairs such that *if* a certain event *e* occurs then a certain consequence/s *c will* (or might) occur. The rating (R) is then a negative or catastrophic assessment of this conditional state of affairs. For example, suppose you are anxious about making a public address tomorrow. Here, the intentional object, more fully articulated, will consist of a conditional statement regarding what will or might happen if the public address does not go well. For example, this statement might be that, "If I screw up tomorrow, then I will make a laughing stock out of myself, and no one will ever take me seriously again." Moreover, you may be ruminating about how devastating this would be if it actually happened. Here it is easy to identify the emotion, based on (O + R); for as you can see, the intentional object (O) would be the prediction that, if you screw up, you'll be a laughing stock whom no one will ever take seriously. The rating (R) would then be your negative rating or catastrophic assessment of this conditional state of affairs. The emotion (E) in this case would clearly be anxiety because it satisfies the (O + R) parameters of anxiety provided in Table 1.1.

As described here, anxiety can be distinguished from fear by virtue of the conditionality of the intentional object. For example, fear of a bear attacking you involves the perception of the actual attack; whereas anxiety about the bear attacking you is along the lines of *what if* the bear attacks you.

SADNESS

The intentional object (O) of sadness is an event or state of affairs. It may be a loss or turn of events that one rates (R) negatively on the basis of its perceived negative effect on one's own life, or on that of others, or on the world as such, or on some part of the world. The event could be anything from a natural disaster where many people lose their lives, the assassination of a president, the death of a friend, to the loss of a job or a poor grade on an exam. The rating of this event or state of affairs is "seriously negative," which means that its perceived negative effect/s is/are viewed as more than relatively minor or nonconsequential life changes. The sadness can be more or less intense based on the strength of this serious negative rating of the event or state of affairs in question. For example one can be sad about something "unfortunate" happening, but much sadder about something thought to be "horrible." Sadness may be intermittent, for example, one is sad only when one thinks about the event or state of affairs in question, but may be relatively contented otherwise. As a mood, it involves a tendency or disposition to be sad, but still may be interspersed with occasional moments of contentment. It is often a healthy response to undesirable things that happen. It often engages our powers of empathetic regard and compassion for others as when we feel sad about the misfortunes of others. However, sadness can also be unhealthy as when it takes the form of depression.

DEPRESSION

In contrast to anxiety, the intentional object of depression is typically a past or present event or state of affairs; or it is perceived to be, or imagined as such rather than as a future possibility. For example, you can be depressed about the loss of your job or over having been divorced.[12] And, while you can also be depressed about a *possible* job loss or divorce, you typically imagine the possible future state of affairs as though it were actual or imminent. Moreover, the rating of such an intentional object is catastrophic on the basis of which you devaluate your own existence and/or the world itself as devoid of worth or hope. There are, accordingly, two major levels of rating: (1) the negative rating of a particular event or state of affair, and (2) the negative rating of one's own existence and/or the world itself. Thus, in the case of the divorce, there may be a catastrophic rating of the event as so devastating that one's own existence is perceived to be without value or hope for future happiness. "There will never be anybody else for me, and I will spend my life alone. What kind of life is that anyway!?" Such *Existential Damnation* is also distinct from *Self-Damnation*. Thus one can perceive one's existence as being hopeless without necessarily believing that one is a bad or totally worthless person. In the case of the divorce, one might even perceive oneself as a good person who has suffered a grave injustice, for which one's existence has been forever destroyed.

While sadness can sometimes involve a devaluation of self (Self-Damnation) and/or devaluation of one's life (Existential Damnation), depression *always* involves such devaluation. Moreover, depression tends to be persistent from moment to moment rather than occasional, fleeting, or interspersed with moments of positivity. As mentioned, I might be sad on occasion when I think of a particular event or state of affairs, but contented otherwise when I am not thinking about it.

Sometimes people say, "I'm depressed" when they really mean they are very sad at the moment. For example, in hearing bad news, say that one didn't get a promotion, a person might report being depressed. However, her attention may soon shift to some other matter and she may no longer feel and act despondently. Such a looser, colloquial use of the term "depression" needs to be disambiguated from the stricter sense of clinical depression defined in the *Diagnostic and Statistical Manual* of the American Psychiatric Association (APA).

According to the APA, the common feature of all "depressive disorders" is "the presence of sad, empty, or irritable mood, accompanied by somatic and cognitive changes that significantly affect the individual's capacity to function."[13] For example, a diagnosis of Major Depressive Disorder may include cognitive changes such as "diminished ability to think or concentrate" as well as somatic changes such as weight loss or gain, fatigue, or psychomotor agitation.[14] This strict clinical definition of depression is detailed in the introduction to this book under the set of indications for referral by philosophical consultants (under "Bipolar and Depressive Disorders").

It is worth mentioning at this juncture that not everyone who is depressed is necessarily *clinically* depressed. For example, a person may be depressed, according to the (O + R) definition given above, but still not have undergone "somatic and cognitive changes that significantly affect the individual's capacity to function." Thus, all or most of us have gone through extended periods of hard times in which we were depressed about things in our lives—job loss, inability to make ends meet, medical expenses, a sick child, being passed over for a promotion, going through a divorce, and so forth. Yet we may not have satisfied the APA's strict standards of clinical depression. For example, we may have irrationally come to the conclusion that our future was, indeed, in the toilet, felt down about life for weeks or even months, but still continue to function effectively as an employee, parent, spouse, or student.[15]

One particular concern about depression is the danger that one may attempt suicide.[16] Not all people who become depressed have suicidal ideation or make a decision to kill themselves; however, because there is a sense (rating) of hopelessness or bleakness that pervades depression, a person in a depressed state may be prone to drawing the further inference that one is better off dead or that one *should* kill oneself. Drawing such an inference does not necessarily mean that one will act on it; however, there is a quasi-logical connection to carrying out the lethal act. If one seriously believes that one should do something, and nothing prevents one from doing it, then one will do it. This is why intervention in the case of depression is important, particularly where there is such an inference drawn. This is also why LBT practitioners, who are not themselves mental health practitioners (those who are philosophical consultants), should have a referral network of mental health practitioners with whom they work.

GRIEF

Grief is an intense form of sadness. The intentional object of grief is always the loss of a loved one. This can be a significant other. It can also be a pet. The strong, negative rating of this loss leads one to look upon one's own life through bleak lenses. That is, the bereaved tends to view life without the deceased as overwhelming, intolerable, unmanageable, or meaningless. However, as in other forms of sadness, this negativity tends to be interspersed with occasional pleasant moments as, for example, in recalling memorable occasions in the life of the deceased. Grief also tends to have a social dimension since bereavement tends to (although does not necessarily) take place in the company of others such as family or friends. This is in contrast to depression, especially in the clinical sense, in which the depressed individual tends to isolate himself from others, or becomes noncommunicative.[17]

Grieving is essential to "working through" the loss, and is therefore a healthy response to it. This is because, through grieving, one can eventually come to see the irrationality of one's beliefs about loss of hope for future happiness. Without going through the pain of grieving, one can harbor these beliefs for many years or even a lifetime without ever dealing with them. In such a case, one never works through the grief and the irrational beliefs play out as part of one's "life script." That is, one never does, in fact, find future happiness. Still, even when one does work through the grief, there typically remains the residue of sadness when one is reminded of the loss.

Inasmuch as grief is a healthy part of living and not a mental illness, it is grist for the assistance of philosophical practitioners, who can amply help to provide constructive philosophical insight into questions about the meaning of life. However, grief can also involve depression when one constantly, without intermittent positive thoughts, casts one's existence as devoid of value or hope, entertains suicidal ideation, damns oneself, and/or withdraws from social interaction. In such cases, philosophical consultants should refer the depressed client to a psychological practitioner.

GUILT

Guilt can be characterized as a moral emotion. This is because guilt is always about the perception of having done something that is morally wrong. This "guilty act" can include having had certain thoughts as well as having performed some overt, publicly observable action/s. Thus, the intentional object of guilt is always a past (or ongoing) action/s that the guilt-ridden individual perceives himself to have committed. The rating of this intentional object is, in turn, a strong condemnation of the guilty act alone or of the guilty act along with oneself for having done it. In cases of extreme guilt, the rating of the guilty act is of catastrophic proportions. "What I did was horrible." Where the rating also includes oneself, there is typically self-damning thoughts of near or total worthlessness. Guilt of the latter sort, where there are also self-damning thoughts, can be associated with depression when the negative attitude becomes all pervasive and persistent over time.

Guilt can also be concomitant with sadness that does not rise to the occasion of depression, as when one feels guilty of a perceived moral transgression and condemns oneself for it when one is reminded of the perceived moral transgression. This quiet sort of guilt can last many years unless the self-damning belief that perpetuates it is identified and worked through. This sort of guilt is popularly referred to as "having skeletons in the closet." Unless the proverbial closet is opened and emptied of these skeletons, the guilt will persist, even over a lifetime.

"What I did was so awful that I am totally worthless." Guilt, involving such self-damning thoughts, tends to be self-defeating as the perception of oneself as worthless forecloses the possibility of doing anything constructive about the moral transgression. Since, by definition, worthless people cannot perform worthy actions, such a guilty person perceives no chance of rectifying the situation in the future, or of redeeming oneself as a worthy person.

ANGER

In anger, the intentional object is a perceived present or past action performed by someone other than the agent, or the anger can also sometimes be directed at oneself. Where there is a perceived moral transgression, self-anger is a form of guilt. The rating in anger can be of the person performing the action or of the action itself. Anger that damns the doer rather than the deed is the most volatile form of anger. Road rage is a good example of how volatile this form of anger can be. Thus, someone cuts a motorist off on the highway and the motorist becomes enraged. "That no good, rotten piece of shit almost killed me!" Here, the devaluing of the offending motorist to the status of excrement is tantamount to granting the angry motorist self-permission to "dispose of" the other motorist. This is the context in which regrettable acts of violence are perpetrated on our roadways—anything from embarking on high speed assault on the other vehicle, to committing murder with a firearm. In contrast, anger that rates the deed rather than the doer is less likely to generate this sort of violent response inasmuch as a measure of respect for the human worth or dignity of the perceived offender can remain intact.

Anger as a secondary emotion needs to be disambiguated from anger as a primary emotion. Thus, someone who steps on your foot when you are on a cafeteria line, waiting your turn to be served, may provoke anger. Such anger may be sustained by strongly rating the individual performing the action. "Stupid idiot, can't you watch where you are stepping?" Without such evaluative processing of the intentional object, the anger will fade along with the perceived threat.

Unlike depression, which is always irrational, anger need not be irrational. For example, you can become "indignant" (rationally angry) about a friend having lied to you; which can motivate you to let your friend know how you feel about what he has done; which, in turn, can promote a constructive, heart-to-heart discussion. On the other hand, *intense anger or rage* is ordinarily fueled by irrational thinking and tends to lead to self-defeating behavior. It is such anger that LBT addresses. It does not, therefore, seek to eliminate *all* (secondary) anger, but instead affirms that anger can sometimes be a rational emotional response.

Formulating Emotional Reasoning in LBT

According to LBT, not only can (O + R) be used to define particular emotions as described above; it can also be used to formulate the client's emotional reasoning. Thus, the emotional reasoning of an emotion is, in a sense, embodied in the emotion itself. But what, exactly, does this mean?

According to LBT, the intentional object (O) of an emotion, when articulated, constitutes the minor premise of the (primary) emotional reasoning; whereas the rating (R) constitutes its conclusion. So when Willy Witherspoon becomes angry about his roommate, Johnny, having eaten the entire cake he bought, leaving none for him; having rated him as a "selfish pig," his (incomplete) emotional reasoning goes like this:

Johnny ate the entire cake I bought, leaving none for me.

So, he's a selfish pig.

The (incomplete) form of the above reasoning is then, as such:

O

So, R

Logicians refer to such reasoning as "enthymematic," which means that it is missing a part needed to validly deduce the conclusion from the premise.[18] In the present case, Willy is *assuming* that, if Johnny ate the entire cake without leaving any for him, then he is a selfish pig. Thus, the missing part is the "major premise," such that, when made explicit, the full argument is formally valid:

If Johnny ate the entire cake I bought, leaving none for me, then he's a selfish pig.

Johnny ate the entire cake I bought, leaving none for me.

So, he's a selfish pig.

Saying that the above argument is formally valid means that it has a logical form such that, it is impossible for the premises to be true and the conclusion false. The logical form of an argument is a kind of skeleton of the argument consisting of logical components such as "if...then..." with all statements removed and replaced with variables (letters that are placeholders for statements).[19] For example, the logical form of the above argument can be represented as follows:

If p then q

p

Therefore q

Here, notice that the statements "Johnny ate the entire cake I bought, leaving none for me" and "He's a selfish pig" have been respectively replaced with the letters p and q. This argument is formally valid because, any statements substituted for the statement variables p and q that make the premises true will also make the conclusion true.[20] For example, let p = George Washington was an American president; and q = George Washington was a primate. The argument obtained by consistently plugging in these statements for the statement variables would then be:

If George Washington was an American president then he was a primate.

George Washington was an American president.

So, he was a primate.

The premises in the above argument are both true. Notice that the conclusion is therefore also true. Since the form of this argument is valid, any statements substituted for p and q making the premises true automatically make the conclusion true. Indeed, the form of this argument is the commonplace valid argument form known as *modus ponens* or "affirming the antecedent."[21]

According to LBT the standard form of (primary) emotional reasoning is itself *modus ponens*:[22]

(Major Premise Rule) If O then R

(Minor Premise Report) O

(Conclusion) So, R

Consequently, once an LBT practitioner finds the O and R that identifies a client's emotion, it is easy to construct the *primary emotional reasoning* that undergirds the emotion; for this reasoning, constructed out of the O+R formula, takes the above (*modus ponens*) form.[23]

The (Suppressed) Major Premise Rule

According to LBT, the conditional premise (If O then R) of the primary syllogism provides an inference rule, which validates the inference. LBT calls this premise the "Major Premise Rule." Because this rule is typically assumed, rather than stated, LBT holds that this premise is a "suppressed" premise, and distinguishes it from a *repressed* premise or belief.[24] Classically, a repressed belief is one that a person has hidden away in the unconscious because it is too threatening at the time to consciously accept. In such a case, if a repressed idea were suggested to the person who is repressing it, this person would likely emphatically deny its veracity and become very defensive, even about

the mere suggestion that it may be true. This defensive demeanor is sometimes metaphorically referred to as "hitting a nerve."

In contrast, when a suppressed belief or premise is suggested to someone
who is assuming it, the person typically immediately and emphatically owns
and accepts it. Thus, the responses for repression and suppression tend to be
the exact opposite. It is therefore usually very easy to distinguish a suppressed
premise from a repressed one.[25] LBT ordinarily addresses suppressed premises rather than repressed ones. However, it may happen that, in the course of
LBT, a client may eliminate the basis for keeping a belief repressed. For example, a client who was sexually abused by her father may have repressed the
abuse. She may also have had nothing but nice things to say about her father.
However, she may also subscribe to the rule that, "If a man sexually abuses
her child, then he is a horrible monster." In the course of LBT, the client may
come to see that, although a person may have committed a very bad act, the
person is still a person and not a monster. Thus, by giving up the tendency to
damn persons (rather than their actions), such a client may eliminate the block
that has heretofore kept her sexual abuse repressed.

THE MINOR PREMISE REPORT

LBT refers to the second premise of the client's reasoning as a "Minor Premise Report," which is filed under the rule. To say that it is a report means that
it tends to be descriptive in character, describing or reporting on a particular
event or state of affairs. Thus it is an empirical claim that is typically based on
observation, testimony, or otherwise inductively inferred from other empirical beliefs. For example, the report that "Johnny ate the entire cake, leaving
nothing for me" was an inference from Willy's finding the cake box in the
garbage. However, there were other explanations for this purported fact such
as, the dog ate it.

Accordingly, reports are subject to mistakes in *inductive logic*, that is,
mistakes in probabilistic inferences drawn from experiential data. As in the
case of the missing carrot cake, the empty cake box in the garbage seemed to
point to someone who had direct access to the cake, namely Johnny. However, when Johnny explained that Marv the dog also had direct access and
that he was found in the kitchen with the empty cake box on the floor, "lickin'
his chops," with cream on his snout, this information made it unlikely that
Johnny was the culprit and highly probable that it was Marv who had eaten
the entire cake. Of course, Johnny could have been using the old "the dog ate
it" routine to get out of trouble; so it is still possible that Johnny did, indeed,
eat it. On the other hand, if Johnny has consistently been a reliable witness in
the past, then this possibility is not a very strong one. As such, minor premise

reports are never established with certainty. They can be "highly probable," "justified," and "reasonable," but not certain.

The classic example of the probabilistic nature of reasoning about "matters of fact" was well noted by eighteenth-century philosopher David Hume. In his famous example, even though the sun has always risen in the past, the proposition that, it will rise tomorrow, is still not certain, notwithstanding that we may be habituated to believe it. This is because the denial of this proposition is still conceivable.[26] For example, it is conceivable that the sun will be destroyed by a cosmic event, such as a giant meteor striking it.

EMOTIONAL REASONING AS PRACTICAL SYLLOGISM

When such an inductively ascertained minor premise report is filed under a rule, a client deduces a conclusion that "activates" an emotion. That is, the conclusion does not simply describe or report the intentional object; instead it rates or evaluates it. As discussed earlier in this chapter, this means that it *does* things like condemn, condone, reject, accept, discommend, commend, admonish, recommend, proscribe, prescribe, demand, request, and so forth. According to LBT, these so-called illocutionary acts (speech acts performed *in* saying things)[27] performed by the conclusions of such "syllogisms" are the linguistic mechanisms that produce and sustain our secondary emotions.

These linguistic acts also make such syllogisms practical.[28] In fact, according to Aristotle, in the case of practical syllogisms, "the two premises result in a conclusion which is an action."[29] That is, their conclusions tend to lead, not only to belief, but to overt or physical action. For example, when Willy concludes that Johnny is a "selfish pig," he is condemning or denouncing him and he will therefore also tend to act in certain condemnatory ways toward him.[30] What exactly these ways are will depend on the "behavioral rules" he has accepted. Willy appears to have embraced a rule of confronting friends whom he believes have done him an injustice. But Willy could have responded differently had he embraced a different set of behavioral rules. For example, someone else might have requested a new roommate or even threatened retaliation. In extreme cases, verbal condemnations can promote very aggressive behavior, including commission of violent, even lethal actions.

BEHAVIORAL REASONING

Behavioral rules occur as major premises in *behavioral reasoning*. This sort of reasoning includes a minor premise that "justifies" the behavior prescribed by the major premise rule, and a conclusion that prescribe the behavior. For example, Willy's behavioral reasoning would be along the following lines:

(Behavioral Rule) If Johnny is a selfish pig, then I *should* tell him off.

(Justification) Johnny is a selfish pig.

(Conclusion) So, I *should* tell him off.

Notice how the justification in the minor premise gives Willy a reason (or justification) to apply the behavioral rule given in the major premise, that is, "telling Johnny off" (scolding him). As such, Willy deduces the conclusion that he *should* tell Johnny off. In general, all behavioral reasoning (including moral reasoning) uses prescriptive terms such as "should" or "shouldn't" (or similar terms such as "ought" or "oughtn't") to prescribe the behavior in question.

As discussed previously, the conclusions of emotional reasoning tend to lead to action. This is because emotional reasoning interfaces with behavioral reasoning. For example, notice how Willy's emotional reasoning links to his behavioral reasoning:

(Major Premise Rule) If Johnny ate the entire cake I bought, leaving none for me, then he's a selfish pig.

(Minor Premise Report) Johnny ate the entire cake I bought, leaving none for me.

(Conclusion/Justification) So, he's a selfish pig.

(Behavioral Rule) If Johnny is a selfish pig, then I *should* tell him off.

(Justification) Johnny is a selfish pig.

(Conclusion) So, I *should* tell him off.

Notice how the conclusion deduced from Willy's emotional reasoning is also the justification premise of his behavioral reasoning. Accordingly, you can see how emotional reasoning is linked to behavioral reasoning, which, in turn, tends to lead to action,[31] in the present example, that of Willy telling Johnny off.

Multitiered Emotional Reasoning

According to LBT, all emotional reasoning contains a primary syllogism. While the conclusion of the primary syllogism is always a rating or evaluation, there may, and typically are, "higher order" syllogisms from which this conclusion is deduced. Consider again Willy's primary syllogism:

(Major Premise Rule) If Johnny ate the entire cake I bought, leaving none for me, then he's a selfish pig.

(Minor Premise Report) Johnny ate the entire cake I bought, leaving none for me.

(Conclusion) So, he's a selfish pig.

The major premise rule of this syllogism might itself be deduced from a further syllogism. For example, Willy might hold that people must never treat him unfairly by unfairly favoring themselves over him, and that eating the entire cake he bought, leaving none for him, is to treat him in such an unfair way. As such, the more complex structure of the emotional reasoning in question would look like this:

(Second Major Premise Rule) People must never treat me unfairly by unfairly favoring themselves over me.

(Bridging Premise) If people must never treat me unfairly by unfairly favoring themselves over me, and Johnny ate the entire cake I bought, leaving nothing for me, then he's a selfish pig.

(Original Major Premise Rule) So, if Johnny ate the entire cake I bought, leaving nothing for me, then he's a selfish pig.

(Minor Premise Report) Johnny ate the entire cake I bought, leaving nothing for me.

(Conclusion) So, Johnny is a selfish pig.

The formal structure of this chain of reasoning can be clearly represented as follows:

(Second Major Premise Rule) R2

(Bridging Premise) If R2 then if O then R

(Original Major Premise Rule) So, If O then R

(Minor Premise Report) O

(Conclusion) So, R

Notice how the Original Major Premise Rule is now itself a conclusion deduced from a Second Major Premise Rule utilizing a Bridging Premise.[32] The purpose of the latter Bridging Premise is simply to connect the Original Major Premise Rule to the Second Major Premise Rule.[33] All multitiered structures include bridging premises in all but the *prim*ary syllogism, which is the syllogism that is formulated using the (O + R) formula.

THE IMPORTANCE OF
IDENTIFYING BASIC RULES IN LBT

Take a look at the rules in the above structural representation of Willy With-erspoon's belief system. Notice how one rule can be defended by deducing it from a further rule. Of course, this deductive process cannot go on forever, so there must be some *basic rules* from which all other rules are deducible but which are not, themselves, deducible from any further rules. One important advantage of the logic-based approach is that it can provide a methodological framework for identifying these basic rules. Since all other rules are deduc-ible from them, LBT can help people get at the "root" of all other rules they may be using to upset themselves.

Perhaps an analogy can help to illustrate this point about the importance of helping clients identify their basic rules. I have had several large evergreen shrubs on my property. Each year, during the spring and summer months, a rather aggressive vine would invade these shrubs ensconcing them in a network of vibrant green weeds; and I would spend several hours on each occasion pulling the vines off the shrubs in an effort to protect them. How-ever, these vines would regenerate rapidly making this a constant chore. With much frustration, I would inspect the ground underneath the shrubs in search of a root system that I could pull out and thus end the reign of the unrelenting vine. Unfortunately, each time I looked, I could not locate the root.

Then on one great day in the morning, I looked more carefully at a network of straw-like twigs lying underneath one of the bushes. To the untrained eye, these looked to be lifeless and dead. Nevertheless, I scraped the outer coating off one of these twigs, and low and behold there was a luxuriantly green and very much alive vine. Delighted by my discovery, I pulled out the root system and the vines attacking the shrub died in a matter of a day or two. No longer did I have to spend hours pulling these vines off my shrubs. I only needed to find the root and pull it out to end the reign of this destructive weed.

In an analogous way, identifying and getting rid of the basic (irrational) rules in a person's belief system can be more effective than simply addressing the rules that are deduced from these basic rules. The Buddha himself once made the same rational prescription using the same analogy. "Just as a tree," he said, "though cut down, sprouts up again if its roots remain uncut and firm, even so, until the craving [read as "demand"] that lies dormant is rooted out, suffering springs up again and again."[34] Thus Willy can get some temporary relief from his stressful responses to people who treat him unfairly *just* by working on his tendency to damn others (such as calling them "selfish pigs"). But a more effective and far-reaching way of getting such relief would also be to work on his tendency to demand that others always treat him fairly. This is because, once he stops demanding that others always treat him fairly, he will have eliminated at least one of the "roots" of his tendency to damn others. It does not follow from this that Willy does not have to work on his tendency to damn others. Indeed he does. However, a robust and efficacious way to do this is to get at the (deductive) root of this tendency, namely, his demand that others always treat him fairly.

So, as you can see, Willy's getting angry at Johnny is more than a visceral churning. According to LBT, it also involves a complex, hierarchical structure of emotional and behavioral reasoning (consisting of a set of interfacing practical syllogisms), which is intrinsic to the nature of the emotion itself. The ancient dichotomy of reason versus emotion is therefore at odds with the conception defended here.

It should also now be apparent that there can be some rather destructive emotional "weeds" that can infect the premises of one's emotional and behavioral reasoning. So, for instance, Willy angered himself by using "must" to *demand* that people always treat him fairly. Then, because he thought that Johnny did not do what he "must," he relegated him to a "selfish pig," which, in turn, led Willy to erroneously tell Johnny off instead of politely asking for an explanation for the missing carrot cake. Here, Willy committed two "Fallacies of Emotional Rules," namely, Demanding Perfection and Damnation of Others, respectively. In the next chapter, these and other related faulty thinking errors will be more carefully explored.

NOTES

1. Antonio Damasio, *Descartes' Error: Emotion, Reason, and the Human* Brain (New York: Penguin Books, 2005).

2. Damasio, p. 139.

3. William James defined emotions themselves in terms of such awareness of biopsychological changes. See William James, *The Principles of Psychology*. Vols. 1–2. (Cambridge, MA: Harvard University Press, 1981).

4. Damasio, pp. 174–75.

5. See Elliot D. Cohen *What Would Aristotle Do?: Self-Control through the Power of Reason* (Amherst, NY: Prometheus Books, 2003).

6. Cited in Albert B. Hakim, *Historical Introduction to Philosophy*, 4th Ed. (Upper Saddle River, NJ: Prentice Hall, 2001), p. 562.

7. American Psychiatric Association, *Diagnostic and Statistical Manual of Mental Disorders,* 5th Edition (Arlington, VA: American Psychiatric Publishing, 2013), p. 222.

8. Robert C. Solomon, *The Passions: The Myth and Nature of Human Emotions* (Garden City, NY: Anchor Books, 1977), 258.

9. Solomon, *The Passions*, 267.

10. P. H. Nowell-Smith, *Ethics* (New York: Penguin Books, 1964); J. L. Austin, *How to Do Things with Words* (Cambridge, MA: Harvard University Press, 1975).

11. Charles L. Stevenson, *Ethics and Language* (New Haven, CT: Yale University Press, 1964).

12. You can also be depressed about a possible divorce, so depression can also sometimes be about conditional states of affairs as well as actual ones.

13. American Psychiatric Association, *Diagnostic and Statistical Manual of Mental Disorders* (Arlington, VA: American Psychiatric Publishing, 2013), p. 155.

14. Ibid, p. 161.

15. Unless otherwise noted, the use of the term "depression" in this book is the one defined by the (O + R) definition given above. Whether a client in the case studies presented in this book is also clinically depressed is a further matter.

16. This concern should not be limited to cases in which a person is depressed in the clinical sense. It is presumptuous to assume that a person who is not clinically depressed according to the criteria of the DSM5 is beyond the pale of attempting suicide or of having suicidal ideation.

17. Joseph Nowinkski, "When Does Grief Become Depression?" *Psychology Today*, March 21, 2012 https://www.psychologytoday.com/blog/the-new-grief/201203/when-does-grief-become-depression.

18. Elliot D. Cohen, *Critical Thinking Unleashed* (Lanham, MD: Rowman & Littlefield, 2009).

19. Ibid.

20. Ibid.

21. Ibid.

22. *Modus ponens* can generally be used to capture the logical structure of the primary emotional reasoning that undergirds all emotions whose minor premise is a nonconditional statement. However, with respect to emotions such as anxiety, which have a conditional intentional object, the logical structure of its primary emotional reasoning is, more exactly, a pure conditional syllogism, that is, reasoning of the following form:

If q then r

If p then q

So, r

For example, this is a pure conditional syllogism:

1. If this is a fruit, then this has pits.

2. If this is an apple, then this is a fruit.

3. So, if this is an apple, then this has pits.

Notice that, not only is the major premise (line 1) a conditional (if…then…) statement but the minor premise (line 2) and the conclusion (line 3) are also conditional. This is why this form is called a pure conditional syllogism: both premises are conditional, and so also is its conclusion.

The conditional syllogism fits the characterization of the emotional object in anxiety because, as discussed earlier in this chapter, anxiety has a conditional emotional object. For example, imagine a student is anxious about not passing the next exam. Suppose the full emotional object of his anxiety is, "If I flunk the next exam then I won't pass the course." And suppose his rating is that he would be a loser. In this case, the student's primary emotional reasoning that sustains his anxiety would be:

If I don't pass the course then I will be a loser.
If I flunk the exam then I won't pass the course.
So, if I flunk the exam then I will be a loser.

Notice that this reasoning has the form of a pure conditional syllogism. Both of its premises are conditional statements, and so too is its conclusion. For further discussion of pure conditional syllogisms as well as the other forms of conditional syllogism, see Cohen, *Critical Thinking Unleashed*, ch. 3.

23. Except in the case of emotions with conditional intentional objects such as anxiety, where the logical form is a pure conditional syllogism rather than *modus ponens*. See note 22 for details.

24. Elliot D. Cohen, "Critical Thinking, Not Head Shrinking," in Peter B. Raabe, Ed., *Philosophical Counselling and the Unconscious* (Amherst, NY: Trivium Publications, 2006).

25. Ibid.

26. David Hume, *Treatise of Human Nature*, Part 3, Section 11.

27. John R. Searle, *Speech Acts: An Essay in the Philosophy of Language* (Cambridge, UK: Cambridge University Press, 1970).

28. A syllogism is a deductive argument with two premises. A practical syllogism, in the form of emotional reasoning, is a syllogism whose conclusion rates or evaluates an intentional object or some aspect of it.

29. Aristotle, *On the Motion of Animals*, trans. A. S. L. Farquharson, ch. 7. Accessed September 1, 2013. http://ebooks.adelaide.edu.au/a/aristotle/motion/.

30. Ibid. I say "tend to" because, as Aristotle acknowledges, something might prevent one from acting accordingly or there might be an overriding reason. For example, Johnny might be my boss and my job might depend on my acting toward him in favorable ways only.

31. The term "action" here refers to deliberative or intentional actions, which need to be distinguished from bodily changes that occur as a result of automatic processes, for example, changes in heart rate or other so-called knee jerk responses.

32. Other formulations with more general tiers are also possible. For example, the more general rule "People must never treat me unfairly" might be the anchor for the more specific rule "People must never treat me unfairly by unfairly favoring themselves over me." In such a case, the following more complex structure would emerge:

(Third Major Premise Rule) People must never treat me unfairly.

(Bridging Premise) If people must never treat me unfairly, then if anyone treats me unfairly by unfairly favoring themselves over me, then he's a selfish pig.

(Second Major Premise Rule) So, if anyone treats me unfairly by unfairly favoring himself over me, then he is a selfish pig.

(Bridging Premise) If Johnny ate the entire cake I bought, leaving nothing for me, then he treated me unfairly by unfairly favoring himself over me.

(Original Major Premise Rule) So, If Johnny ate the entire cake I bought, leaving nothing for me then he's a selfish pig.

(Minor Premise Report) Johnny ate the entire cake I bought, leaving nothing for me.

(Conclusion) So, Johnny is a selfish pig.

33. By "connect" is meant "validate" by constructing a formally valid argument.

34. Buddha, *The Dhammapada: The Buddha's Path of Wisdom* trans. Acharya Buddharakkhita, Buddha Dharma Education Association, 1985. http://www.budd hanet.net/pdf_file/scrndhamma.pdf.

Chapter Two

Getting at the Root of
Your Emotion

Fallacies of Emotional Rules
and their Guiding Virtues

As you have seen in the case of Willy Witherspoon, fallacies in emotional reasoning can lead to self-defeating behavior and emotions. Practically speaking, a fallacy is "a kind of thinking or reasoning that has a proven track record of frustrating personal and/or interpersonal happiness."[1] In fact, LBT identifies and addresses eleven Cardinal Fallacies, a core set of irrational ideation which is especially prone to frustrate personal and/or interpersonal happiness, as based on clinical evidence and research gleaned from both LBT and REBT.[2] Some of these troublesome types of thinking or reasoning tend to be found in the major premise rules of emotional reasoning, which LBT appropriately calls, *Fallacies of Emotional Rules.* As you will see, these fallacies can be behind very destructive forms of emotion such as intense and debilitating guilt, sadness, anxiety, worry, and anger. Table 2.1 provides succinct definitions of these emotionally disturbing fallacies.

This chapter, in turn, looks carefully at each. As you will see, LBT not only shows why these (as well as all eleven Cardinal Fallacies) are irrational, it also introduces a set of corresponding "Guiding Virtues" for systematically overcoming them, and aspiring toward attainment of excellence in living.

DUTIFUL WORRYING

In many instances, Dutiful Worrying is undertaken by individuals whose loved ones are perceived to be imperiled. Commonplace scenarios include

Table 2.1. Fallacies of Emotional Rules

Fallacy	Definition
Dutiful Worrying	Dutifully and obsessively disturbing oneself and significant others until one is certain (or virtually certain) that an ideal (or virtually ideal) solution has been found to one's perceived problem.
Demanding Perfection	Demanding that a fundamentally flawed reality exist in a state of ideality or perfection.
Damnation	Complete or almost complete devaluation, based on a perceived defect, of one's own person (Self-Damnation) or existence (Existential Damnation), that of another person (Damnation of Others), or of the world itself (Global Damnation).
Awfulizing	Reasoning from bad to worst either by catastrophically magnifying risks of bad things happening, or by exaggerating just how bad something really is.
The-World-Revolves-Around-Me Thinking	Dictating what another *must* accept based on one's own subjective beliefs, values, desires, or preferences.

parents who worry about the welfare of their children. The following example is a case in point:

> Esther looked sternly at her husband, Fred. "We need to have a long talk about what to do about Lynn!" exclaimed Esther. "She failed another math quiz because she still doesn't know how to multiply. Imagine, third grade and she doesn't even know her times tables. God knows how hard I tried to teach her how to multiply but she keeps confusing the six and four times tables."
>
> "Well, why don't we get her a math tutor? This is not a big problem. I was always bad in math myself," responded Fred with a smile.
>
> "Right, and look where it got you!? Don't you want our daughter to be someone important, maybe a doctor or a lawyer?"
>
> Fred's smile turned inside out. "Of course, I want her to be someone important, but you are worrying too much. She'll get through this."
>
> "How can you be so sure? And how do we know for sure that a tutor will help? What if we can't find a good tutor? It takes time to find someone, and we have to interview them first; and we might not find the right person in time."
>
> "Just relax, Esther, we'll get someone on Monday. We can call the community college and ask if they can recommend someone. It's a weekend and we can't do anything about it now anyway. Hey, I've got a great idea! Why don't just the two of us go to a movie tonight? Why don't I call the babysitter to see if she can sit for us tonight? That movie you wanted to see starring Meryl Streep is playing too. We can have a romantic dinner too, before the show, make a night of it! What do you say, Esther?"

"I don't believe you! You are thinking about romance and the movies when our child's future is at risk! Are you serious!? UNBELIEVABLE!!"

ESTHER'S FALLACY

As this drama plays out it is easy enough for an outside observer to get the sense that Esther is overreacting. However, for those like Esther who perceive a potential threat to the welfare of a loved one, it's not wrong to worry so much about it. To the contrary, it's a *moral duty* to upset oneself unrelentingly until a perfect or near perfect solution is found. According to LBT, this form of chronic worrying is called *Dutiful Worrying*. It is a fallacy because it tends to frustrate the happiness, not only of the dutiful worrier, but also of anyone else (such as Fred) who might be perceived by the dutiful worrier (such as Esther) to share the same duty to worry.

ESTHER'S FALLACIOUS EMOTIONAL REASONING

Dutiful worrying is worrying about not worrying enough (a sort of "meta-worry" worrying), and it is perpetuated by guilt when the dutiful worrier thinks she is not worrying enough to discharge her duty to worry. It is a rather disruptive, pervasive, and debilitating form of anxiety.[3] Like all anxiety, the intentional object of dutiful worrying is a conditional state of affairs. For example, in the case of Esther, the intentional object is along these lines: "If I don't keep worrying about the problem, then Lynn's entire future will be at risk." When this object is inserted into the emotional reasoning that drive's Esther's dutiful worrying, her reasoning is along the following lines:

(Rule 2) I must (it is my moral duty to) constantly worry about how to help Lynn whenever there is a problem that could (potentially) put her future welfare at risk.

(Bridging Premise) If I must constantly worry about how to help Lynn whenever there is a problem that could put her future welfare at risk, then if I don't help her learn to multiply and (consequently) her future welfare is at risk, I will be a horrible person.

(Rule 1/Conclusion) So, if I don't help her learn to multiply and her future welfare is at risk, I will be a horrible person.

(Report) If don't keep worrying about how to help Lynn learn to multiply, then I won't help her and her future welfare will be at risk.

(Primary Conclusion) So, if don't keep worrying about how to help Lynn learn to multiply, I will be a horrible person.

As you can see, Rule 2, which contains the fallacy of Dutiful Worrying, is the basis of Esther's deducing Rule 1, which connects her failure to keep worrying with being a "horrible person." So, once Esther adds her intentional object that, if she doesn't worry about it, Lynn won't learn to multiply and her future welfare will be at risk (as stated in the Report), she deduces that she will be a horrible person if she doesn't keep worrying (Primary Conclusion). As such, whenever Esther tries not to worry, she is overcome by intense guilt about not worrying. "How can I not worry when Lynn's future is on the line? What kind of person would do that to her baby!?"

A GUIDING VIRTUE FOR ESTHER: DON'T WORRY, BE PRUDENT!

So why do dutiful worriers like Esther connect worrying with solving problems and preventing harm to loved ones? It is because they think that if they worry enough they will eventually come up with the "perfect" (or "most perfect") solution. They also think that by forcing themselves to ruminate and turn the problem over and over again in their minds, that they will, indeed *must*, eliminate all doubt about what will work and be certain (or near certain) about it. Unfortunately, for the dutiful worrier, rather than helping to solve their problems, it creates high levels of stress that interfere with rational deliberation of what will or might work. True, some dutiful worriers eventually figure out what to do about their perceived problems; but it is only after putting themselves and others through the ringer. After a lifetime, such chronic worry takes an incredibly heavy toll on well meaning and caring people. Unfortunately, many dutiful worriers do go through their entire lives needlessly stressing out themselves and their beloved ones.

So, Dutiful Worrying, as a chronic habit, is indeed a vice. But, as Aristotle would confirm, for every vice, there is a virtue, and it is no different with Cardinal Fallacies such as Dutiful Worrying. Accordingly, LBT holds that each of its Cardinal Fallacies has a corresponding "Guiding Virtue" that counteracts or replaces it, that is, redirects a person toward a rational, aspirational end or "ideal." These virtues thus provide a way of giving people, who have cultivated self-defeating and destructive habits of emotional reasoning, a new approach to living; one that has the potential to confer new hope for a brighter future by replacing fallacious emotional reasoning with sound emotional reasoning directed toward such "self-actualizing" goals.

Since Dutiful Worrying misguidedly prescribes worry as the morally incumbent means to dispose of one's problems of living, the Guiding Virtue of this Cardinal Fallacy, according to LBT, is that of *Prudence*, which involves a realistic grasp of problems of living and manner of addressing them. In its particulars, Prudence is the contrary or opposite of the vice of Dutiful Worrying. Whereas the dutiful worrier has a misguided idea that worrying is the moral route to problem solving, the prudent individual has a philosophically enlightened grasp of morality and moral standards regarding the welfare, interests, and needs of others (as well as of oneself). Whereas the dutiful worrier demands certainty in solving perceived moral problems, the prudent individual has tolerance for the ambiguity and uncertainty of moral choices, and is not averse to taking reasonable "moral risks" by trying out novel ways of confronting the challenges of living. Whereas the dutiful worrier tends to see reality in terms of dilemmas ("Damned if I do and damned if I don't"), thus tending to ruminate about the negative consequences of choosing one way or the other, the prudent individual has a helpful ability to frame life in constructive, relatively unproblematic ways.

As such, in contrast to dutiful worrying, prudential reasoning is *proactive*. This means that it is directed toward solving a problem rather than worrying about solving it. As you have seen, the conclusion deduced from Dutiful Worrying (that one would be a horrible person for not worrying enough) promotes guilt, which, in turn, perpetuates more worrying rather than constructive action. Whereas, the conclusions deduced in the practical reasoning of prudent individuals is that of how properly to dispose of the problem at hand.[4] For example, Fred's reasoning was proactive in this manner inasmuch as he concluded that getting a math tutor for Lynn on Monday would be a reasonable way to address her difficulty with multiplication.

Moreover, the prudent person tends to be worldly; that is, not merely prudent about this or that, but possesses an ability to rationally address problems of living in general. The prudent individual, Aristotle says, is "able to deliberate well about what is good and expedient for him, not in some particular respect, e.g., about what sorts of thing conduce to health or to strength, but about what sorts of thing conduce to the good life in general."[5] In contrast, the dutiful worrier's ability to resolve problems of living tends to be sidetracked due to a persistent habit of worry.

While dutiful worriers have strong moral consciences and want, in fact demand, that they do what is morally right—as part of an absolutistic, unflinching duty to do so—they are out of touch with morally correct standards. In the history of philosophical ethics, there has never been a recognized ethical theory that contended that people have a duty to upset and torment themselves whenever they have a problem they deem significant. In fact, all of the historical currents of ethical theory, from utilitarian and Kantian ethics to virtue and care-based ethics would militate against doing such a thing. Thus, classical utilitarianism stresses doing that which maximizes happiness as defined in terms of pleasure. But Dutiful Worrying neither promotes overall pleasure for the agent nor anyone else. In fact, because it produces needless stress, it actually works against promoting overall happiness. Kantian ethics says quite bluntly to treat oneself, not just others, as "ends in themselves" and not as "mere means."[6] But dutiful worriers treat themselves as mere means (or vehicles) to the promotion of the happiness of others about whom they worry by needlessly tormenting themselves. Virtue ethics, such as that of Aristotle, stresses avoidance of extremes in the way of emotions in favor of moderation, but dutiful worriers go to the extreme in worrying, which, according to Aristotle, would be a vice, not a virtue. And the ethics of care emphasizes caring for everyone, which includes empathetically seeing the perspective of others, including that of family members who are not disposed to upset themselves with worry.[7] But dutiful worriers force others who are relevantly situated to worry, even against their will, as the case of Esther and Fred plainly illustrates. So, Dutiful Worrying is anything but ethical according to these prominent traditions of ethics.[8]

As is evident from the definition included in Table 2.1, Dutiful Worrying can be viewed as a particular type of Demanding Perfection. This is true because the fallacy prescribes a duty to attain a state of affairs that is seldom if ever attained in this imperfect world, namely that of being certain (or virtually certain) that one has found a perfect (or near perfect) solution to a perceived problem. It is such a search for the ideal that can, indeed, undergird a host of other emotional problems and disturbances.

DEMANDING PERFECTION

This fallacy is commonly a "basic premise" at the root of many emotional disturbances as is illustrated in the following confessions of James, a college freshman and baseball player, aspiring to be in the Major Leagues:

> Ever since I can remember, it's been my dream to play pro baseball. As a little boy my dad and I would play catch and we would often go to the park to practice batting. The most memorable experience I had was when I was five years old and my dad took me to Shea Stadium to see the Mets. It was probably then that I decided that I was going to be a pro ball player. I never really cared much for school except phys. ed., especially when it was baseball season. I always did my best when I was playing. I was really good at it too! I had to be perfect if I was someday to play in the Big Leagues. This is why I took it so hard when I messed

up last week when I was playing second base. I fielded a grounder and hesitated before passing it to first base. I could have had a double play but instead I kind of froze up and then it was too late! The batter made it to first and by the time the first baseman passed the ball to me the guy on first slid into second and the ref said safe! It was a close call but I really didn't move fast enough. This is unacceptable. I felt like such a loser. I don't care if I do poorly on exams, but this is what I plan to do with my life! If I screw up playing ball, then I'm a complete failure. I always have to be at the top of my game if I am going to be drafted! It's been really hard, though. Sometimes I am playing great and I'm so stressed out about screwing up, because I know that if I mess up, then it's all over for me!"

Like many athletes, James experiences a great deal of anxiety about his performance on the field. For him, a single screw up will mean that he has not only failed to meet his career goal, but that he himself is a failure. It is analogous to walking a tight rope without a net, where he (metaphorically) will plunge to his death if he does not remain surefooted at every turn. Quite stressful!

JAMES' UNDUE STRESS

Many athletes I have known who take James' perspective argue that this stress is necessary for them to perform well. However, this is a hypothesis contrary to fact for which there is no evidence. In fact, such constant stress can and often does lead to just the opposite. Indeed, intense stress such as that described by James can have negative effects on performance by impairing the ability to concentrate as well as preventing one from getting a restful sleep. It is even possible that James' hesitation in throwing the ball to first base was a consequence of the slower processing of information due to intense stress![9]

Here, there is a difference between James' level of stress and the primary emotional responses that can accompany the play-by-play exchanges on the field, where adrenalin is up and the "fight or flight" response is engaged. James' stress is ongoing both on the field and off. It involves rumination and catastrophic conclusions about the end of self-worth if there is even one false move. This is not just a lower brain process where the amygdala is responding to an immediate stimulus, which, in turn, engages the hypothalamus, which, in turn, engages the adrenal glands to pump adrenaline into the bloodstream. There is an additional level of stress that can impair the ability to execute skillful behavior such as required in ball playing. It debilitates rather than enables by working against such other brain processes.

This additional and self-destructive level of stress is not merely reflexive. It is, instead, a product of a chain of emotional reasoning that, not only prevents

James from playing his best, but also prevents him from enjoying the game. For him, it is more like escaping being eaten by a den of hungry lions than it is taking joy in the comradely of fellow teammates working harmoniously together through the pooling of skillful, cooperative efforts to score the most runs.

James' Fallacious Emotional Reasoning: It's in the Absolutistic "Must"

James' emotional reasoning appears to have two levels of interfacing syllogisms along the following lines:

> (Second Major Premise Rule) I *must* realize my dream of playing professional ball.
>
> (Bridging Premise) If I must realize my dream, then if I don't, then I'm a complete failure.
>
> (First Major Premise Rule/Conclusion) So, if I don't realize my dream, then I will be a complete failure.
>
> (Minor Premise Report) If I screw up then I won't realize my dream (of playing professional ball).
>
> (Primary Conclusion) So, if I screw up, then I will be a complete failure.

As you can see by examining his basic premise (Second Major Premise Rule), James' dream to play professional ball is not just a desire or wish, it is an absolutistic "must" or demand, which he has placed on himself. From this premise, he deduces that he will be a complete failure if he messes up (Primary Conclusion). Consequently, he is the author of his own stress. Either he realizes his "dream" or he is reduced to a worthless thing. His value as a human being is, on this view, a function of whether or not he is successful in reaching the Big Leagues, which is not very probable, even for an excellent player. Notice that James' intentional object (Minor Premise Report) is a conditional state of affairs—*if* he screws up then he won't realize his dream. It is the constitutional "iffyness" of his object that keeps him in a suspended state of anxiety. Change the conditional to a statement about what actually happened or will (definitely) happen—that he did, or will, definitely, screw up—and the character of his emotion will shift to a depressive or saddened state. In the latter case, he would perceive himself as *actually* being worthless, or destined to be so. This explains the high rate of comorbidity between anxiety and depression, with, about 50 percent of people who suffer from anxiety also having symptoms of depression, according to some surveys.[10]

In the case of intense anxiety, such as James', as well as other irrational secondary emotions (including depression, anger, and guilt), the genesis of the emotional problem tends to lie in an absolutistic, perfectionistic "must" within the basic major premise rule of emotional reasoning. Indeed, an inspection of the myriad of cases presented in this book will confirm that such a "must" is at the root of much needless human stress. This "must" is both prescriptive and descriptive in character.[11] Thus, in James' saying that he *must* realize his dream, he is expressing a quasi-law-like expectation that this state of affairs actually happen. Perhaps an analogy will help. Just as there is a lawful necessity that, what goes up must come down (it is a corollary of the universal law of gravity), so too does James "expect" to fulfill his dream. From this perspective, the universe is inexplicable and turned upside down if it fails to deliver—much as one would be utterly shocked if the law of universal gravity ceased to operate. Second, James is prescribing this expectation, that is, not only is it necessary; it *should* or *ought* to happen. This gives such a "must" its evaluative force. Here, there is a conceptual bridging of "is" and "ought." What *is* (must be) *ought* to be. This is natural law theory with a vengeance. The stakes are quite high, indeed, if nature fails to deliver—total self-devaluation, and in the case of depression, the potential for self-harm.

A GUIDING VIRTUE FOR JAMES

According to LBT, the Guiding Virtue of Demanding Perfection is *Metaphysical Security*. This is the habit of accepting imperfections in reality. Routinely, the metaphysically secure person is prepared for and accepts the imperfections of the world of space-time objects he inhabits. He accepts the inescapable fact that he as well as other human beings are fallible in judgment and perception, not always rational, limited in their knowledge and power to affect change; he accepts that bad things can and do happen, that people, nations, and even world communities are not always fair or just; that natural disasters happen, and that risk is a part of life. He remains hopeful about realistic possibilities, is humble in the face of the uncertainty of the universe, and has a strong desire for knowledge, but is not frustrated by his inability to know all. Such a person does not attempt to control what is beyond his ability to control but stays focused on excelling in what he can control. This does not mean that the metaphysically secure person is complacent with the status quo or does not aspire to do an excellent job. Indeed, such a person can shoot for the stars, but does not demand that she land on them. It is the latter demand that leads to needless stress, and the metaphysically secure individual, while preferring to reach her mark, avoids the stress of demanding it.[12]

Clearly, James' challenge is to overcome his metaphysical *insecurity*[13] inasmuch as he demands perfection in his athletic performance, and, thereby, needlessly and self-defeatingly stresses himself out over it.

DAMNATION

Notice that, in James' case, the "must" feeds the self-damning provisional conclusion that "If I screw up then I will be a complete failure." Damnation is indeed frequently a deduction from Demanding Perfection. There are principally four kinds of damnation: (1) Self-Damnation; (2) Damnation of Others; (3) Global Damnation; and (4) Existential Damnation. Self-Damnation is often embedded in the emotional reasoning of anxiety, as you have seen in James' case; and in guilt, as in Esther's case. Damnation of Others is often embedded in anger. Existential Damnation and Global Damnation are often in depression or sadness. Existential Damnation involves the perception of the worthlessness or futility of one's own existence, whereas Global Damnation involves the perception that the entire universe is devoid of worth. All four kinds of Damnation are versions of the so-called Fallacy of Composition, that is, inferring something about the whole of something based on a part. Clearly, the inferential leap from the badness of a part of something to the badness of the whole thing is a *non sequitur*.

Of course, while the conclusion does not necessarily follow, it is tempting to think that the conclusion can follow in some cases. Thus, doing something horrible does not necessarily make someone a horrible person; but what if the act in question is something extremely bad such as mass murder? Would that not make the person a horrible person? For example, wasn't Hitler a horrible person, even though he might have had some positive attributes, such as his artistic ability or his vegetarianism?

It is important to notice that, in such a context, calling someone a "horrible person" amounts to a *moral* condemnation of the person. But even morally condemnable people can have some *non-moral* virtues (such as Hitler's artistic ability), which means that they are not *totally* devoid of value. Further, even if it is granted that Hitler was a horrible person, the use of such labels is itself of little or no value. Indeed, the purpose of moral judgment is to guide people's actions. As such, moral evaluation should be as precise as possible. Calling someone, even Hitler, a horrible person does not give us any action-guiding information. In contrast, saying that Hitler ordered atrocious acts such as the extermination of millions of people is quite action guiding. It proscribes actions that we, as a global community, should never again tolerate.

Not uncommonly, people engage in damning judgments without claiming that the total individual or thing they are condemning is bad or worthless. For example, someone may say that the world is *mostly* bad or *bad enough*. Such judgments as these still qualify as fallacious inasmuch as they still exaggerate the degree of bad things in the world. So, there are murders, rapes, and natural disasters, among other bad things. But there are also such good things as love, charitable giving, friendship, and warm sunny days, among other good things. Accordingly, we must take care not to throw the proverbially baby out with the bath water. Better to stick to evaluating the deed rather than the doer, and the event rather than the world.

Existential Damnation follows suit. But this does not mean that there are no rational judgments about the futility of someone's existence. A person who is in the late stages of a terminal illness, such as colon cancer, may prefer to die rather than suffer the indignity of loss of control of bodily functions, irremediable and excruciating pain, or loss of consciousness. In such a case, the judgment that one's existence is futile or not worth preserving need not be fallacious. Here, it is important to distinguish between disagreement in values and disagreement about what is rational. While some may consider life precious, even under the most adverse conditions, this does not mean that those who disagree are being irrational. Thus, the concept of "rational suicide" is not a contradiction, even if those who object to suicide, say on religious grounds, adamantly disagree. Indeed, within the sphere of rationality, there is considerable room for disagreement in values.

However, there are also limits to rational disagreement. Thus, the bleak existential outlook of an individual who is depressed about the loss of a job is not the same as that of a person who is suffering from a terminal illness. While the former's conclusions about the futility of life, based on the job loss, typically make false or unjustified assumptions (for example, "I have nothing left to live for" or "It is not possible for me to ever find future happiness"), the latter need not make any such assumptions. For example, consider the case of Martin Gregory, a former CFO of a technology firm.

"I had a beautiful house, two BMWs, a cushy job, a beautiful wife, and many friends. Since losing my job, I had to sell everything; now I rent an apartment on the Lower East Side; my "trophy" wife left me when I lost my shirt; and I now live alone. My so-called friends don't want to associate with me and are embarrassed even to be seen with me. No one in the firm will even look at me; my savings are about depleted; and I will need to find work doing something menial if I am to survive. I really got a raw deal! Instead of promoting me, they fired me and hired some hotshot, just two years out of Wharton. What the hell! What's the point of living now!

Martin Gregory's case is not uncommon. The vicissitudes of life are, indeed, a part of living on earth. While some of us experience a chain of bad luck, a so-called pileup effect, others of us have occasional downsides. Of course, some of us tend to land on our feet, but virtually none of us are strangers to some measure of misfortune, whether it is loss of material possessions, or loss of friends or family. However, the dynamic quality of existence is that it can change for the better, especially when we are motivated to make constructive changes in our lives. For those of us who assess the quality of life purely in terms of money and possessions, Martin's situation is a tragedy of colossal proportions. He "had it all" and now he has "nothing"—that is, none of the things that money can buy. But for others of us who assess the quality of life in terms of meaningful interpersonal relationships and good works, Martin's situation is still unfortunate but not hopeless. His interpersonal relationships—his wife and friends—were based on opportunism and inauthenticity. His job paid well, but did the money bring him self-fulfillment? Indeed, possibilities for existential change for the better were not destroyed when Martin suffered his financial and interpersonal losses; for there were still other things that he could attain in his life that could add new meaning and value to his existence if he were open to such possibilities. This is why Martin's Existential Damnation is a fallacy. It assumes that, because some coveted aspects of his existence were lost, that the value of his whole existence is hopelessly, forever damned. Martin's emotional reasoning is, accordingly, along the following lines:

(Major Premise Rule) If I lost my job, wife, friends, cars, and house, then my (whole) existence is forever meaningless and hopeless.

(Minor Premise Report) I lost my job, wife, friends, cars, and house.

(Primary Conclusion) So, my existence is forever meaningless and hopeless.

As you can see, the edifice of Martin's emotional reasoning rests on the basic rule that, if he loses his job, wife, friends, cars, and house, then his existence is forever meaningless and hopeless (Major Premise Rule). However, the fallacy is glaring in this rule; for it supposes that there can never be anything else to fill the void left by the loss of the present values. But, as discussed, when these values are dismantled it is seen that there are significant possibilities left to be desired such as friends who are not fair weather friends, and a wife who is authentic and not looked upon (or treated) as a "trophy." Indeed, as you will see, there are diverse philosophical perspectives that can help a depressed person, who deduces the meaninglessness and hopelessness of his life from such fallacious rules, to attain greater Existential Respect, that is, a more rational, uplifting view of the possibilities for finding meaning and value in life after a significant loss.

AWFULIZING

"It's so terrible!" one might exclaim, when a tragedy happens. But bad things come in degrees, and a difference in degree can sometime equate to a difference in kind. For example, it is unfortunate if one loses one's job; but it is not nearly as bad as mass murder or a tsunami. The upshot is that badness is a relative concept, so that things could always be worse. Thus, even mass murder or a tsunami could be "topped" by a larger mass murder or a more destructive tsunami. This means that nothing, yes nothing, is absolutely terrible, horrible, or awful; nothing can be rightly thought to be the worst thing that could possibly happen. Yet, in a relative sense, one can reasonably say that the mass murder or the tsunami is (relatively speaking) awful; but the same cannot be said about many other things that people commonly say are awful such as getting into a fender bender, being late for class, or losing one's job. Psychologist Albert Ellis referred to such exaggerations as "Awfulizing" and he admonished others to use words like "unfortunate," "tough break," and "too bad" instead of words like "awful," "horrible," and "terrible" to characterize the bad things that happen. However, while Ellis recommended that the latter words never be used, LBT tolerates their use to characterize the clearly tragic events in one's life, but only in a nonabsolutistic, relativistic sense. With respect to other ordinary language uses of such terms, LBT agrees with Ellis. Thus, the loss of a loved one, say the death of a child due to illness, is awful in this tragic sense, but getting a failing grade on a final examination is not.

It can be useful to think of relative degrees of negative values ("badness") on a scale of one to ten, where a ranking of ten is reserved for extremely bad things like a tsunami or genocide; and a ranking of one is reserved for small inconveniences like having your TV remote break or missing your favorite TV show. Of course, while reasonable people can disagree about where something like job loss or divorce would be situated on such a scale, it would not be reasonable to list it as a nine or ten; nor would it work as a seven or eight, for then where would one reasonably place the death of a child, the murder of a loved one, or dying of starvation? I have found that, clients who Awfulize tend to give rankings anywhere from seven to ten to things that are easily shown to be less serious than many other things that they would rank just as high. As a result, these clients usually see just how much they have exaggerated the degree of badness. The upshot is that it is easy enough to inflate just how bad something is until one examines it comparatively with other bad things.

There are two types of Awfulizing. One type is *retrospective* or *occurrent*. Here, one awfulizes about the inherent badness of things that have already happened; or which are presently occurring or ongoing; for example, ranking the unfaithfulness of a girlfriend or boyfriend on the same par with an earthquake having a magnitude of ten on the Richter scale. The second type of Awfulizing is *predictive*. In this type, sometimes called catastrophic reasoning, one awfulizes about the *consequences*, or possible consequences, of an event; for example, thinking that if you don't get into a top notch university, you will end up working at a menial job for the rest of your life, which, you conclude, would be the worst thing that could ever happen to you. In the case of such reasoning, first you make unjustified predictions about bad things happening; or you exaggerate the probabilities of bad things happening; and then you give unreasonably high negative ratings to these consequences (such as nine or ten on the badness scale). One faulty thinking error leads to another. You make unrealistic empirical claims about what consequences will or probably will happen, or you take remote possibilities and catapult them into high probabilities; you then awfulize about these unrealistic predictions. The first empirical fallacy sets the stage for the second evaluative fallacy wherein you brace for a nine or ten on the badness scale, akin to the tsunami or the literal end of the world.

Retrospective or occurrent Awfulizing tends to be associated with sadness. "It's *so* awful that I devoted my life to her and she cheated on me with my best friend! Now, my life is over!" In contrast, the predictive kind of Awfulizing, (particularly the kind that involves "what ifs") tends to be associated with anxiety. "If she breaks up with me, I will never be happy again."[14]

Consider the case of Winston, a computer scientist who works for a large advertising company:

> I prefer to keep to myself at work. Most of my team members think that I'm weird. Whenever I try to talk to them about my ideas—I believe I have found a way to upload the contents of the human brain to the cloud and thereby attain immortality in cyberspace—they walk away from me. All they are interested in is trying to create applications that help to sell products for our corporate clients. True, that's what our team is supposed to be doing, but they don't seem to care about anything else. I know what they are saying about me because I overheard several of them talking about me last week. They mockingly called me "Super Cyberman," and said that I was "weird." It's not that I am judging myself based on what they are saying about me. I don't believe, for one moment, that I am weird or that my ideas are silly. It's just that they won't listen to me.

Sometimes they try to talk to me about their families and their kids. I really don't care to talk to them about these things—I find such small talk to be utterly boring—so I generally try to avoid talking to them except when we have meetings about logistical matters that call for my programming expertise. As a result, I have also gained a reputation for being unfriendly, even antisocial. Well, I might be willing to put up with their small talk if they would give me a chance to discuss my ideas too. I just need them to listen and be more open-minded; but they don't get it. And I really feel very down about it!

Clearly, Winston is disturbed about his not being able to control the way his team members respond to his theory about human brains and cyber-immortality. Given his strong negative emotional response to this inability to control others, it is evident that he is ranking it very high on the badness scale, perhaps a nine or ten.[15] Here Winston's Awfulizing is with respect to an ongoing state of affairs, namely that of his not being able to control others' responses to his theorizing. So, for him, such inability to exercise control is, *in itself*, awful, not that he necessarily thinks it could have consequences that are awful. Accordingly, in Winston's case, it is such occurrent, nonconditional Awfulizing that promotes his sadness.

WINSTON'S EMOTIONAL REASONING

But not being able to control others' responses to one's ideas would not be perceived as something awful unless one also *demanded* such control. As such, notice that Winston says "I just *need* them to listen and be more open-minded." So, Winston's emotional reasoning appears to be along the following lines:

(Second Major Premise Rule) I must control the way others respond to the ideas that are important to me.

(Bridging Premise) If I must control the way others respond to the ideas that are important to me, then if I am not able to control the way my team members respond to these ideas, then it is awful (magnitude of nine or ten on the badness scale).

(First Major Premise Rule/Conclusion) So, if I am not able to control the way my team members respond to the ideas that are important to me, then it is awful (magnitude of nine or ten).

(Minor Report Premise) I am not able to control the way my team members respond to my ideas. In fact, they, walk away from me when I try to discuss them.

(Primary Conclusion) So it is awful (magnitude of nine or ten).

Notice how the occurrent Awfulizing in the First Major Premise Rule is a deduction from the perfectionistic demand for control in the Second Major Premise Rule. Such a deductive hierarchy is commonplace in cases of sadness or depression. The sense of powerlessness over what one deems important can be seen as "devastatingly" bad, thereby promoting and sustaining the sadness. Indeed, people who feel powerless over their own lives tend to be sad. Often, however, this sense of powerlessness is misconceived because one may be demanding to control things that are not truly in one's control in the first place. This includes the responses of others.

A GUIDING VIRTUE FOR WINSTON

Quite evidently, Winston's Awfulizing is a function of his metaphysical insecurity, in particular, about not being able to control the responses of others. Thus, an important Guiding Virtue for Winston is that of Metaphysical Security. Further, according to LBT, the Guiding Virtue of Awfulizing is that of *Courage* in the face of perceived danger. In Winston's case, the perceived threat is to his ability to maintain control over what is important to him. His perception of his team members appears to be that they are rejecting, belittling, or refusing to dignify his ideas, which, for Winston, are very important. However, just as it is unreasonable to *demand* that others respect or agree with one's ideas, it is also irrational to fear others' rejection of these ideas. Indeed, the courageous person is not afraid of opposition to even his or her deepest convictions. Such an individual may even welcome dissent as a way of strengthening those convictions.

According to LBT, the courageous person is prepared to confront adversity, neither underestimating nor overestimating it. Such a person is afraid of things to the extent that it is reasonable to fear them and, in the face of significant danger, judges the situation on its own merits. This person appropriately perceives the relativity of badness according to which things could always be worse and are never absolutely bad (not "the worst thing in the world"). Such a person tends to learn from and derive positive value from his misfortunes and is willing to take reasonable risks in order to live well.[16] In Winston's case, this means not retreating from others because they do not take some of his ideas seriously. It means his not being afraid of others' negative opinions, even of highly prized things such as his theory about brains and cyberspace.

To aspire to such virtuous stature, Winston might apply some Stoic wisdom, particularly that of Epictetus, who astutely admonished, "keep before your eyes day by day death and exile, and everything that seems terrible but most of all death; and then you will never have any abject thought, nor will you yearn for anything beyond measure."[17] Here, the relative disvalue of having one's ideas dismissed by team members can be easily identified in relationship to things much worse, such as death. Accordingly, with this added perspective, Winston can more reasonably, without "abject thought," confront such relatively minor things.

THE-WORLD-REVOLVES-AROUND-ME THINKING

While Winston did not demand that others believe or accept his ideas (he demanded only that they respect them), there are some who make such a demand on others, and, as a result, awfulize when others do not comply. LBT refers to this Cardinal Fallacy as The-World-Revolves-Around-Me (WRAM) Thinking. According to this way of thinking, if one has certain beliefs, desires, preferences, likes, dislikes, affections, passions, or values, then others must also share them too. For example, if I believe that horror movies are the best genre of movie, then you too must think so, and if you don't, then there is something wrong with you, or it is awful and unacceptable.

From an epistemic perspective (view about the nature of knowledge and truth), WRAM Thinking is the opposite of the Correspondence Theory of Truth. This theory was famously expressed by Aristotle. "To say of what is that it is not, or of what is not that it is, is false, while to say of what is that it is, and of what is not that it is not, is true."[18] In other words, beliefs that do not correspond to fact are false and beliefs that correspond to fact are true. In a manner, WRAM Thinking turns this view upside down and holds that something is false when it does not correspond to my belief and true when it does. As such the WRAM thinker sets himself up as a sort of reality guru whose beliefs, desires, values, preferences, and so forth set the standards of truth.[19] This is a very hard "philosophy" to practice in a social context. Indeed, interpersonal relationships fashioned on it could only endure under very oppressive or conflictive conditions. Typically such relationships are short-lived and lead to regret.

However, WRAM Thinkers may be willing to tolerate difference of perspective in some circumstances while not in others. Thus, there are degrees of the commission of this fallacy. In fact, because human subjectivity always starts with the "I" or ego having the experience, it is understandable how all of us can fall into this pitfall, at least sometimes. Indeed, we all perceive the world from our own subjective perspectives, so what seems right or good for oneself may be inferred to be right or good for others. But what seems right or good for oneself may not be right or good for others; and it is failure to appreciate this distinction that can and does often lead to much needless conflict in interpersonal relationships. Consider, for example, the case of Dr. Longley, a single, forty-five-year-old physician.

"Hello, Dr. Longley," I said, as Dr. Longley entered my office.

"Nice to meet you, Dr. Cohen," he said, as he extended his hand to greet mine.

"I have heard that your LBT works like a charm."

"Well, not exactly. Charms are magical. LBT works when clients put in the effort to make constructive life changes. Nothing magical about that!"

"Well, I could certainly use some constructive changes in my life."

"Tell me more about that."

"I am forty-five years old, married and divorced three times, and haven't had much luck playing the field either."

"Tell me more about that."

"All three of my wives walked out on me. They all had the same line."

"And what was that?"

"They said that I never spent enough time with them. The third one was the worst."

"Tell me about that."

"She accused me of emotional abuse. Said I neglected her because I was never home. I'm a physician, for God's sake! I save lives! Why couldn't she understand that!"

"So you think she just didn't understand your situation."

"That's correct. That was pretty much the case with everything else too."

"Tell me about that."

"Take her strange dietary habits. She was vegan."

"Vegan?"

"Yes, she ate carrot sticks and lentil beans. I told her she needed to eat meat and fish if she was to be healthy but she refused to listen to me. I'm a doctor and she wouldn't even listen. Can you imagine?"

"So you are obviously not a vegetarian."

"I like a nice steak, medium rare. I tried to get her to taste it several times and she refused. What kind of person doesn't like steak? I'm a doctor and I eat it. And she was extremely boring."

"Boring?"

"Yes, she liked to go for walks at night. Told me that it was romantic! But when I asked her to do something exciting like going rock climbing, she refused. The last time I saw her she told me that I was selfish. Imagine, me selfish! I spend my life saving lives and I'm selfish? You've got to be kidding! These gals are just too much! Imagine talking to me like that!"

Indeed, Dr. Longley's view of the world was different than that of his three wives, and undoubtedly each of his wives had world views that were different from each other. However, Dr. Longley thinks that his view is The Truth, whereas all other views are false. He is, after all, a physician, and he believes that his medical credentials make his perspectives more enlightened and true than anyone else's. But notice that, while knowledge of internal medicine can make Longley an authority about the practice of internal medicine, this does not make him an authority about what foods taste good, what activities are more pleasurable, how much time to spend at home, and a host of other matters of personal preference, opinion, values, and taste. Unfortunately Dr. Longley fails to intellectually and emotionally realize this point, and, as a result, he refuses to make any changes in order to make his relationships work.

Clearly, Dr. Longley's emotional frustration stems from his demand that reality conform to his subjective perspectives over that of others. Accordingly, his emotional reasoning appears to be along the following lines:

(Secondary Major Premise Rule) Others must always agree with me.

(Bridging Premise) If others must always agree with me, then if my (former) wife does not agree with me, then she is not treating me as she must.

(First Major Premise Rule/Conclusion) So, if my wife does not agree with me, then she is not treating me as she must.

(Minor Premise Report) My wife does not agree with me—for example, she wants me to go on walks, doesn't eat beef, and expects me to spend more time with her instead of devoting it to practicing medicine.

(Primary Conclusion) So, my wife is not treating me as she must.

As tends to be true in interpersonal dysfunctions stemming from WRAM Thinking, Longley's emotion appears to be one of self-righteous indignation, the intentional object of which is Longley's wife's disagreement with him over various things; and his rating is the negative one that she is not treating him as he *must* be treated. Clearly, Longley has a sense of entitlement that others must agree with him or else they are somehow violating his rights, treating him unfairly, or in a way that they must never do. For, after all, he has set himself up as the reality doctor to whom all others must conform. It is this demanding sense of reality entitlement that has led Longley down a lifelong road of unsuccessful personal relationships.

The Secondary Major Premise Rule of Longley's emotional reasoning—that others must always agree with him—is the source of this demanding sense of entitlement from which he deduces the Primary Conclusion that his wife is not treating him as she must. Such a demanding conclusion closes off the lines of interpersonal communication because, as such, he thinks his wife is violating his right to be recognized as the bearer of truth.

Inasmuch as the basic premise from which such self-righteous indignation stems is a "must," WRAM Thinking can be regarded as a species of Demanding Perfection. Thus, like all forms of Demanding Perfection, this fallacy turns a preference into an unrealistic requirement. This inference, "I *prefer* that others agree with me, therefore they *must*," is a *non sequitur*, whose refutation is the veritable fact that others do not always agree with you. Indeed, if it were true that people *must* agree with you, then no one would ever, in fact, disagree with you. But the latter is plainly false to fact.

Such an unrealistic demand for agreement interferes with a person's ability to understand where others are coming from. If I think that I am always right, I will not be motivated to look into anyone else's views. Since I am right and others, who disagree with me, are wrong, I summarily dismiss their views and therefore never try to see the truth in what they are saying. Such closed-mindedness tends to make WRAM Thinkers very *un*-empathetic. Accordingly, the Guiding Virtue of WRAM Thinking, which counteracts it, is Empathy.

A GUIDING VIRTUE FOR DR. LONGLEY: EMPATHY

If Dr. Longley is to transcend his own ego-centered universe and become open to others' points of view, then he needs to try to connect (cognitively, emotionally, and spiritually) with others' subjectivity. However, in order to connect in these ways with another's subjectivity, the Doctor will need to give up the self-defeating idea that only his own values, interests, preferences, and beliefs carry import and validity. He will accordingly need to work at bracketing this idea and push himself to try to see the truth in what others are saying, even if their views do not comply with his own. Indeed, as long as he approaches the perspectives of others with incredulity and a desire to discredit them, he will not be able to "connect" with the subjective worlds of others to gain an understanding. This does not mean that he need, in the end, always agree with such different or opposing perspectives; for there is a difference between understanding where another is coming from and accepting it. The former, not the latter, is requisite to empathizing with another.

Here, Cartesian doubt is not likely to advance the virtue of empathy, for while you are in a state of doubting what another is saying, you are separating or detaching yourself from the other. Philosophically, Empathy is nicely aligned with philosophies that promote tolerance for alternative perspectives and styles of living. For example, John Stuart Mill's treatise on liberty emphasizes freedom of expression:

> As it is useful that while mankind are imperfect there should be different opinions, so is it that there should be different experiments of living; that free scope should be given to varieties of character, short of injury to others; and that the worth of different modes of life should be proved practically, when anyone thinks fit to try them. . . . Where, not the person's own character, but the traditions or customs of other people are the rule of conduct, there is wanting one of the principal ingredients of human happiness, and quite the chief ingredient of individual and social progress.[20]

So Longley's insistence on his own mode of living and thinking, to the exclusion of others', crushes the very fabric of human happiness and leaves in its stead a flat and dead conformity. Longley's WRAM thinking is therefore self-defeating because his oppressive reality regimen preempts the happy coexistence with others. As he should have learned through past experience, neither he nor his intimate relations can live happily, under one roof, when one of the "principle ingredients of human happiness," and of "individual and social progress," is lacking, namely the freedom and diversity of self-expression.

Empathy, as a virtue, is not to be confused with a weepy feeling for others. It is not devoid of cognitive import. Thus, the more one knows about a person's life situation, the better situated one is to empathize with the person. This means that *listening* is an important part of being able to empathize. Dr. Longley's WRAM thinking has, unfortunately, prevented him from listening intently to the stories of his intimate relations because he has assumed from the start that they have nothing meaningful and important to add. This has, in turn, prevented him from understanding their perspectives.

Psychologist Carl Rogers has defined empathy from a therapeutic perspective as "a moment-to-moment sensitivity that is in the 'here and now,' the immediate present. It is a sensing of the client's inner world of private personal meanings 'as if' it were the therapist's own, but without ever losing the 'as if' quality."[21] According to Rogers, the therapist's ability to key into this subjective set of private and personal meanings of another is a primary vehicle of constructive, forward-moving change. But, more generally, it is for Rogers also a condition for the thriving of interpersonal relationships.[22] Indeed, if Longley had been able to so key into his former wives' subjective worlds in this manner, and express to them this understanding, the probability that he would have had functional interpersonal relationships with them would have been substantially increased.

This does not mean that one's own personal subjective meanings and values are irrelevant to empathetic understanding. Indeed, empathetic understanding can also be heightened through the sharing of subjective meanings and values. For example, Longley may have had experiences that have bearing on the way his former wife is feeling. Indeed, Longley, like the rest of us humans, have had a diversity of overlapping human experiences. Thus, we all know what it is like to be in emotional or physical pain. We have all been subject to unfair treatment at one point or another in our lives. We all eventually experience the death of loved ones. We know what it is like to experience hardships of one form or another. Clearly, by sharing one's own experiences as relevant to what the other is experiencing, the empathetic resonance can be augmented and its unifying value increased.[23] Indeed, it is precisely the ability of empathy to unify and bring people together that makes its human worth of inestimable importance to the flourishing of human interpersonal relationships and happiness.

Like the other Guiding Virtues, empathy is acquired and improved through practice. Thus, Longley would need to be committed to working on his empathetic powers. This is not to say that there are not differences between individuals in their abilities to be empathetic. Nevertheless, while all WRAM thinkers may confront greater challenges in this area, all or most of us[24] are capable of improving.

And, like the other Guiding Virtues, empathy is also an Aristotelian mean between extremes of excess and deficiency. That is, one can get too close to the subjective worlds of others as well as too far. This is what Rogers means when he says that empathetic understanding involves sensing the subjective world of the other "as if" it were one's own "but without ever losing the 'as if' quality." Clearly, being empathetic does not mean losing oneself in the subjective world of the other. For example, Longley is not expected to experience the same exhilarating passion for going on "romantic walks" as his former wife; or to feel similarly disposed to vegetarian meals. Nevertheless, Longley does know what it is like to enjoy an activity (like rock climbing); and he knows how it feels to eat foods he likes. Thus, he can resonate with her subjective world without exactly being in it. He is still, after all, an individual, with different preferences. He is not her and she is not him. But they can still share and be brought together through this deep interpersonal *inter*-subjective relating. On the other hand, loss of the "as if" quality would be tantamount to losing of one's own individuality. This would be precisely what Longley expected of his wives, and probably why they divorced him.

From a therapeutic or helping perspective, maintaining the right distance (neither too close nor too far) can be edifying. In fact, as you will see in chapter 5, the effective LBT practitioner also needs to exhibit Empathy if the client is to open up and disclose to the practitioner. In particular, as you will see, empathetic listening and reflection can help the client to elicit and clarify her intentional object, which comprises the minor premise report of the client's emotional reasoning.

Eliciting the minor premise report is an essential aspect of the LBT process. This is because, like the major premise rule, this report can also contain self-defeating fallacies. Accordingly, the next chapter will examine further Cardinal Fallacies that frequently occur in the minor premise report of people's emotional reasoning.

NOTES

1. Elliot D. Cohen, *Caution: Faulty Thinking Can Be Harmful to Your Happiness* (Fort Pierce, FL: Trace-Wilco, Inc., 1994).

2. See, for example, Elliot D. Cohen, "Critical Thinking Beyond the Academy: Using Interactive Software to Help Students Cope with Problems of Living," *The Successful Professor*, Spring 2002; "Is Perfectionism a Mental Disorder," *International Journal of Applied Philosophy*, Vol. 26.2, Fall 2012; K. Robert Bridges and Richard J. Harnish, "Role of irrational beliefs in depression and anxiety: a review," *Health*, Vol. 2, No. 8 (2010).

3. Elliot D. Cohen, *The Dutiful Worrier: How to Stop Compulsive Worry without Feeling Guilty* (Oakland, CA: New Harbinger Press, 2011).

4. Elliot D. Cohen, *The Theory and Practice of Logic-Based Therapy* (Newcastle upon the Tyne, UK: Cambridge Scholars Publishing, 2013).

5. Aristotle, *Ethics* trans. W. D. Ross (New York: Oxford University Press, 2009), Book 6, Ch. 5.

6. Immanuel Kant, *The Fundamental Principles of the Metaphysics of Morals*, Gutenberg e-book, Section 2. http://www.gutenberg.org/cache/epub/5682/pg5682-images.html.

7. Carol Gilligan, *In a Different Voice: Psychological Theory and Women's Development* (Cambridge, MA: Harvard University Press, 1982).

8. Cohen, *The Dutiful Worrier*.

9. Roger Covin, "How Stress Can Affect Athletic Performance," in *Huffington Post*, September 7, 2011. http://www.huffingtonpost.ca/roger-covin/stress-sports_b_892562.html.

10. Hara Estroff Marano, "Anxiety and Depression Together," *Psychology Today*, January 20, 2011. http://www.psychologytoday.com/articles/200310/anxiety-and-depression-together.

11. See Cohen, *Theory and Practice of Logic-Based Therapy* (Cambridge, UK: Cambridge Scholars, 2014).

12. Elliot D. Cohen, *The New Rational Therapy: Thinking Your Way to Serenity, Success, and Profound Happiness* (Lanham, MD: Rowman & Littlefield, 2007).

13. Elliot D. Cohen, "Metaphysical Insecurity," *Practical Philosophy*, January 2008. http://www.society-for-philosophy-in-practice.org/journal/pdf/9-1%2031%20 Reflection%20-%20Cohen%20-%20Metaphysical%20Insecurity.pdf.

14. Not all predictions are conditionals with if-clauses, however. For example, the prediction, "I will never amount to anything," which may have been precipitated by a prior event such as loss of a job, can support depression.

15. In a similar case, the client actually gave such an inability to exercise control over others a rating of ten.

16. Cohen, *New Rational Therapy*.

17. Epictetus, "Encheiridion," in Forrest E. Baird and Walter Kaufmann, Eds., *From Plato to Derrida*, 4th, Ed (Upper Saddle River, NJ: Prentice Hall, 2003), 261.

18. Aristotle, *Metaphysics*, trans. W. D. Ross, 1011b26. http://classics.mit.edu/ Aristotle/metaphysics.mb.txt.

19. Cohen, *New Rational Therapy*.

20. John Stuart Mill, *On Liberty*, Chapter 3. https://ebooks.adelaide.edu.au/m/mill/ john-stuart/m6450/.

21. Carl Rogers, *Dialogues*, Eds. Kirschenbaum and Henderson (London: Constable, 1990) p. 15.

22. Carl Rogers, *On Becoming a Person: A Therapist's View of Psychotherapy* (New York: Mariner Books, 1995).

23. Elliot D. Cohen, "How to be Empathetic," *Psychology Today*, May 17, 2015.

24. The exception may be those with certain forms of brain damage. Phil Newton, "Traumatic Brain Injury Leads to Problems with Emotional Processing," *Psychology Today*, January 3, 2010. https://www.psychologytoday.com/blog/mouse -man/201001/traumatic-brain-injury-leads-problems-emotional-processing.

Chapter Three

Getting the Object of
Your Emotion Straight

Fallacies of Reporting and
Their Guiding Virtues

As you have seen in the previous chapter, the emotional reasoning of ir-rational (secondary) emotions such as anger, sadness, depression, guilt, and anxiety can contain fallacies in their major premise rules. These include such Cardinal Fallacies as Dutiful Worrying, Demanding Perfection, Awfuliz-ing, Damnation, and The-World-Revolves-Around-Me (WRAM) Thinking. These fallacies might also be called evaluative or rating fallacies because they evaluate or rate particular objects of emotion. Thus they use terms such as "must," "awful," and "rotten" to rate objects of emotion (or aspects of objects of emotions) such as actions, events, and persons.

However, there is also another class of fallacies that *report* or *describe* par-ticular objects of emotion. Logic-Based Therapy refers to this second class of fallacies as "Fallacies of Reporting." These fallacies make empirical claims, that is, claims that can be confirmed or disconfirmed empirically—through inductive inference or sense perception. These fallacies are typically con-tained in the minor premise report of emotional reasoning, which accordingly reports or describes the object of emotion.

For example, what if Sally angrily concluded that John was a rotten person because he cheated on her, then her emotional reasoning would include the minor premise report that John cheated on her. This would be an empirical claim inasmuch as it could either be confirmed or denied by adducing evi-dence, gleaned from sense perception, for or against John having cheated on Sally. For example, John having lipstick on his collar might be evidence of John's having cheated on Sally. However, what if the lipstick on John's collar was the same color worn by Sally? And what if Sally had no other reason to suspect that John was cheating on her? In such a case, we could speak of a fallacy of reporting in the minor premise rule of Sally's emotional reasoning.

LBT distinguishes between three general kinds of fallacies of reporting. They are: (1) Oversimplifying Reality, (2) Distorting Probabilities, and (3) Blind Conjecture. This chapter considers each in its turn.

1. OVERSIMPLIFYING REALITY

There are at least three ways to oversimplify reality: Overgeneralizing, Pigeon-Holing, and Stereotyping. Often, intense, self-defeating emotions can be sustained as a result of these types of cognitive distortions. The following discussions show how this can happen.

Overgeneralizing

This fallacy arises when you draw an inference about all or most of a given class from an inadequate sampling of its members. Such an inference can and often does help to sustain sadness or depression due to a perceived loss or other negative experience. Consider the case of Jordan Gerstein, a New York stock trader:

> You know the saying, "Riding high in April, shot down in May." That's the story of my life. I was on top of the world in April. Then came May; Monday, May 4, to be exact. The market seemed stable, and then it happened. The announcement came about that med company I had put all my life savings into. They had produced a truckload of data showing that they had found a way to electronically control blood sugar, making daily self-monitoring for diabetics a thing of the past. No more meds; no more needles; no more meters; no more insulin treatments: just a tiny transceiver injected under the skin on an outpatient basis, and a reasonable service fee for electromagnetically monitoring and stimulating the body to regulate blood sugar on its own. I had everything riding on this tech stock. Then that bloody headline came out from under a rock and the shit hit the fan: "Company Falsifies Data." These were words that would live in infamy. They were the words that ended my life. Everything I had worked for—money to do and go wherever I wanted, an early retirement, a new house, new car, and a new lease on life—all gone in an instant. All my savings, every last dollar, gone! Now I have nothing whatsoever left to live for. I might as well be dead!

Mr. Gerstein's own words—"*everything* I had worked for," "*nothing whatsoever* left to live for"—mark out the Overgeneralizing inferences that feed his deep dark suicidal depression. In saying that he has lost "everything" he worked for, he is denying that there is anything else besides money to which he has devoted his time and effort. In saying that there is "nothing whatsoever" left for him to live for, he is saying that there is nothing left in his life that could give meaning and purpose to his life. Accordingly, his fallacy becomes quite blatant when we learn that Mr. Gerstein has a wife and two adult children along with four grandchildren, all of whom love him. While Gerstein did, indeed, spend much of his life working and saving, he also spent much of his time as a devoted husband and father. So, while he has lost his money, he has not lost *everything* he has worked for; consequently it is also false that there is *nothing whatsoever* left to live for—that is, which can give meaning and purpose to his life. To make the latter claim, however, Gerstein must claim that the family to which he dedicated himself in the past can no longer provide *any* meaning or purpose to his life; and he must maintain this because he has lost his money. But this would make the value he attached to his family contingent upon his having money, which would fly in the face of his genuine, intrinsic regard for his family. Therefore, just because he has lost his money does not mean there is *nothing* left to live for.

This is not to dismiss the magnitude of Gerstein's loss. Money is not everything, but, as Aristotle himself maintained, a moderate amount of "external goods" (including money) is necessary to be happy.[1] However, this means that he and his family now have an unanticipated financial problem to address. This would involve proactive thinking about how to address it; in particular, what options are available in order to make ends meet. Such are the vicissitudes of life. Like the ocean tide, it retracts and can take back what it has brought to shore.

But Gerstein's emotions are not adjusting to the tide; for his emotional reasoning clearly supports depression, inasmuch as he damns his existence (although not necessarily himself) based on his having lost his money. This emotional reasoning appears to be as follows:

(Rule) If I have lost everything and now have nothing left to live for then I might as well be dead.

(Report) I have lost everything and now have nothing left to live for

(Conclusion) So I might as well be dead

The Major Premise Rule in Gerstein's reasoning may be quite seductive for a person who has suffered a major setback. However, its seductive force trades on the assumption that one who has lost all things that give meaning and purpose to one's life cannot find anything else to give meaning and purpose to one's life. So, for example, an athlete who has lost the use of her limbs and can no longer play her sport might believe she has nothing left to live for and might as well be dead. But there is always the possibility of finding new meanings and purposes, such as teaching others about the values inherent in sportsmanship.

As emphasized in chapter 2, even if, contrary to fact, Gerstein lost all things that presently gave meaning and purpose to his life, this would not mean he could not find new meanings and purposes. For example, he might cultivate his artistic talents or donate his time helping others who are destitute and in need of guidance. Of course, he might decide that he prefers to die than to seek out new meanings and purposes to his life. But notice that this is different than saying that he might as well be dead; for the latter assumes that there are no options left whereas he is choosing not to pursue any new avenues that may still be open to him.

As such, even if the Minor Premise Rule in the above reasoning were true, the Major Premise Rule would still commit the fallacy of Existential Damnation examined in chapter 2. But, the Minor Premise Rule is not true because it is an Overgeneralization:

> I lost my life savings.
>
> So, I have lost everything and now have nothing left to live for.

Behold the *inductive leap* by which Gerstein attempts to justify his Minor Premise Rule.[2] The inference is a "leap" because it draws a conclusion about *everything* in his life based on just *some* things. Thus, although Gerstein has lost his money, he can still have other things in his life that (continue to) give meaning and purpose to his life, such as the love of family. Unfortunately, such inductive leaps, teamed with the seductiveness of a complementary major premise rule committing Existential Damnation, are often at the root of depression.

Pigeon-Holing

This fallacy involves falsely bifurcating or "pigeon-holing" reality into two alternatives without due recognition of other possibilities. This form of Over-simplifying can also sustain depression when it supports the Minor Premise Rule of emotional reasoning. Thus, Gerstein might also have told himself that either he has his money or he has nothing left to live for. Notice that this logic would lead to the same conclusion:

1. Either I have my life savings or I have nothing left to live for
2. I lost my life savings

So I have nothing left to live for.

Here, in contrast to Overgeneralizing, the inference is *deductive*. That is, the conclusion necessarily follows. However, it is based on a false dichotomy because both alternatives in Premise (1) are false: Gerstein does not have his life savings yet he still has some things left to live for. And this is precisely the problem with Pigeon-Holing. It leads one to perceive one's possibilities in a narrow and circumscribed manner, thereby preventing one from exploring alternative possibilities or options. Often, this can lead to a debilitating sense of futility about managing one's life challenges.

Take the case of Jaspers Delano, a salesperson "stuck" in a "dead end" job:

> I have been working for "The Really Big Shoe" retail shoe store for almost a decade. Not once, in all this time, did my boss tell me I am doing a good job or how much he appreciated my dedication and my expertise in fitting shoes and dealing with some very difficult customers. I am a professional shoe salesman and I really take pride in doing a good job and it has gone unappreciated, to say the least. But that is not the only thing. My boss has not given me a raise in five years. Last week I confronted him on it and he told me that I need to be patient and that I would be getting a raise soon enough. But this is exactly what he told me last year when I asked for a raise. I have three daughters and a wife who's a stay-at-home mom, so it is all up to me to bring home the bacon; and the bills have been piling up lately with not enough coming in to pay them. Maria, my wife, has been really good about trying to cut back on expenses but we both refuse to cut back on buying healthy food, and it costs more than junk.
>
> Other salesmen with my experience in the field are getting much better salaries than me. My friend Sal works for a less prestigious outfit and he is getting much higher pay and better benefits. While the store I work in is in this swanky town mall with much better clientele, this is no consolation for the amount I get paid. We are barely living above poverty level, and it's not going to get any better unless I do something about it.
>
> I have thought about applying for a job at another store, but what if I don't get it? It's a small community and the shoe shop owners know each other. If I don't get the job, and my boss catches wind that I applied for a job at another shoe store, I am sure he will fire my ass. But if I stay at this dead-end job, then I will end up stuck here. So, no matter what I do, I'm f-ed.

Jaspers' thinking is what is commonly called "dilemma thinking." This is thinking that involves seeing things in terms of two alternatives (*di*lemma) such that no matter which one of these two options is taken the results are negative. This is Jaspers' dilemma thinking:

1. I can either remain at my present job selling shoes or try to get another job selling shoes.
2. If I remain at my present job then I won't make enough money to support my family; and if try to get another job selling shoes, then my boss will find out and fire me.
3. So I will either not make enough money to support my family or my boss will fire me.

As you can see, given Premises 1 and 2, Jaspers sets himself up to deduce the negative outlook in conclusion 3. Then, he files this negative outlook under an existentially damning rule, in the following emotional reasoning:

(Major Premise Rule) If I will either not make enough money to support my family or my boss will fire me, then I'm f-ed.

(Minor Premise Report) I will either not make enough money to support my family or my boss will fire me.

(Primary Conclusion) So, I'm f-ed.

See how Jaspers' drives his own emotional gloom and doom and sense of futility by pigeon-holing his prospects for the future under two equally gloomy forecasts—either he doesn't support his family or he gets fired (in which case he still won't support his family). So he is "f-ed" no matter what he does. But notice that this existentially damning conclusion follows only if Jaspers pigeon-holes his options as expressed in premise 1—either remaining at his present job selling shoes or trying to get another job selling shoes. That is, he takes a needlessly confining view of reality by thinking only in terms of getting another shoe sales job in his same community. What about looking for a job somewhere else? And does he need to sell shoes? Indeed, his sales experience may qualify him to sell something other than shoes. What about going back to school, perhaps at nights at the local community college, to train in another field? What if his wife got a part-time job to supplement the family earnings? Indeed there are more than just two alternatives, but it is only by pigeon-holing reality into two slots that Jaspers is able to drive himself to experience a pervasive sense of futility.

Notice also that as long as Jaspers continues to engage in his dilemma thinking, he is not likely to make any constructive changes. Instead, he will focus his energies on telling himself how he is stuck in a dead end job with no way out—damned if he does and damned if he doesn't. As such, he is likely to make his *decision by indecision*. That is, instead of doing something constructive—for example, applying for a different sort of job or going to night school—he will self-defeatingly bring about what he does not want, namely staying where he is without making any constructive advances.

Indeed, Pigeon-Holing is often associated with dilemma thinking, which quite often leads to decision by indecision. Fortunately, by avoiding this form of Oversimplifying, one can avoid such thinking along with its self-defeating consequences.[3]

Stereotyping

Still, there is another type of Oversimplifying Reality that is associated with defeating one's purposes. This is to engage in Stereotyping. While Pigeon-Holing oversimplifies reality by putting things into categories that are too narrow, Stereotyping goes to the other extreme with regard to lumping reality, especially human beings, into categories that are too broad through the use of universal (and quasi-universal) quantifiers such as "all," "every," "none," "no," and "most." "All blacks are lazy," "No white man can jump," "All Italians are in the Mafia," "All Jews are rich." How many times have you heard such crystallized portrayals of diverse groups of people? And how often have *you* used such a broad brush to paint a picture of a diverse group of individuals? The latter question is not an indictment but rather a request to fess up. For, undoubtedly, you (and I both) *have* stereotyped. Our stereotypes may and often are different, but it is beyond question that we have stereotyped to one extent or another. How do I know this? It is because Stereotyping is a human tendency.

The term "stereotype" was first used by media scholar, Walter Lippman, in his classic work, *Public Opinion*, to characterize the manner in which human beings attempt to deal with the complexity of reality and its impending risks and dangers. The term "stereotype," literally referring to a printer's stamp, was used by Lippmann to suggest the manner in which human beings go about "stamping out" or homogenizing reality as a mode of self-protection. According to Lippmann, stereotypes provide

> an ordered, more or less consistent picture of the world, to which our habits, our tastes, our capacities, our comforts and our hopes have adjusted them-selves. . . . In that world people and things have their well-known places, and do certain expected things. We feel at home there. We fit in. We are members. We know the way around. There we find the charm of the familiar, the normal, the dependable; its grooves and shapes are where we are accustomed to find them. . . . it fits as snugly as an old shoe.[4]

As such, through stereotypes, we bring order and consistency to a world with which it would be much harder to cope. This orderliness makes the world more predictable and relieves many of the anxieties of not having a preformed coping mechanism. According to Lippmann, this systematic or-dering is acquired through enculturation: "we pick out what our culture has already defined for us, and we tend to perceive that which we have picked out in the form stereotyped for us by our culture."[5] Here, then, are cultural blinders which, while making the world tidier and more approachable, also oversimplify reality. In the case of stereotyping of other human beings, it tends to conceal the distinctiveness and individuality behind a general form. Moreover, while these forms may sometimes be positive (for example, it is not a bad thing to be rich, or have rhythm), stereotypes of human beings invariably, whether they are positive or negative, insult the integrity of those to whom they apply—and we are all subjects of stereotypes to one extent or another. Thus, it is insulting, not complementary, to assume that a Chinese person is good at mathematics, just because he is Chinese.

So stereotypes are always forms of prejudgment or prejudice. As such, they prevent people from judging others on their own merit. As in the case of negative stereotypes, which abound across cultural divides, they tend to widen the cultural gaps and chill off interpersonal relationships by preventing people from getting to know each other as individuals. Employment, education, housing, and other social contexts have suffered greatly as a result of Stereotyping. Programs and laws that militate against prejudice such as affirmative action programs have successfully countered some amount of prejudice due to stereotypical thinking, but such formal mechanisms cannot be expected to counter much of the damage that is done quietly with the tacit stamp of legality. Thus, people may be treated differentially because of their race, ethnicity, religion, gender, or sexual orientation in the workplace or other cultural settings in more nuanced and subtle ways without the outward and obvious modes of discrimination, for example, making jokes behind the backs of others. And, of course, in private contexts, it is easy enough to avoid befriending others whom one views through jaundiced stereotypical eyes. The range of available legally allowable exclusionary or degrading manners of treatment that are protected by the First Amendment are quite numerous and abundantly practiced.

This is not to discount the persistent illegal acts that are still perpetrated based on Stereotyping. Consider the case of Joseph and Georgia Silva. In July 2007, on a Lake Tahoe beach, the couple attacked a thirty-eight-year-old Indian American man, Vishal Wadhwa, after calling him, his fiancée, and her cousin "terrorists," "relatives of Osama Bin Laden," and other racial slurs. Wadhwa suffered several broken bones in his face.[6] The Silvas, who mistakenly thought that these three Indians were "Iraqi, Iranian, or Middle Eastern," were motivated by hatred moved by Stereotyping:

If anyone is Iraqi, Iranian, or Middle Eastern, then he or she is a terrorist.

Wadhwa and company are Iraqis, Iranians, or Middle Eastern

So, Wadhwa and company are terrorists.

With this minor premise report in mind—that they are, all three of them, terrorists—the Silvas concluded that they were rotten, dangerous, creatures, thereby giving themselves permission to attack and harm them. Armed with stereotypes, the Silvas were patriotically attempting to avert another terrorist attack. The only problem was that Wadhwa, his fiancée, and her cousin were not terrorists; nor were they Iraqis, Iranians, or Middle Easterners. And this is precisely what is wrong with Stereotyping. In aiming at self-protection stereotyping tends to get it wrong by prejudging and lumping distinct individuals together under one rigid class designator, in this case, "terrorists." As a result, Stereotyping underwrites blind hatred and its offspring is often the perpetration of violent, unjust, and regrettable acts.

As Lippmann maintains, Stereotyping is often the result of enculturation, teaching children at a young age to classify various target groups under rigid, unflattering, or degrading categories. Thus, stereotypes are often not the result of a process of Overgeneralizing. For example, one who believes that all blacks are criminals will generally have been brought up to believe this. As a result, when a black person fits this description, one uses this coincidence to corroborate the stereotype. Lippmann explains,

> If what we are looking at corresponds successfully with what we anticipated, the stereotype is reinforced for the future, as it is in a man who knows in advance that the Japanese are cunning and has the bad luck to run across two dishonest Japanese.[7]

On the other hand, if one comes upon an individual who does not fit the preconceived stereotype, then one may be inclined to see it merely as an exception. Lippmann continues,

> If the experience contradicts the stereotype, one of two things happens. If the man is no longer plastic, or if some powerful interest makes it highly inconvenient to rearrange his stereotypes, he pooh-poohs the contradiction as an exception that proves the rule, discredits the witness, finds a flaw somewhere, and manages to forget it. But if he is still curious and open-minded, the novelty is taken into the picture, and allowed to modify it.[8]

The second case Lippmann distinguishes, wherein a person actually gives up the stereotype, happens more often when one gets to know well someone from the target group. This is why integration of schools, beginning in the 1960s, proved to be relatively successful in helping to decrease the stereotypical misconceptions held by both blacks and whites about each other. Unfortunately, because stereotypes tend to be taught at a young age, they take the form of mindsets that are resistant to contrary evidence. Indeed, empirical

evidence is to stereotypes what garlic is to a vampire. If we are predisposed
to accept beliefs only to the extent that they are supported by the evidence,
then we are likely to question and work toward relinquishing our stereotypes.
Because Logic-Based Therapy promotes evidence-based thinking, it is, by its
nature, an antidote to Stereotyping.

So, do people ever derive their stereotypes from Overgeneralizing from an
insufficient sample of individuals rather than from enculturation? After the
attacks on September 11, 2001, many people appeared to use these attacks
as a reason to think all Arab Americans were terrorists. In reality, however,
negative stereotypes of Arab Americans, as reflected in media portrayals,
existed well before the 9-11 attacks. In fact, in one study there appeared to
have been an incremental increase in such stereotypes in the years after 9-11,
which suggests that the stereotypes were reinforced by the 9-11 attacks; but it
would be contrary to this evidence to suppose that the stereotypes were themselves spawned by these attacks since they existed well before these attacks.

While it is reasonable that at least some people may have derived their
negative stereotypes of Arab Americans as a result of generalizing from the
few Arabs who committed these atrocities, the evidence appears to support
that the attacks, instead, reinforced *pre-existing* stereotypes.[9] This suggests
that people whose emotional reasoning is based on Stereotyping are most
likely to give up their stereotypes only if they are exposed to the target group.
This would involve giving individuals, whose emotional reasoning is based
on stereotyping, "homework assignments" that bring them in close proximity
with members of the target group. For example, in one service learning program offered as part of a world religions course at Indian River State College,
students are required to visit several different houses of worship, including a
mosque and a synagogue, and write a paper analyzing the experience. Many
students have reported that these visits have helped to change favorably their
impressions of religions to which they had previously little or no exposure,
save for popular stereotypes reinforced through watching certain television
shows and movies.

Still, while many—perhaps most—stereotypes are the products of enculturation and are reinforced by the popular media, there also appear to be
stereotypes that some people come to accept from their own negative experiences with a small sampling of the target group. For example, a woman
whose boyfriend broke up with her because she turned down his sexual over-
tures may come to believe that "All men are after just one thing." Of course,
she may have been exposed earlier in life to such a popular stereotype but
still did not accept it until it happened to her. In such a case, the woman may
not have held the stereotype before having the negative experience with her
former boyfriend, so she did not use the latter experience merely to prove to

herself what she thought she already knew ("See, I told you they were all like that!"). As such, one could say in such a case that the stereotype in question was a result of an overgeneralization from an insufficient sample, for it was based on a negative experience with only one man, namely her boyfriend, who seemed to her to fit the stereotype. Yet, even in such situations, it is hard to deny the role of culture in influencing the adoption of the stereotype. Indeed, in her vulnerable situation, she is then likely to cave to social pressures to adopt the stereotype as her own, even though she may have not held it prior to her negative experience with her former boyfriend.

The Guiding Virtue of Oversimplifying: Objectivity

In any event, all stereotypes, as well as all other forms of oversimplifying, involve some form of irrational bias and loss of objectivity. Thus, when Gerstein overgeneralized from loss of his money to loss of everything, he was basing his conclusion on a biased sample; and when he told himself that either he has his money or he has nothing left to live for, he failed to take into account the other things he cherished in life. When Jaspers Delano narrowed his options to remaining in his present job or seeking another shoe sales job in the same community, he failed to look objectively at the range of job options that might be open to him; and when the Silvas assumed that all Middle Easterners are terrorists, they were driven by an anti-empirical mindset. In each of these cases there was bias and loss of objectivity. Accordingly, what was needed in each case was *Objectivity*.

Objectivity, as the Guiding Virtue of Oversimplifying Reality, trumps biased judgment. It is the ability to make *un*biased judgments in practical matters. In contrast to Stereotyping, it means equitable or fair judgment. Objective people avoid global judgments of others on the basis of broad anti-empirical generalizations. They avoid the use of labels in place of empirical evidence. This would, for example, preclude calling people "terrorists" where there is no empirical evidence that they have committed any acts of terror. Objective people are especially careful about applying universal quantifiers like "all" and "none," and quasi-universal quantifiers like "most" without a representative sample from which to generalize. This means having a sample of group members that is both sufficient in number and diversity to support such a strong inference. For example, you can reasonably infer that all people are mortal because, out of the countless number of people throughout recorded history, across all geographical regions, races, creeds, and colors; male and female, alike; there has, so far, been no person encountered who hasn't eventually died. Indeed, such a generalization is inductive, which means it is still only probabilistic, and therefore it is always possible, at some future time, that a person is discovered who, like the proverbially Energizer Bunny, simply refuses to give up the ghost. Nevertheless, such a generalization is strongly supported by a representative sample, which makes it worthy of belief. In fact, from the universal law of gravity to the laws of genetic biology, all laws of nature are in the same boat—highly probable, not certain, yet worthy of belief.

Compare such scientific laws to the universal (or quasi-universal) claims captured in everyday stereotypes, and it should be evident that there is no science behind such judgments inasmuch as they are not based on representative samples. And the same can be said of any and all overgeneralizations or universal claims that are not so supported.

Objective people are accordingly scientific about what count as a credible generalization. This means that they do not accept such judgments unless they are supported by representative samples. It also means that they are realistic in the face of evidence to the contrary and reject generalizations for which there is contrary evidence. Thus, objective people avoid stereotypes inasmuch as there is evidence to falsify them—for example, many peace-loving Arab Americans who denounce terrorism.

Objective people, as scientific, are also open-minded and are, therefore, prepared to entertain the possibility that beliefs long held to be true may someday be disconfirmed or falsified by new evidence. As such, they are not dogmatic and hold no "sacred cows." For example, they do not allow their religious convictions (or lack thereof) to prevent them from proportioning their beliefs (such as in evolution) according to the evidence. The latter point is eloquently underscored by W. K. Clifford:

> If a man, holding a belief which he was taught in childhood or persuaded of afterwards, keeps down and pushes away any doubts which arise about it in his mind, purposely avoids the reading of books and the company of men that call into question or discuss it, and regards as impious those questions which cannot easily be asked without disturbing it—the life of that man is one long sin against mankind.[10]

And Clifford succinctly drives home the ideal or virtue of Objectivity thus: "it is wrong always, everywhere, and for anyone, to believe anything upon insufficient evidence."[11]

2. DISTORTING PROBABILITIES

Objective people are also disinclined to commit other reporting fallacies such as Distorting Probabilities, since this fallacy is also anti-empirical. It involves making predictions about the future that are not probable relative to the evidence at hand. There are three different varieties of this reporting fallacy: (1) "Murphy's Law," (2) Insisting on the Past; and (3) Magnifying Probabilities.

1. Murphy's Law

"If anything can go wrong, it will." This is what is popularly called a "law," one that bears the name of an aerospace engineer, Edward Murphy, who would have been insulted by the association of this fallacy with his good name. Murphy's job was to safety proof systems whose failure could result in death or serious injury. In 1949, he was testing a U.S. Air Force rocket-sled to see how much acceleration a human subject could withstand. One test involved attaching sixteen meters to the subject's body. There were two ways to attach the meters, one correct and the other not. As it happened, someone attached the meters incorrectly, and in response, Murphy said, "If there are two or more ways to do something, and one of those ways can result in a catastrophe, then someone will do it." This was the original version of Murphy's Law. A few days later, Maj. John Paul Stapp, who was the test subject, gave a press conference in which he misquoted Murphy as saying, "If something can go wrong, then it will." So came to be the infamous "Murphy's Law!"

Quite clearly, in Murphy's line of work, it makes sense to assume that something will go wrong. After all, his job was to imagine, in advance, all possible permutations that might play out over time and use of a product, and to safeguard the product against the unwanted possibilities. But most of us are not in Murphy's line of work, so it is taken grotesquely out of context when applied to everyday life. For example, you know that it is possible to be struck by lightning if you venture outside on a cloudy day. But this doesn't mean that you *will* get struck by lightning if you do venture outside. Indeed, there are many things that *can* go wrong that never actually *do* go wrong. So, if you were to curtail your activities based on the so-called Murphy's Law, then you would never do anything; for virtually everything you do has some amount of risk, even if it is a minute amount. The practical question is therefore not what can go wrong but rather what will *probably* go wrong. Consider the case of Juan Gomez:

My wife really wants to have a baby but I don't think we should try. When I was married to my first wife, we tried to have a baby and she had a miscarriage. Before then we were happy. We had friends, great sex, and a whole future to share. This all came to an end after the miscarriage. She fell apart, became depressed, and we were never the same. I know how hard this must have been for her, but it was hard for me too. We started to fight and one thing led to another. Finally, she walked out, went to live with her sister, and filed for a divorce. I was very depressed until I met my second wife-to-be, Marta. She and I really have a nice life together. But now she has this thing about having a baby. I understand how she feels. Her biological clock is ticking and she wants a bun in the oven before the oven times out. I get it. But we're really good, just the two of us. Why look for trouble. You know what they say, "If anything can go wrong, it will." That includes miscarriages! If we try it will end up just like what happened to my first marriage; and I am just not willing to go through that again.

There is little question that miscarriage is a significant risk of pregnancy, with roughly about fifteen to twenty percent of verified pregnancies miscarrying.[12] Still this is a risk that most people are prepared to take in order to have children. Ironically, if Juan were right that trying to have children is not worth the risk of miscarriage, then Juan himself would have to also agree that his parents took a risk not worth taking in trying to conceive him!

But Juan's anxiety about getting pregnant is even more specious, for he is claiming not merely a fifteen to twenty percent risk but rather a certainty or virtual certainty. Behold the words: "If anything can go wrong, *it will.*" So even a one hundred billionth of a percent chance would, according this "Law," imply that it *will* happen. Here, the implication is that everything you might try will go wrong, because, in this material world of ours, everything you might try *can* go wrong. This is a self-defeating cop out; for nothing ventured, nothing gained; and unless one is prepared to (literally) do nothing (which means cease to live, for even staying alive is doing something), one must resign oneself to taking risks of things going wrong. This is the human condition, but this doesn't mean you are doomed before you try. It is only by taking the fatalistic position that, whatever can go wrong will go wrong, that you will be left with such a self-stultifying conclusion. Message to Juan: Get pregnant. There is, *a priori*, an eighty to eighty-five percent chance that you won't miscarry. Those are reasonable odds. And if a miscarriage does happen, unfortunate as that would be, you will have the consolation of knowing that, at least, you are trying.

2. Insisting on the Past

But the unsavory road to fatalism about the future is paved with other misconceptions besides Murphy's Law. In rational judgment about the future, there is a healthy acceptance of probability rather than certainty of outcomes. Indeed, we humans have our feet anchored in the here and now, and as the now passes into the past, we can add it to our repertoire of information about the world. However, short of a time machine (not impossible given the relativity theory of space and time[13]), we are not able to catch the future in the here and now before it turns into the present and then passes into the past. So we can only make probabilistic inferences about the future, which always falls short of certainty. As David Hume so aptly surmised, "there is no probability so great as not to allow of a contrary possibility; because otherwise it would cease to be a probability, and would become a certainty."[14] And that the past can only provide us with probability, Hume was quite clear. All predictions about the future, he maintained, can never be certain, for otherwise we could not imagine their falsehoods, which, indeed, we can. So, for example, states Hume, "That the sun will not rise tomorrow is no less intelligible a proposition, and implies no more contradiction than the affirmation, that it will rise. We should in vain, therefore, attempt to demonstrate its falsehood."[15]

That the future will resemble the past is thus, according to Hume, an assumption that human beings are prone to make, even though they can't prove it. It is, he says, "derived entirely from habit, by which we are determined to expect for the future the same train of objects, to which we have been accustomed."[16] But this expectation can and is sometimes dashed, much like the chicken who expects to be fed as usual but is instead sent to the slaughter.[17] Indeed, as Hume emphasizes, it is quite natural for us humans to expect the past to define the future. But this comfort zone of expectations about the future can be a profoundly disabling habit if we turn it into a fatalistic denial of future happiness. Consider, in this regard, the case of Su Jen, a thirty-year-old librarian in Taipei.

> I have wanted to be a philosophy professor ever since I took a course in philosophy as a young undergraduate student; but I am instead a librarian. I would have loved to earn my doctorate from the university, but I have been a librarian at the public library for six years, and that is where I must stay. I am also single, and I am thirty years old too, so I expect I will always be a single librarian. It's not so bad. I make enough money to pay for food and I live at home with my parents who take very good care of me. But sometimes I am very sad because I imagine myself a professor of philosophy, and it is hopeless. I read many books in the library on philosophy and I am very knowledgeable; but I am and always will be a librarian. I must just learn to accept that this is what I am and will always be.

Su Jen's reasoning proceeds thus:

> If I have been a librarian for five years and am still single at the age of thirty, then I must (of necessity) remain a single librarian and cannot be a philosophy professor.

> I have been a librarian for five years and single at the age of thirty.

> So, I must (of necessity) remain a single librarian and cannot be a philosophy professor.

Sadly, Su Jen, in turn, uses her deduced conclusion to spearhead her emotional reasoning:

> (Major Premise Rule) If I must (of necessity) remain a single librarian and cannot be a philosophy professor then it is hopeless.

> (Minor Premise Report) I must (of necessity) remain a single librarian and cannot be a philosophy professor.

> (Conclusion) So, it is hopeless.

As you can see, Su Jen's hopelessness, as expressed in the above conclusion, stems from her Minor Premise Report. As a result she experiences remorse—a sense of futility and the hollowness of being resigned to a life she deeply regrets. She feels trapped by her past and its perceived superimposition onto her future. There is nothing she can do because it is fated. She is a cog in the machine of time that plays out a future out of her hands, out of her control. But this sense of hopelessness and loss of control over her life is a perception, or, more properly, a misperception founded on an irrational conception about the nature of reality, in particular, about possibility and necessity, potentiality and actuality. Su Jen is under the spell of the fallacy of Insisting on the Past. This is the Humean fallacy of fatalistically inferring the *necessity* of the future resembling the past. It flies in the face of Hume's admonition against assuming that the future must, *necessarily*, resemble the past. As a result, Su Jen does nothing to advance her career because she thinks she must remain a single librarian. The problem here is that she is fulfilling her own prophecy. The future is not foreclosed by her past since she can always make choices that can change both her (future) pasts and her (future) future. There is no necessity to wallow in the past, to regret her past decisions, yet do nothing to change her future. If Su Jen's future is to resemble her past, it will largely be because she will have decided that it be so. The royal route to making changes in one's future is action. By doing nothing, Su Jen does nothing to change the probabilities of the future being different. As Jean-Paul Sartre eloquently stated, "possibilities are to be reckoned with only to the point where my action comports with the ensemble of these possibilities, and no further."[18] In other words, it is not enough to want something. Possibilities do not turn into actualities unless one acts on them.

As long as Su Jen fails to act is as long as she will remain in her same place—unless something else happens to change things for better or for worse. Su Jen can return to the university to pursue graduate studies in philosophy. She can, as a result, meet new and interesting people with whom she may have things in common—such as the study of philosophy. She can take a fresh look at life and the possibilities that are open to her. She can take responsibility for who she is and becomes by defining her future self through her actions. As Sartre expresses, one's "essence" precedes one's "existence," meaning that people do not have pre-established purposes like manufactured items (for example, paper cutters) for which they have been created. Rather they create their own purposes through the existential choices that they make.[19] So, Su Jen is responsible for having defined herself as a librarian who has remained single. And she is responsible for not redefining herself according to a new plan. In not acting, Sartre would admonish, she has negatively defined herself, "as a disappointed dream, as miscarried hopes, as vain expectations."[20]

So probabilities become actualities only by acting upon them. Indeed, living is largely about taking risks in order to attain one's goals. The universe is pregnant with possibilities but they are stillborn unless brought to fruition through implementation of the choices one makes in the myriad contexts of human existence.

3. Magnifying Risks

But taking risks in order to attain one's end or purpose is a rational process that assumes rational assessment of the risks. As such, from an Aristotelian perspective, there are two extremes to avoid, underassessing risks and overassessing them. According to Aristotle, the person who underassesses the risks or dangers inherent in seeking an end or goal, or acts without due caution in taking these risks, is foolish; whereas the person who overassesses the risks, or is too afraid to act in the face of them, is cowardly. Still, the person who avoids such extremes, reasonably assesses the risks—neither underassessing nor overassessing them—and acts *on principle* with due consideration of these risks, is a courageous person. It is a mark of the courageous person, states Aristotle, "to feel and act according to the merits of the case," and to face danger "as he ought and as the rule directs."[21]

In Su Jen's case, if she is to act courageously she needs to reasonably assess the risks inherent in seeking a new career as a philosophy professor. It is possible that the pursuit might be unsuccessful. She might not succeed at getting a job at a university after investing much time and expense of attaining a doctorate in philosophy. Yet, looking at the matter from a broader perspective, the education would never be wasted, given the intrinsic value of philosophy, its utility for addressing problems of living, and the marketability of the analytic skills it teaches. Moreover, teaching philosophy is a noble profession since it aims at the happiness and well-being of others by helping them to gain valuable thinking skills and insights. Thus, fear of not realizing her dream, even if this is a significant possibility, should not deter her from trying. Indeed, not to take the risks would be cowardly; but to take them, for the sake of such a worthy end, would be courageous.

Unfortunately, many of us fail to act, or act precipitously, because we magnify the risks. And this is precisely the problem with commission of this fallacy. We subvert our own well-being through self-defeating emotional responses (such as worry, anxiety, guilt, depression, and anger) precipitated by a propensity to Magnify Risks. Take the case of Todd Steiner, an injured war veteran.

> I did two tours of combat duty in Afghanistan. It was one week before I was going to be back in the States when it happened. A land mine exploded blowing my leg off and blinding me. Two of my buddies didn't make it, so I'm supposed to be the lucky one. I have flashbacks; I wish I was the one who lost his life, not just a leg and my eyesight.
>
> I joined the service so that I could get my tuition paid on the GI Bill. I wanted to go to business school, get my MBA and eventually be a corporate CEO in a major corporation. I thought the combat duty would look good too on my resume, but now look at me! Who would ever hire a one-legged blind guy as a company CEO! Who would ever hire me for any decent job, period! They tell me I can be fitted for a prosthetic leg, but how's that really going to help. Even if I can hobble about on it, that's not going to make me see! I will be lucky if I can get a job flipping burgers. I used to be real popular with the women too; but now what woman is going to look at me. What's the point in even trying! I already know I'm screwed.

The sad plight of many combat vets fits this description. Many, like Todd, suffer from post-traumatic stress disorder (PTSD) and, as a result, develop substance abuse habits in order to cope. Many with serious injuries like Todd's become addicted to pain medication, and end up giving up on life. This is the disquieting reality. It is a harsh reality, to say the least. Anyone who discounts the challenges of putting one's life back together after going through such an ordeal is not connecting with the subjective worlds inhabited by those in Todd's situation. Still, the assessment of probabilities is a key to constructive change. In Todd's case, he has inflated the probabilities of not being able to accomplish career or personal life goals. From his perspective, he is "screwed" before he even tries so there is no point to even trying. Clearly, he is depressed about his prospects for the future. Inasmuch as he perceives himself as *already* "screwed," he experiences depression or extreme sadness. He thinks he doesn't have any real or significant chance for future happiness, and so perceives himself as existentially damned from the get-go. Such predictions of future failure are what drive his sadness. Accordingly, the following appears to be Todd's emotional reasoning:

(Major Premise Rule) If I fail to accomplish my career/life goals, then I will be screwed (there will be no point to my existence).

(Minor Premise Report) If I try to accomplish my career/life goals then I will fail—no one is likely to hire a one-legged, blind guy, and no woman is likely to be interested in me.

(Conclusion) So, if I try to accomplish my career/life goals, I will (still) be screwed.

Since, even if he tries to accomplish his career/life goals, Todd still thinks he will be screwed, he perceives himself to be screwed no matter what he does or doesn't do. This reasoning therefore supports the sense of futility that can potentially propel him into a depression. But notice also that the iffyness of the above Minor Premise Report can also promote anxiety. As long as Todd views failure as a future possibility conditional upon his trying to accomplish his goals, then he can also experience anxiety about trying. So Todd's emotional state is likely to be dually charged with depression (or at least intense sadness) as well as anxiety about his future.

However, notice that the Minor Premise Report, upon which both these emotional states rests, ignores the relative nature of probabilities themselves; for what is probable is a function of evidence, and evidence is itself subject to change as one takes further steps to make positive changes in one's life. Thus, Todd could allow himself to be fitted for a prosthetic leg. He could avail himself of a service dog. He could undergo physical therapy. He could seek counseling for his PTSD.[22] These and other changes could substantially change the probabilities of reorientation into a constructive lifestyle and thus dramatically increase his chances at accomplishing his career/life goals. This is obviously labor-intensive requisite but very few worthwhile things in life are achieved without putting in the effort. Further, it is a feature of forging life goals that they can also change as new possibilities emerge by making positive changes in one's life. So Todd might not, in the end, choose being a corporate CEO as his dream job. Instead, he might find something else quite different than he had ever envisioned. For example, he might decide to get a job in which he can help other wounded veterans like himself get back on track; and he might come to find great worth and dignity in the new life he will have forged for himself. Indeed, many of us end up doing things we never at first envisioned ourselves doing. I never imagined, when I started out as an accounting major in undergraduate school (it lasted one semester), that I would become a philosopher, no less a philosophical practitioner. But with new experiences come new discoveries about one's abilities, talents, and interests. And with these changes come new possibilities. Unfortunately, Magnifying Risks tends to blind us to the openness of the future and the many exciting avenues that we can travel down in the course of our lives. For some, in Todd's boat, this realization never takes root; and their lives become self-fulfilled prophecies of drug addictions and lives of crime to support the drug habits. But, for others like Todd, there is eventually the perception of light at the end of a dark tunnel. This way out of the darkness is illuminated through the cultivation of Foresightedness, the Guiding Virtue of Magnifying Risks.

A Guiding Virtue for Todd: Foresightedness

As Hume so aptly noted, there is no necessity about the future resembling the past, and it is in vain that we try to prove this by our past experience. For, no matter how many times we see past resemblances, we never get to confirm future ones until they too slip into the past. Still, I do think most of us would agree that some predictions about the future are more reasonable than others. For example, believing that you will win the lottery on the next purchase of a lottery ticket is wishful thinking—unless you happen to have some inside information! There are a vast set of permutations of numbers and the odds are that you won't have the lucky number. In contrast, it is more reasonable to believe that it is less risky to diversify your stocks, that is, "by not putting all your eggs in one basket." This is because it is less likely for many stocks to fall than just one or two. Again, if you have inside information that the stock market is going to crash, then that added information changes these probabilities. The person who is foresighted thus makes predictions about the future that are probable relative to the facts as known. Such a person also makes a reasonable effort to be sufficiently informed before acting on a prediction. This does not mean going to extremes, however. One extreme is demanding certainty about the future before acting, and the other is acting without due regard for the facts. The foresighted person chooses the mean between these extremes and is not afraid to take reasonable risks. Such a person is so able to cope effectively in this material universe, where there are degrees of probability, not certainty.

"Probability" here means a measure of how reasonable a belief is. While a probability calculus is possible in some cases, such as computing the probability of getting heads on the toss of a two-sided coin, in the mainstream of life there is often no mathematical means of calculating reasonability of belief. This is especially true in predicting human behavior, which is a lot less predictable than the weather! How likely is it that the editor of your blindly reviewed manuscript will accept it for publication? How likely is that your boss will give you a raise—or let you go? When will you meet your mate? Will your landlord raise your rent for next near? These and many other questions about the future, where there is human intervention, are not easily answered with precision. Nevertheless, the foresighted person can make reasonable predictions based on past performance of the individuals in question; knowledge about what often motivates human beings; and other relevant information. They are also cognizant of alternative possibilities in case things fall through, for example, of getting a job in a new line of work in case one's present job dead ends.

Foresighted people are also selective in their acceptance of the testimony of others as a basis for making predictions. They value expert testimony to the random and uninformed (often misinformed) assurances of the lay person. So, for the foresighted person, the lay medical advice of a friend does not count as much (if at all) in comparison to that of a physician. But, even here, such a person is privy to qualifications of the individual physician. Is she a board certified cardiologist? How often has she performed the procedure? What is her track record? Where was she trained? How long has she been practicing? If the stakes are quite high (for example, the procedure in question is invasive surgery), then a second opinion (or third) from another well qualified expert tends to be better than one. As Sartre would admonish, in the end you must decide and act on it. Procrastination is not generally a good idea when the stakes are high—and when time is of the essence; nor is impetuosity. The foresighted person is good at aiming at the mean between these extremes.

This mean, as Aristotle notes, "is relative to us,"[23] which means that one size does not fit all, and what may be reasonable belief in one context may not be in another. So, what worked for you might not work for me, and conversely. Thus, penicillin might be the drug of choice to eradicate streptococcus, but it may not be much good for you if you are allergic to it. Again, the foresighted person considers the reasonability of a prediction within the context of further relevant information.

Judgments of probability are, as such, defeasible. A prediction p is probable relative to e but it may not be probable relative to the larger set of evidence e & e'. For example, it may be probable that the nanny, who has applied for the job for which you advertised, is trustworthy based on the several references she has produced. But if a background check subsequently turns up that she has been arrested twice recently for drunk and disorderly conduct (or worse), then this further information would lower the probability that she is a good risk to watch your little ones. Foresighted people are attuned to the defeasibility of predictions.

As with all Guiding Virtues, Foresightedness is not cultivated in a day. It is a habit strengthened by practice. As Aristotle eloquently expressed, "For one swallow does not make a summer, nor does one day; and so too one day, or a short time, does not make a man blessed and happy."[24] And this is true of Foresightedness and the other Guiding Virtues, which are acquired and improved by practice over time.

In Todd's case, the antidote to his Magnifying Risks is to strive toward Foresightedness in fashioning his plan of life. This means working diligently, both cognitively and behaviorally, in changing the probabilities of success. He has disabilities, but they are in walking and seeing, which can significantly be compensated. Indeed, I have often noticed how some of us with serious physical disabilities have worked harder and more ambitiously for their life goals than many of us who do not have such disabilities. In particular, I have found that some of my most serious-minded and avid students have had serious physical disabilities. The challenge to overcome their disabilities has often incentivized them to strive to achieve their life goals. They have often exercised determination coupled with foresight in a manner that reflected a cognitive and emotional maturity well beyond their chronological age. These are the unsung heroes to be emulated. They even (or surpass) the playing field by going the additional miles to make changes that enable and maximize their potentials.

Let me offer one example: the case of Jerry. Here was a young man with a rare degenerative neuromuscular disease. He was quadriplegic with limited motion in both of his hands when I had him as a student. This student never missed a class. He refused to accept a note taker and managed to take his own notes with the aid of braces on his hands. He participated regularly in class, and performed among the highest in the class on his examinations. His goal was to become a human services professional. He graduated undergraduate school with honors and went on for his master's degree. While in graduate school he passed away. I often think about him and how he never lost perspective. I believe he knew well what the probabilities were of finishing his degree. As I reflect, I realize that it was the activity of striving to meet his goal that was, in the end, what he valued the most. He lived the remainder of his life doing just what he wanted to do: learning and growing, intellectually and emotionally. He had the foresight to realize that this goal was within his reach by making a concerted, single-minded effort. As a result, he altered the probabilities of reaching his goal, which he attained, magnificently so. For those like Todd, who are understandably disillusioned by their plights, there is still potential for significant change through cultivation of the virtuous habit of foresight, the priming and compensating of their capacities, and the perseverance and courage to succeed. This is, again, not to disregard the magnitude of the behavioral and emotional challenges inherent in such a feat. Still, as evident in the case of Jerry, through striving to overcome these obstacles, there can be an immensely gratifying sense of purpose.

3. BLIND CONJECTURE

Clearly, such a sense of purpose, and the potential for success in confronting the obstacles and vicissitudes of life, is guided largely by a rational appreciation and openness to future possibilities. But this rational grasp regarding the future should not be at the expense of forgetting about how one's perception of *current*, here and now, events can affect the quality of one's life. Indeed, most human beings spend considerable amounts of time anguishing about what has *already* happened. Often, this anguish stems from anti-empirical causal judgments, contrary-to-fact claims, and unsupportable explanations regarding these events. "I didn't do well on the exam because I'm stupid," "I had bad luck because I'm jinxed," "If I had been better in bed, he wouldn't have cheated on me." Such claims are speculative and lack adequate empirical evidence. Thus, you may have not done well on the test because you didn't study effectively for the exam; your partner may have cheated on you regardless of your sexual performance for reasons entirely unrelated to it; your bad luck may have been mere happenstance, not the work of some unverifiable, diabolical force. The *Fallacy of Blind Conjecture* involves the construction of such unscientific, anti-empirical causal judgments, contrary-to-fact conditionals, and explanations. It can take its toll on your happiness by supporting self-defeating emotions such as depression, extreme sadness, intense anger, and self-deprecating guilt. In the following, I will examine some popular offenders: *post hoc* reasoning, self-blaming contrary to fact conditionals, and unsupported explanation.

1. *Post Hoc* Reasoning

Blind Conjecture is often committed in the context of making causal judgments, that is, judgments about the causes and effects of things. Causation is, inescapably, part of the human condition. We invariably see the world of space-time objects in terms of causes and their effects.[25] Indeed, you are not likely to live a single day without making causal judgments. Driving a car, you stop short to avoid a collision; avoid foods that might upset your stomach; lock your doors to prevent intruders; turn up the heat when you are cold; seek shelter when it rains; use sunscreen to prevent skin cancer; and so on. Causation permeates every aspect of our material existence. Good causal judgments can mean the difference between life and death, happiness and despair. One very common form of *bad* causal judgment is that known by the Latin phrase, *post hoc ergo propter hoc*.

The Latin phrase above means "after this because of this." In other words, you see one thing followed by another and designate the first the cause of the other. But this can lead to some very unfortunate conclusions about what causes what. This manner of establishing causal connections is very prevalent in the case of bad experiences. For example, about twenty-five years ago I was in a serious accident when a small Honda motorcycle collided with my car, a sporty, light blue Cougar. I was listening to my radio at the time and the song

"You Can't Hurry Love" by the Supremes was playing. I approached a busy intersection while the light was still green and was making a left turn as the light turned to amber and then to red. The cyclist attempted to get through the light and broadsided me on the passenger side. I can recall the cyclist flying up in the air and falling to the ground, getting up for a bit, and then laying back down. All this time, "You Can't Hurry Love" played in the background. My car was totaled by the motorcycle. The good news was that the cyclist broke some ribs but was okay. He was given a citation for going through a light on red. I was physically okay but it took me a while to feel secure on the road again. The residue of the experience was having built up a causal connection between "You Can't Hurry Love" and the accident. As a result, whenever I heard the song play while driving, I anticipated being struck by another vehicle. The share trauma of the event had created a rather stubborn cause and effect connection between the two events—the playing of the song and the collision. Time has softened the connection and I no longer expect a collision when I hear the song, although it does still remind me of the accident.

Overcoming *post hoc* obstructions to happiness is largely a cognitive behavioral process of reframing causal reality. For example, I often reminded myself that the mere sequence of events, the particular song playing in the background and the motorcycle broadsiding me, cannot establish a causal relationship.[26] If it did, then I might as well have focused on some other condition present at the time, designating it as the cause. For example, at the time I was wearing a certain shirt. Well maybe that was the cause of the accident! Clearly not! The rest of the reframing process involved engaging in the problematic behavior, namely listening to "You Can't Hurry Love" while driving. Consequently, I refused to turn off the song when it came on the radio while I was driving. As a result, I was able to weaken the tendency to draw the inference. In any event, it did not prevent me from continuing to listen to the song while I drove (although I must confess that I enjoyed it more before the accident).

Of course, *post hoc* reasoning can have a lot worse consequences than not enjoying a song. Consider the case of Jenny Cooper, who blamed herself for the death of her mother. Jenny was a senior in high school at the time of her mother's death. One school day, instead of going to history class, she decided to go out for pizza with a group of friends. When she came home, she received the tragic news. Her mother was killed when a drunk driver blew a stop sign and collided with her car's driver side. Jenny connected not going to class with her mother's death even though the two events had nothing to do with one another. Somehow, because she *should* have been in class, she was responsible for the fatal accident. Jenny is now in her thirties and she still feels the guilt swell up inside of her when she thinks about the last time she saw her mom. "I let her down. She thought I was in school, and instead

I was out getting pizza. And then she was gone forever. I just keep thinking that she would be alive today if I had been in school where I was supposed to be."[27] And while the two events—cutting class and her mother's fatal accident—were not causally related, the one followed the other. This made it *feel* to Jenny like they were connected as cause and effect. In reality, her guilt about cutting class made this event stand out from all other events that preceded the accident. After all, she was also doing other things before the accident—-drinking water, talking on the phone, combing her hair, laughing, etc. However, feeling guilty about having cut class does not mean that cutting class was what caused the accident. This was plainly irrational. And while she eventually realized this, she was never able to fully get beyond her cognitive dissonance. So, as you can see, such Blind Conjecture, about causality can stubbornly take its toll on one's happiness.

2. Self-Blaming Contrary to Fact Conditionals

Effectively, Jenny impeded her own happiness by *blaming* herself for her mother's death. Such self-defeating use of causal judgment to blame oneself, or others,[28] for untoward events, abounds in ordinary life. The making of causal judgments to cast blame and hold others responsible is also commonplace in legal contexts.[29] Inasmuch as people's welfare, even their freedom, may hang in the balance, it is important that such judgments avoid commonplace pitfalls. One context in which fallacious causal judgment can be especially pernicious is in the context of domestic abuse. For example, meet thirty-six-year-old Brittney Jankowsky:

> Jim is really a good man. He gets angry sometimes because I don't always act sweet the way he wants me to be. It's my fault and I feel like I have let him down. When he drinks he can get really violent, though. Yesterday he beat me so hard that I had to go to the emergency room for stitches over my left eye. I told them that the door slammed in my face, but I don't think they believed me. I felt so uncomfortable. I don't want anyone to get the wrong idea about Jim. He takes good care of me most of the time. I'd be out on the street if it weren't for him. Today, he even brought me flowers when he came home from work. I know he's really sorry for what happened, but I am no angel. Before he hit me, I said something really unkind to him. I called him a drunk. He has a good job, and everybody loves him. It really wasn't right of me to say such a terrible thing to him. If I had kept my big mouth shut this wouldn't have happened. So I guess I got what I deserved!

Looking at the case of Brittney from an objective perspective, it is easy for most of us to admonish her to "dump this guy." Unfortunately, such advice would fail to recognize the dynamics of domestic abuse and the complex set of beliefs that often keep someone like Brittney attached to someone who physically and/or emotionally abuses her. Her case is classic in that it exemplifies a cycle of abuse involving the actual abuse (the beating); ritual and undoing (giving flowers, telling her how much he loves her); walking on eggshells (where the honeymoon is over); and, once again, an act of abuse perpetrated.

Here, Brittney acquiesces in the cycle of abuse by being a willing subject, having what social workers commonly call a "victim mentality." She allows her abuse to continue because she is able to blame herself for what Jim does to her. This is because she has invented a set of causal excuses, a reason that lets Jim off the hot seat and places the blame largely on her. According to the causal narrative Brittney has constructed, Jim's ordinary powers of self-control are compromised when he drinks. In such cases, he succumbs to his anger toward her. And what has she done to deserve his wrath? Well, she sometimes says "unkind" things to him—like calling him "a drunk," she is not as "sweet" as she should be to him, and so on. Thus Brittney rescues Jim from taking responsibility by blaming herself.

So, Brittney experiences self-deprecating guilt about having provoked Jim into beating her, which enables her to remain in the dysfunctional relationship and cycle of abuse. However, this causal judgment, which is the object of her guilt, is based on a *contrary-to-fact conditional*. The latter is a statement about what could or would have happened if things had been otherwise.

In practical life contexts, contrary-to-fact conditional statements (also known as counterfactuals) are often speculative and fallacious. This is because they make claims about things that did not actually happen. In doing so, they are prone to make assumptions that are questionable. In cases of abuse such as Brittney's, the abuse victim blames herself because she thinks that the abuse would not have happened if she had done something different.

In particular, Brittney's stated contrary-to-fact conditional is, "If I had kept my big mouth shut, this wouldn't have happened." Notice that she is *assuming* that, contrary to fact, Jim would not have beaten her if she didn't call him a drunk. As such, she is, in effect, *arguing* that, given the assumption that she does not call Jim a drunk, the conclusion follows that he does not beat her:

(Assumption 1) I do not call Jim a drunk.

(Conclusion) So, Jim does not beat me.

However, notice that the conclusion in the above argument does not follow given the assumed premise (Assumption 1) unless another assumed premise is added, namely, Jim does not find some other reason to beat her:

(Assumption 1) I do not call Jim a drunk.

(Assumption 2) Jim does not find some other reason to beat me.

(Conclusion) So, Jim does not beat me.

Clearly, Assumption 2 is needed for the conclusion to follow. However, this assumption is purely speculative because Brittney has no rational basis to believe that it is true. What if Jim thought that Brittney was just not being "sweet" enough? As you can see, her contrary-to-fact reasoning is based on speculation and is, as such, irrational.

There is considerable value in being able to refute such irrational contrary-to-fact conditionals in the above manner (by setting them up as arguments and then checking the veracity of their assumed premises). This is because these statements can and often do serve as minor premise reports in people's emotional reasoning. For instance, the following appears to be Brittney's emotional reasoning, by which she continues to blame herself for the abuse:

(Major Premise Rule) If Jim would not have beaten me if I had kept my big mouth shut, then I got what I deserved.

(Minor Premise Report) If I had kept my big mouth shut, this wouldn't have happened.

(Conclusion) So, I got what I deserved.

In the above emotional reasoning, the contrary-to-fact claim in the Minor Premise Report supports Brittney's self-deprecating guilt. Thus, its refutation can be instrumental in helping her to work through this guilt.

It can also be helpful to weaken contrary-to-fact claims by substituting "might" or "might not" for "would" or "would not." Thus, it is less speculative for Brittney to say "If I had kept my big mouth shut, this *might not* have happened." But then again it *might still* have happened! So, by substituting the word "might," you can deflate somewhat the self-blaming force of such a contrary-to-fact claim.[30]

"If I had invested in that stock, I would be a rich man today," "If you weren't talking to me, I wouldn't have gotten into that accident," "If I didn't eat in that Italian restaurant, I wouldn't have gotten sick," "If you didn't complain so much, I wouldn't be so volatile," "If the professor was a good teacher, then I wouldn't be failing this course." Indeed, contrary-to-fact conditionals like these abound in ordinary parlance. And they are typically stated in a matter of fact voice, without using "might" (or "might not"). LBT emphasizes the importance of identifying and refuting the Fallacy of Blind Conjecture inherent in such claims so that their self-destructive behavioral and emotional tendencies can be addressed.

3. Unsupported Explanation

Another prevalent version of this fallacy is that of Unsupported Explanation, which involves attempting to explain a set of facts in an unscientific manner. This may mean that there are not enough convergent or confirming facts (for example, that you have weakened immunity does not adequately confirm that you have HIV); there are divergent or disconfirming facts (that the earth is 5,000 years old is inconsistent with carbon dating results of bones and other archeological findings); or the explanation is "magical" and therefore incapable of being confirmed or disconfirmed by the facts (for example, that the devil made you do it).[31]

A little logic about explanations can be helpful. An explanation is generally invoked when a set of facts is bewildering. You want to know how this could be! So you start to "hypothesize," that is, come up with reasons for why what is bewildering is actually true. Say you park your car at a large shopping mall, you do your shopping, and, after you are all shopped out, you exit the mall through the east exit to return to your car. But your car is not to be found! Wandering up and down the long parking lot isles, you still can't find it. This is a situation that many of us sometimes find ourselves in. "Where is it!?" you say, with exasperation. Then you start to hypothesize about what's going on. "Someone stole my car! Now what am I going to do. I need that car. I loved that car!" This would be a fine example of Unsupported Explanation because you do not yet have enough confirmation of this explanation. Why? It is because there are lots of other explanations that could equally as well explain why you are unable to find your car in the east parking lot. Maybe you didn't park in the east lot; maybe you parked in the west lot and simply exited the mall through the wrong exit. Maybe you parked illegally and it was towed; maybe you are looking in the wrong part of the east lot; maybe you forgot what your car looks like; maybe you forgot that you took the Ford Mustang and are looking for the Volkswagen Jetta. Maybe your car drove away autonomously.

Obviously, some of these explanations are less likely than others. In the not so distant future it may become commonplace for parked cars to leave on their own, but at present cars do not have this capacity, so the explanation that it drove away on its own is not very likely. Still this explanation is a logical possibility. This is because the set of facts to be explained can be inferred from it. That is, if the car drove away on its own, then it would no longer be parked where you left it.

In the end, the best explanation will be the one that has the most predictive and explanatory power. That is, it explains the most facts, and you are able to confirm other facts that can be inferred from it. For example, if you parked in the west parking lot, instead of the east, then if you went back into the mall and exited from the west exit, you would find your car in the west parking lot. So, you test your hypothesis by seeing if the prediction inferred from it holds true. Problem solved!

Oftentimes, people focus on the explanation that is the worst case scenario: someone stole my car! As a result, they needlessly upset themselves; for just because an explanation is the least desired does not mean that it is the most probable. The probability of an explanation is a function of its predictive and explanatory power, not its desirability or undesirability. Unfortunately, people often confuse probability with desirability and tend to think the worst instead of exploring alternative possibilities, focusing on the most probable explanation.

Magical explanations are also quite commonplace among people. A magical explanation is anti-empirical: it can neither be confirmed nor disconfirmed because there is no evidence that could count in favor or against it. As a result, such explanations are held as mindsets, that is, regardless of the evidence adduced for competing explanations. Such is the case of Edgar Casper, a forty-two-year-old, unemployed heavy drinker:

> The odds are stacked against me. I can't hold down a job. I have health problems. No one wants to be my friend. I have no one special in my life. I'm just one of those hard luck people: born to lose. I had a great job, and I thought that I was on the right track; but then, wouldn't you know it, I got the ax. I was just set up to be knocked down. It was some kind of cruel joke, but I'm not laughing. I don't know why life has treated me so badly but it has, and now I'm ready to throw in the towel. What's the use in trying! I will just get knocked down again.

Like Edgar, all or most of us have streaks of bad luck. Things go poorly and you ask, "Why me?" as though you were being singled out for cruel and unusual treatment. But who or what, then, is controlling the show: Life, Nature, Lady Luck, Fate, or Destiny? Notice how transparently these and similar constructs can be blamed for the bad luck. Since they are abstractions that cannot be disconfirmed, they can be invoked as explanations without running the risk of being proved wrong. For how can one prove that Life didn't play a bad joke on you? In reality, such explanations are no explanations at all because no evidence can count for or against them. Instead, words like "Life," "Nature," "Lady Luck," "Fate" and "Destiny" are abstractions, not persons of sorts with magical powers. Unfortunately, linguistic confusions like this can be the source of much human misery and suffering. This is because they can help to sustain untenable life styles instead of seeking out more realistic, empirically testable hypotheses. Explanations like "This must have been the work of the Devil" follow suit. Such religious or quasi-religious conceptions as the Devil or other representatives of evil are not verifiable and are therefore not proper candidates for rational hypothesizing. In reality, the Devil, along with Freddy Krueger, will do you in only if you believe in him!

Paradoxically, Edgar is downcast about nothing. That is, the intentional object of his melancholia does not exist; for there is no verifiable life force that is pursuing him with a vengeance. Yet it is this nonexistent object that pilots his gloom. Edgar's emotional reasoning is along the following lines:

(Major Premise Rule) If life is plotting against me then I might as well give up on life (not try to succeed at life pursuits).

(Minor Premise Rule) Life is plotting against me.

(Conclusion) So, I might as well give up on life.

Edgar's mistake lies in believing in the malicious power reported in his Minor Premise Rule. Its refutation is that there is no way of confirming or disconfirming it. Instead of explaining his bad luck by appealing to such an anti-empirical, unscientific hypothesis, he can examine his life with an eye toward making constructive changes in it. Maybe his employability problems were due to his heavy drinking. Maybe it was due to cutbacks and a bad economy. Maybe it was his attitude. Maybe his problem with maintaining interpersonal relationships was related to similar attitudinal issues. Maybe he was bleak and cynical. Maybe his health problems have been exasperated by lifestyle, for example, excessive alcohol consumption. Maybe a combination of these explanations is the most likely explanation. Indeed, by open-mindedly considering probable explanations for his life problems, he can then take suitable steps to test them out; for example, change his attitude, pursue a new line of work that has a greater market demand, seek help for his heavy drinking, etc.

A Guiding Virtue for Edgar: Scientificity

In short, what Edgar (and others who tend to commit the various forms of Blind Conjecture) can benefit from is a new goal for keeping on the straight and narrow: *Scientificity*. This is the ability to apply a critical, scientific method in accounting for present, here and now, realities. A scientific person avoids superstition, magical thinking, and other forms of unscientific thinking, and relies, instead, on empirical evidence.

There is a popular misconception that scientific people cannot be religious. However, belief in the existence of God can be quite compatible with science as long as it does not deny the evidence of science. Thus, that the earth is 5,000 years old is incompatible with science. However, that God created the universe through an evolutionary process is not necessarily inconsistent with science.[32] Believing that diseases like AIDS are due to the wrath of God brought down on gays and other sinners is magical thinking that can neither be proved nor disproved by empirical evidence. It is not different in kind from claiming that there are invisible, undetectable gremlins in your gas tank that account for your quickly depleting gas supply. Looking for the causes of diseases through empirical means, no less than looking for a leak in your tank or other mechanical failure, are rational ways to address questions of causality. Religious fanatics who substitute superstition, fear, or blind hate for scientific inquiry are consistent neither with the spirit of religion, nor with that of science. Religious institutions are purposed to foster values such as love and peace, while science seeks to improve human life through the control of nature. Fanatic or dogmatic adherence to anti-empirical claims does neither.

Conversely, scientificity does not mean that science is the only reasonable perspective one can take. This absolutism is inconsistent with the idea of tolerance, which is an important part of Scientificity. By its nature, science is open-minded, open to the possibility of alternative explanations. Secular absolutism whereby one denounces religious perspectives is inconsistent with the spirit of science as tolerant of alternative possibilities. Instead, science and religion can and should work together. So, prayer is not crazy when you've done everything you can do, medically, to save the life of a loved one. Nor is it crazy when you are in the process of doing these things. But, praying, while at the same time refusing to perform life-saving surgery, defeats the point of the prayer in the first place. Playing on Immanuel Kant's famous dictim, "Concepts without percepts are empty; percepts without concepts are blind," Albert Einstein famously stated, "Science without religion is lame; religion without science is blind."[33] Science not moved by respect for the orderliness of the universe, its mysteries, and the inability of science to explain its own explanations (What are the origins of matter and energy?) is mechanical, empty, and without purpose. Religion without science is dogmatic, blind, and self-defeating. The Guiding Virtue of Scientificity accordingly synergizes both.

This synergy embodies the goal of human happiness, for religion and science both aim at it in their respective ways. Scientificity thus aims to improve life through the use of evidence-based thinking. It is not the pathological, cold-hearted respect for technology for its own sake, the dispassionate drive to create Frankenstein's monster simply because one can. The scientific person is philosophical and reflective about what conduces to human happiness and what may not. While it is commonly claimed that technology is neutral; how it is used is not; this does not quite do justice to those who possess the virtue of Scientificity. Such individuals do not bifurcate science from its intended uses. Creating an atomic weapon is different from creating a nuclear reactor; and although the knowledge to create the latter (splitting the atom) can be used to create the former, the inherent goal of Scientificity is to promote life, not its destruction, through scientific means.

So, a scientific Edgar would look at life—his own and that of others—through lenses that illuminate ways to improve life. He would see through such fictions as "Life," in the abstract, as a vindictive force waiting to do him in, and would look at the specific things that are not working in practice, with an eye toward improving his life. Such a virtuous habit would be consistent with making constructive changes, not with giving up the ghost.

It is at this juncture that Scientificity and Foresightedness go hand in hand. Scientificity explains the here and now with an eye toward making improvements. Foresightedness applies what science has provided in order to bring these improvements to fruition. So, Edgar may realize that he needs to overcome his alcohol problems; that this is what is largely contributing to his "bad luck." But he also needs to make predictions about what will work for him. Will a twelve-step program work for him? Will he do better in group therapy than individual? What modality would work best for him? Foresightedness here lies in being able to use one's fund of knowledge—about oneself, about what has worked in the past, about one's financial means, about the availability of facilities, etc.—to make reasonable prognostications. Indeed, the Guiding Virtues of Objectivity, Foresightedness, and Scientificity, as discussed in this chapter, are mutually supportive aspects of the same state of human flourishing. Indeed, according to LBT, the avoidance of their respective fallacies—Oversimplifying, Distorting Probabilities, and Blind Conjecture—through the cultivation and exercise of these virtuous habits is paramount to the attainment of human happiness.

NOTES

1. Aristotle, *Nichomachean Ethics*, Book 10, Chapter 8.

2. This inference is an example of an inductive fallacy because the premise does not make the conclusion *probable*. See the discussion of induction provided in Chapter 1.

3. I have not discussed another type of fallacy of reporting that can also be involved in dilemma thinking, which is Distorting Probabilities. Thus, Jaspers may be exaggerating the probability of his boss firing him if he finds out that he has applied for another job. Indeed, this might even lead Jaspers' boss to give him a raise in order to keep him! Distorting Probabilities is discussed later in this chapter.

4. Walter Lippmann, *Public Opinion* (New York: Penguin Books, 1946), Ch. 7. http://wps.pearsoncustom.com/wps/media/objects/2429/2487430/pdfs/lippmann.pdf.

5. Lippmann, *Public Opinion*, p. 61.

6. The Leadership Conference, "Hate Crimes Against Arab Americans, Muslims, and Sikhs," The Leadership Conference website. http://www.civilrights.org/publica tions/hatecrimes/arab-americans.html

7. Lippmann, *Public Opinion*, p. 74.

8. Ibid.

9. Cherie Jessica Parker, *Before And After 9/11: The Portrayal Of Arab Americans in U.S. Newspapers*, Department of Political Science, University of Central Florida. http://etd.fcla.edu/CF/CFE0002041/Parker_Cherie_J_200805_MAST.pdf.

10. William K. Clifford, "The Ethics of Belief," *Contemporary Review*, 1877, Ch. 1. http://myweb.lmu.edu/tshanahan/Clifford-Ethics_of_Belief.html.

11. Ibid.

12. "Miscarriage," MedlinePlus. http://www.nlm.nih.gov/medlineplus/ency/art icle/001488.htm.

13. "Is Time Travel Possible?" NASA. http://spaceplace.nasa.gov/review/dr -marc-space/time-travel.html.

14. Hume, *Treatise of Human Nature*, Part 3, Section 12. https://www.gutenberg .org/files/4705/4705-h/4705-h.htm.

15. Hume, *Inquiry Concerning Human Understanding*, Section 4. https://www .gutenberg.org/files/9662/9662-h/9662-h.htm.

16. Hume, *Treatise*, Part 3, Section 12.

17. Bertrand Russell, *The Problems of Knowledge*. (New York: Oxford University Press, 1972).

18. Jean-Paul Sartre, *Existentialism and Human Emotions* (New York: Philosophical Library, 1985), p. 29.

19. Ibid., p. 13.

20. Ibid., p. 33.

21. Aristotle, *Ethics*, Book 3, Chapter 7.

22. Prolonged Exposure Therapy as well as Cognitive Processing Therapy, which are forms of Cognitive Behavior Therapy, are popularly commonly for combat veterans with PTSD. See, for example, Christopher Bergland, "Two New PTSD Treatments Offer Hope for Veterans," *Psychology Today*, November 23, 2013. https:// www.psychologytoday.com/blog/the-athletes-way/201311/two-new-ptsd-treatments-offer-hope-veterans. New high tech techniques for virtually recreating battlefield scenarios as a means of exposure have also been devised. See, Jared Defife, "New Treatments to Combat PTSD," *Psychology Today*, January 27, 2012.

23. Aristotle, *Ethics*, Book 2, Chapter 6.

24. Aristotle, *Ethics*, Book 1, Chapter 7.

25. "Our judgments concerning cause and effect are derived from habit and experience; and when we have been accustomed to see one object united to another, our imagination passes from the first to the second, by a natural transition, which precedes reflection, and which cannot be prevented by it." Hume, *Treatise*, Book 1, Part 3, Sec. 13.

26. For a discussion of the standards of rational causal judgments, see Elliot D. Cohen, *Critical Thinking Unleashed*, (Lanham, MD: Rowman & Littlefield, 2009)Ch. 13.

27. The statement, "She would be alive today if I had been in school where I was supposed to be" is an example of a *contrary-to-fact conditional*. This aspect of irrational causal judgments is discussed later in this chapter. It is helpful to note here, however, that such conditional statements can combine with other faulty causal thinking such as *post hoc* reasoning to fortify and sustain irrational causal claims.

28. For a discussion of other-regarding blame, see Elliot D. Cohen, "Stop Playing the Blame Game," *Psychology Today*, July 29, 2012. https://www.psychologytoday .com/blog/what-would-aristotle-do/201207/stop-playing-the-blame-game.

29. For example, in legal contexts, finding someone culpable for a crime requires showing a causal connection between one's action (or inaction) and harm to another. Similarly, in cases of malpractice, there must be shown a connection between a breach of a duty and harm to another. The law is rife with such examples of fundamental reliance on causation to assign blame.

30. I am not saying that there aren't any strong contrary-to-fact conditionals, that is, ones that do not require qualification with "might" or "might not." There are, but these are supported by laws of nature. Consider: "If I had dropped my pen, it would have fallen to the floor." Because this is a corollary of the Universal Law of Gravity, it is reasonable. Assuming that the pen is being dropped in the earth's gravitational field it makes no further assumptions that are questionable. However, the contrary-to-fact conditionals that tend to be used in practical contexts (including the ones used to blame oneself or others) are not ordinarily of this scientific variety (that is, corollaries of laws of nature).

31. One explanation can be *better* than another when it is *simpler* and, therefore, makes fewer assumptions. The classical example of this is the sun-centered view of the earth's orbit versus the earth-centered view. The former, which held that the earth revolved around the sun, required fewer assumptions about planetary orbits to account for the positions of the planets than the latter, so it was more reasonable to accept it over the latter. This meant that we had to give up our religiously inspired idea (mindset) that the center of the universe is "mother earth," and that, therefore, human beings, who inhabit the earth, are special. See, for example, Irving Copi and Carl Cohen, *Introduction to Logic*, 9th Edition (New York: Macmillan, 1994), pp. 538–39.

32. Stefan Lovgren, "Evolution and Religion Can Coexist, Scientists Say," *National Geographic News*, October 18, 2004.

33. Albert Einstein, "Science, Philosophy and Religion, A Symposium," Conference on Science, Philosophy, and Religion in Their Relation to the Democratic Way of Life, Inc., New York, 1941. http://scienceandthemedia.weebly.com/uploads/6/9/6/2/6962884/einstein_science_philosophy_and_religion.pdf.

Chapter Four

Acting Rationally

Fallacies of Behavioral Reasoning and Their Guiding Virtues

The previous chapter discussed the fallacies that can and often do occur in the minor premise reports of emotional reasoning. Such reasoning, as you have seen, tends to interface with a further sort of reasoning, which LBT calls behavioral reasoning. The latter sort of reasoning prescribes behavior and is linked to action. Like emotional reasoning, it can also contain fallacies in its premises. This chapter will discuss three major kinds of fallacies that often infect behavioral reasoning, especially the kind involved in self-defeating emotions of anger, sadness, depression, guilt, and anxiety. These behavioral fallacies are called: (1) Can'tstipation, (2) Bandwagon Reasoning, and (3) Manipulation. Also discussed are the respective Guiding Virtues of the stated fallacies. Table 4.1 provides definitions of each.

CAN'TSTIPATION

"I can't stand it when she puts me down like that," "I can't get up in front of a large audience," "I just can't help feeling terrible about how she ignored me." These statements illustrate, respectively, three different types of Can'tstipation: (1) Volitional Can'tstipation, (2) Behavioral Can'tstipation, and (3) Emotional Can'tstipation. These fallacious "can'ts" prevent one from exercising rational control over one's will, actions, and emotions. Instead, they keep a person in states of emotional distress, prevent one from acting in constructive ways, and sustain irrational, self-defeating emotions. LBT seeks to help clients overcome such self-defeating behavioral blocks to happiness.

Table 4.1.

Fallacy	Definition
1. Can'tstipation	Obstructing one's creative potential by holding in and refusing to excrete one's emotional, behavioral, or volitional *can't*.
2. Bandwagon Reasoning	Blind, inauthentic conformity of belief and/or action largely deduced from the demand for approval of others.
3. Manipulation	Using force, intimidation, threats, deception, chicanery, or other manner of control, instead of rational argument, in order to get a person/s to act, think, or feel in a certain way.

Volitional Can'tstipation

This form of Can'tstipation expresses weakness of will to tolerate something in terms such as "I can't stand it," "I can't put up with it," "I can't take it," and similar terms. The idea here is to give oneself permission not to tolerate a situation that is perceived to be intolerable, so that one justifies (to oneself) acting accordingly. In this context, "intolerable" means the situation is so undesirable that it is beyond one's ability to cope with it.

The case of Clara Wilson provides an instructive example. Married with two children, she has a contentious relationship with her mother-in-law, Zelda, whom she perceives as trying to undermine her relationship with her husband, Bob, and to prove that she is a poor wife and mother.

I can't stand it when that woman puts me down. The way she treats me is deplorable! Last week she dropped by unexpectedly and the house was a mess. I admit it. There were cloths on chairs and mail all over the dining room table. She went around the house looking for things that were wrong like some kind of inspector. Then she started. "What's the matter with you," she said. You can't put your things away? I've never seen such a mess in all my life. Did your mother raise you like this? I really feel bad for my son, having to live like this. If you were my daughter you would have learned how to keep your house in order." And then she started with my cooking, which I admit sucks. She said, "What's for dinner tonight? Are you serving the same old, same old again? More Tuna!? Do you always feed this shit to the children too, or just to me? Do you know how much mercury is in this fish?" As if she was even invited for dinner! She just popped in, uninvited, and expected me to have prepared a gourmet meal for her!? Imagine suggesting too that I would do anything to hurt my children! I just lost it. "That's it!" I shouted. "You BITCH! Nobody even invited you! What right do you have marching in here and treating me like this? Why don't you go back to the crypt from whence you came!" Then she started crying, and ran out the front door. Big mistake! Now she has something on me and my relationship with Bob is really strained. Yep, she succeeded in ruining my life!

Indeed, based on what Clara says, it would appear that her mother-in-law has some issues to work through regarding her son's marriage. However, it is also clear that losing her temper and calling Zelda a bitch, in addition to making other unsavory exclamatory statements, was not the way to address these issues. Instead, the sudden role reversal wherein Clara went from the victim to the aggressor only seemed to undermine her position all the more. It was easy enough for this to happen because, in saying, "That's it!" Clara effectively gave herself permission to haul off on her. She told herself that she could not stand it anymore and accordingly let Zelda have it with both barrels.

Clearly, Clara's behavioral response was part of a complex set of cognitive, emotive, and behavioral conditions comprising her anger about being "put down." Of course, people can get angry without becoming physically or verbally aggressive. They may *feel like* squeezing another's head without actually going through with it. Unfortunately, in telling oneself that one can't stand another or what the other is saying or doing, one denies the willpower to hold back. For willpower is a perceived power. Its strength, indeed its very existence, lies in its phenomenological awareness. In denying that you have the power, you effectively relinquish it. That is why, in telling yourself that you "can't stand it," you set yourself up not to stand it.

If I truly cannot stand something, then it is impossible for me to stand it, which means that I won't, as a matter of course, stand it; which, in turn, means it is futile for me to even try to stand it. So, if I declare that I cannot stand something, that it is impossible for me to stand, I perceive no choice but to go with the flow. Thus, when Clara told herself that she could not stand to be put down anymore by Zelda, she perceived no other option but to let her anger go full throttle. Phenomenologically, "I can't stand it" turns off willpower. Physiologically, her fight or flight system is tripped and she is ready to defend herself. Here, the neocortex, the seat of higher order thinking in the brain, engages the amygdala, which triggers the hypothalamus, which engages the pituitary and other glands that call the sympathetic nervous system into action, stepping up endocrine activity, increasing cardio-pulmonary functions, sending blood away from the brain to the gross muscles, and so forth. Of course, so primed, Clara is likely to say things she later regrets because she is in survival mode, not reflective, philosophical mode.

Turning on its head Immanuel Kant's famous insight that "ought" (or "should") implies "can," this logic says "can't" implies "shouldn't." If I can't stand something, then I should *not* stand it.[1] This is where one gives up the struggle to control oneself. So Clara relinquishes self-control and gives Zelda what she "deserves." The only problem is that the sense of vindication experienced at the time wears off rather quickly, and one is often left with the odiferous residue of regret, as in Clara's case.

Here is Clara's behavioral and emotional reasoning at a glance:

1. (Major Premise Rule) If Zelda puts me down, then the way she treats me is deplorable.

2. (Minor Premise Report) She has put me down.

3. (Primary Conclusion) So, the way she has treated me is deplorable.

4. (Bridging Premise) If the way she has treated me is deplorable, then I can't stand her treating me this way.

5. (Conclusion Behavioral Justification) So, I can't stand her treating me this way.

6. (Behavioral Rule) If I can't stand her treating me this way, then I should defend myself against it and get her back by saying nasty things likely to upset her.

7. (Behavioral Conclusion) So, I should defend myself against it and get her back by saying nasty things likely to upset her.

As you can see, the higher order cognitions about appropriate treatment addressed in the primary syllogism (lines 1-3) deductively support Volitional Can'tstipation (line 5), which deductively supports self-defense. At this juncture is where the "fight or flight" system is engaged and the body is primed more for combat than for philosophical dialog. LBT accordingly stresses the importance of avoiding Volitional Can'tstipation inasmuch as it turns off the perception of willpower to control oneself and therewith the opportunity for rational thinking and philosophical reflection.

Notice that, in the conclusion on line 7, Clara tells how to defend herself. So why did Clara defend herself by calling Zelda names like "bitch" rather than, for example, attacking her physically? While accounts that proceed purely in terms of behavioral conditioning are possible, LBT maintains that people adopt their own behavioral rules, which determine their behavioral *modus operandi*. Thus, some people tend to deal with personal threats in a verbal way while others tend more toward physical responses. I do not doubt that there are genetic and environmental bases that largely influence the adoption of one set of rules versus another. LBT does not, however, make any claims about the causal genesis of such tendencies. The central point for LBT is that people can, indeed, clarify their rules of behavioral engagement and even work on changing them. In Clara's case, she appears to adopt a rather aggressive, retributive, verbal set of rules. This does not mean that there is not a common set of biologically-based rules that are prewired. Indeed, if a wild boar were attacking Clara, I doubt she would defend herself by calling it a bitch. The point is rather that there are additional cognitive-behavioral rules that are not prewired just as there are secondary emotions that are not prewired. In fact, according to LBT, these behavioral rules that are not prewired are precisely the ones that work synergistically as premises in the behavioral emotional reasoning of secondary emotions, such as the anger experienced by Clara.

Indeed, it was such an additional set of cognitive behavioral rules for defending herself that was later a source of regret for Clara. Such negative experience, after the fact, can be an eye-opener for making changes in a contentious rule base. It can also signal the value of overcoming one's Volitional Can'tstipation. This is because this fallacy short-circuits a more reflective approach by turning off willpower and engaging a "fight or flight" response. Under these conditions of perceived urgency, loss of control, and need to defend oneself, a rule set such as that given in line 7 above has an allure. Unfortunately, as in Clara's case, this perception is not a veridical one since there truly is no urgency to defend oneself, and the sense of loss of control is itself a result of misconceiving the object of emotion as being beyond one's capacity to stand or tolerate.

LBT accordingly emphasizes the refutation of Volitional Can'tstipation in order to avoid the self-defeating behavior that can ensue from it; and it emphasizes the adoption of behavioral plans of action that align with more reflective, philosophical perspectives on managing difficult or challenging situations. Thus, in Clara's case, the "can't stand it" can be easily refuted by considering that she has managed to withstand similar criticisms Zelda has made of her on other occasions. This does not mean that these criticisms do not merit Clara's response or that she should just tolerate them because she can. Rather, it means that she can more fruitfully approach the matter with an eye toward rationally addressing them without the needless stress brought on by misperceiving the situation as an intolerable one portending imminent danger to be defended against. For example, Clara might say, "Zelda, you are free to make other dinner arrangements this evening if you would prefer to eat something different. The next time you plan to come to dinner, let me know in advance that you are coming, and I will prepare something more to your liking." In this more diplomatic manner, she would have asserted herself while letting Zelda know that she is not being reasonable about her demands. Such a response would align with a more rational set of behavioral rules that recognize her interest in being treated respectfully, while not contradicting this interest by personally attacking Zelda—for example, calling her a "bitch." Indeed, as you will see,[2] in LBT's sixth step, such a rational overhaul of Zelda's behavioral rules could be developed as part of her plan of action for future dealings with the likes of Zelda.

BEHAVIORAL CAN'TSTIPATION

Notice that Clara claimed to lack the capacity to *tolerate or stand* how Zelda treated her. Thus, she rested her case for not putting up with her on the lack of willpower. Sometimes, however, people can'tstipate themselves by judging that they lack the physical capacity to perform particular actions even though they really can. For example I might say, I can't solve a math problem, meaning that I do not have the mental capacity to do so, even though I really haven't given it adequate attention and even though I have been able to solve much more demanding math problems on previous occasions. Other times, in saying "I can't," one may really mean "I won't" or "choose not to." While the former physical sense of "can't" can be empirically confirmed or refuted, the latter involves a linguistic confusion; for there is a difference between saying that I choose not to do something and saying that I can't. Unfortunately, a good number of us commonly say "I can't" when we really should be saying "I won't" or "I choose not to." This is a popular instance of what LBT calls Behavioral Can'tstipation. One tells oneself that one can't do something, hiding behind this "can't" as though it truly applied, concealing from oneself and/or others the very fact that one does not want to do it, or chooses not to do it. This is frequently due to anxiety about undertaking something at which one thinks one might fail. Consider the case of Stanley Stickle, a college student who is taking a theatrical acting class:

> I needed an elective so I took this acting class. I didn't know that the class was going to put on a show, and that I would end up playing Hamlet. I keep trying to perfect my lines but I keep getting hung up on the most famous lines, the "To be or not to be" soliloquy. I start out fine with the, "To be, or not to be: that is the question: Whether 'tis nobler in the mind to suffer the . . ." but then I draw a blank on the word "slings," which throws off the rest of it. Imagine if this happens when I am on stage in front of hundreds of people in the auditorium! Suddenly I start saying stupid words that everybody will know are not the real words. I will make a complete fool of myself up there. Not only is the audience, who paid good money to see this show, going to be disappointed, but also my teacher and the class are counting on me! The show's tomorrow evening and I'm freaking out! How did I get myself into this mess! I just can't do it! I better tell the teacher that I can't do it. He could ask my understudy to take my place.

Stanley's case is a familiar one. Suddenly, you imagine that all eyes are on you and you start to think, "What if I screw up?!" You feel overwhelmed by the anxiety of not knowing if the event will come off without a hitch or you will make that dreaded mistake and end up falling from everyone's grace. This is definitely an awesome weight to carry before one is about to go into the proverbial lion's den. So you start to get cold feet. "I can't do this," you think, as you feel your muscles tighten in your throat. However, there is no lion's den other than the one of your own devices. For, it is you who *demand*s that others' expectations be met. You are also the one who makes your self-worth a function of satisfying this demand.

Stanley's emotional reasoning appears to be along the same lines:

1. (Second Major Premise Rule) I must satisfy the expectations of others (in particular my teacher, my class mates, and the audience).

2. (Bridging Premise) If I must satisfy the expectations of others then if I let everyone down, then I will make a complete fool of myself.

3. (Conclusion/First Major Premise Rule) So, if I let everyone down then I will make a complete fool of myself.

4. (Minor Premise Report) If I make a mistake on stage then I will let everyone down.

5. (Primary Conclusion) So, if I make a mistake on stage then I will make a complete fool of myself.

6. (Bridging Premise) If I will make a complete fool of myself if I make a mistake on stage, then I can't do it.

7. (Conclusion/Behavioral Justification) So, I can't do it.

8. (Behavioral Rule) If I can't do it, then I should inform the teacher.

9. (Behavioral Conclusion) So, I should inform the teacher that I can't do it.

As you can see, Stanley demands that he satisfy the expectations of all concerned (line 1), from which he deduces that he would be a complete fool if he let everyone down (line 3). Accordingly, the object of Stanley's anxiety is the possibility that he will let everyone down if he makes a mistake (line 4), from which he deduces that he would be a complete fool if he made a mistake (line 5). It is this primary conclusion about the possibility of making a complete fool of himself that leads him to deduce that he *can't* go through with the performance (line 7), and that, therefore, he should let his teacher know that he can't (won't) do it (line 9).

Notice that Stanley's behavioral justification (excuse) for not going through with the performance is that he "can't" do it. However, there is a vicious circularity here because he can't because he won't and he won't because he can't. In other words, he has *no* independent justification for claiming that he can't. Clearly, bailing on the eve before the show is self-defeating inasmuch as this would not satisfy the (reasonable) expectation of the teacher and the class, namely that he go through with his commitment to do the show. Once Stanley realizes that, in this context, "can't" simply means "I choose not to" or "I won't," he can begin to deal more realistically with his performance anxiety. Unfortunately, his use of "can't" conceals this confusion from him and therefore keeps him from addressing the true reasons why he does not choose to go on with the show. These reasons are the self-imposed demand that he satisfy the expectations of others and the conclusion he draws from it, that making a mistake would make a fool of him. These ideas feed the bogus conclusion that he can't go through with the performance, and create the undue stress.

Fittingly, Epictetus admonishes against making such external demands that are beyond one's control. He states,

> When I see a man in a state of anxiety, I say, 'What can this man want? If he did not want something which is not in his power, how could he still be anxious? It is for this reason that one who sings to the lyre is not anxious when he is performing by himself, but when he enters the theatre, even if he has a very good voice and plays well: for he not only wants to perform well, but also to win a great name, and that is beyond his own control.[3]

As such, Stanley's nemesis does not lie in his inability to recall the word "slings," but rather in his *demand* to "win a great name." If, in the attempt to perform, he should make a mistake, he would not be the first to do so, nor would he be the last. It is through such effort that one learns and grows. In refusing to take such rational risks, one ceases to gain valuable experience. By covering up one's ability to engage in such life-enriching experiences with the can'tstipating use of "can't," one loses the opportunity to learn and grow.

EMOTIONAL CAN'TSTIPATION

However, can'tstipating "can'ts" can not only stunt behavioral progress, they can also impede emotional well-being. This happens when you say or think that you "can't help feeling" as you do. Indeed, when feeling very sad or downcast, it is easy for one to go with the flow, and to think oneself incapable of feeling otherwise. But this is easily refutable by common human experience. Did you ever feel so down that you wanted to be alone with your misery, away from all human contact, but nevertheless had an unavoidable commitment that would bring you out of your cocoon into contact with others, such as at the workplace or classroom? Did it ever happen that in the process of pretending to be in good spirits you really started to feel better, in fact, really good? "Fake it until you make it" is the popular adage that describes this common potential to alter one's mood or emotion. Through such experiences, we see that the "can't" in "I can't help feeling this way" may be contrary to fact.[4]

An instructive example is the case of Jessica Lessing, a seventeen-year-old high school senior who has fallen out of grace with her classmates:

> They used to be my friends. Now they just ignore me or, even worse, laugh to themselves when I walk into homeroom. When I try to talk to them, they walk away like I didn't exist. They just give me the silent treatment! I'm so upset about it. I go home, lock myself in my room, and cry. I refuse to come out of my room even when my mom calls me for dinner. Yesterday, I told my mom that I was sick so that I could stay home from school, but she took my temperature and made me go anyways. I just can't help feeling like such a loser. All I did was refuse to go along with their stupid prank phone calls to that nerdy kid, and now they treat me just like they treat him. It's making me sooooo sad. I don't know how to get them to like me again so I can feel happy again.

Jessica's situation is one that many of us have experienced at some point in our lives. People whom we thought were our friends turn on us for reasons that make little sense to us. Indeed, we can empathize with Jessica's plight. Here is a young woman who perceives her self-worth to be on the line. If she can get the other kids to like her again, then she can restore her self-worth to its default state; otherwise not. This is not a comfortable set of beliefs to have and they can lead to much emotional stress. Here is the reasoning that appears to be sustaining her emotion:

1. (Second Major Premise Rule) I must have the approval of the other kids.

2. (Bridging Premise) If I must have the approval of the other kids and they are giving me the silent treatment, then I'm a loser.

3. (Conclusion/First Major Premise) So, if the other kids are giving me the silent treatment, then I'm a loser.

4. (Minor Premise Report) The other kids are giving me the silent treatment.

5. (Primary Conclusion/Behavioral Justification) So, I'm a loser.

6. (Bridging Premise) If I'm a loser, then I just can't help feeling like one.

7. (Behavioral Conclusion) So, I just can't help feeling like a loser.

As you can see, the highest tier of Jessica's emotional reasoning proceeds from a demand for approval (line 1), from which she deduces Self-Damnation in terms of being "a loser" (line 5). This conclusion comprises the basis for her behavioral justification for concluding that she just can't help feeling like a loser (line 7).

In telling herself that she "can't help feeling like a loser," that is, feeling down about herself, she is sustaining her emotion by not permitting herself to make constructive changes in her emotional reasoning. Thus, as long as she holds onto this emotional "can't," she will remain distraught. The key to unleashing herself from this emotional bondage is to come to the realization that it is not her classmates that are making her upset, but rather herself. For, she is the one who is reasoning herself into this painful emotional corner, not her classmates. Of course, this is easy enough said, harder to fess up, especially for a seventeen-year-old who carries the baggage of wanting to fit in with her peers.

Notice she says that the way her classmates is treating her is "making her" sad. Such passive terms as "You upset me," "It was aggravating," "That pissed me off," "You made me angry," and the like deny responsibility for one's emotions and tend to support Emotional Can'tstipation. Indeed, if Jessica was *caused* to feel as she does by others, rather than *making herself* sad, then she *can't* do anything about the way she feels. In contrast, the active voice in which one takes responsibility for one's feelings is a useful antidote against Emotional Can'tstipation. Thus, it is more empowering to say that "I pissed myself off" than to say that "You pissed me off."[5]

A GUIDING VIRTUE FOR CLARA, STANLEY, AND JESSICA: TEMPERANCE

Indeed, Clara, Stanley, and Jessica alike have disempowered themselves as a result of holding onto their irrational can'ts. The goal, then, for these individuals is the cultivation of resolve in willing, feeling, and acting in line with what is rational. Such a habit of rational self-control is called *Temperance*, which is the Guiding Virtue of Can'tstipation. By telling oneself one *can't* do, or not do otherwise, one can defeat one's own prospects for happiness. For example, you easily lose your temper, cave to pressure, eat or drink to excess, or keep yourself from advancing by refusing to try. In contrast, in becoming temperate, one can take control of one's life (body, mind, and spirit) by cognitively, conatively, emotionally, and behaviorally overcoming such self-stultifying *can'ts*.

The temperate person embraces challenges and perceives them as making life more interesting and as opportunities to learn and grow. Such a person, like all imperfect humans, can get worked up over mundane things, at times, but she also knows that these feelings are not like bolts of lightning out of the sky, over which she lacks control. Rather, she realizes that she is largely the producer of her (secondary) emotions and that, where there is unreason, there is likely to be emotions that following suit; and that, inversely, if there is reason, there is less likely to be self-destructive emotions. While not perfect at overcoming irrational thinking and its attendant emotions, the temperate person is quite artful at handling the stresses of life and does not easily succumb to the allure of the "I can't" excuse.

Of course, Temperance is an ideal and one can only aspire to it without ever attaining it perfectly. There is always room for improvement in this mortal life of ours. Still, we can draw distinctions between those who are *relatively* temperate and those who are not. Thus, the person who is *generally* disposed to handle the stresses of everyday life without invoking behavioral, emotional, or volitional can'ts is worthy of the appellation "temperate." On the other hand, one who is prone to outbursts, or gets caught up in the herd mentality, or acts in ways he knows he shouldn't, or is deterred by challenges and retreats from them, deserves to be called "intemperate," although not necessarily completely so. This is true because some people may be more adept at controlling their emotions than they are at putting their rational plans into action; or conversely. Still, one form of Can'tstipation tends to give birth to another. For example, Jessica's Emotional Can'tstipation probably spawned Behavioral Can'tstipation, as in telling herself that she *can't* go to class and face her classmates.

It is a mistake to assume that overcoming one's Can'tstipation makes one temperate, however. This is because Temperance also involves a disposition to control oneself as a kind of second nature. For example, one might feel constrained by a "can't," but push oneself to act against this constraint. So you might tell yourself that you can't stand to study algebra yet force yourself to do so notwithstanding. Undoubtedly, this is an important step towards becoming temperate, but one is not temperate simply by virtue of having taken this step. In contrast, Temperance involves not perceiving such a constraint in the first place. So you do not feel constrained by a "can't." You simply study the algebra because you realize that this is the best way to learn it.

Temperate people are also temperate about their intemperance. As imperfect humans we all make mistakes. Temperate people do not come apart at the seams in such cases. They do not tell themselves that they can't make mistakes. This enables such individuals to learn from their mistakes.

So temperate people also tend to be secure metaphysically, and are rationally tolerant of the human imperfections, whether in themselves or others.

Instances of intemperance tend to be noticed more by others than instances of temperance. So, you get angry and "lose your cool," and onlookers stare with condemning glazes. On the other hand, someone insults you and you continue to treat this person in a dignified manner without having a temper tantrum; yet onlookers are not particularly impressed by your composure. As such, temperate people are not likely to be regularly reinforced in their temperate ways by positive responses from others. The reinforcement is likely to be an internal one wherein the fulfillment of a temperate act is subjectively noticed and looked upon by oneself as a source of self-satisfaction. "I can indeed stand this. I just did!"

The most important question is not whether one *is* temperate but rather whether one is aiming at becoming temperate, and whether one is making progress. As Aristotle long ago pointed out, most people do not even connect the idea of their fulfillment with virtue.[6] As such, a major part of LBT's mission is to acquaint the many with this idea by placing it in a practical light. LBT practitioners do not therefore assess their clients on the basis of whether they have attained this virtue, but rather on the basis of whether they have made virtues such as Temperance their end, and are making progress *toward* attaining it. Since this is a lifetime journey, LBT, as a relatively brief and focused form of assistance, does not, and cannot, track a client until she is self-realized. Its goal is instead the more realistic one of helping clients to get on track, and to provide them with the tools they will need in moving forward. This applies to all the other Guiding Virtues LBT addresses through it six-step approach.

BANDWAGON REASONING

Staying on track toward virtue can and often is derailed by pressures from others to conform. I believe that such a common human tendency is one of the chief hindrances to the attainment of happiness in the virtue-based, Aristotelian sense embraced by LBT. As Erich Fromm maintains, the majority of humankind are motivated to conform as an adaptation mechanism in confronting anxiety and fear of the outside world. One closes the gap between oneself and the external world simply by blending into it. However, this security is purchased at an extremely high price: the loss of individuality or self.[7] In common parlance, this tendency often goes by the name of "Jumping on the Bandwagon"[8] or, as developed in the literature on LBT, "Bandwagon Reasoning."[9] This it defines as "Blind, inauthentic conformity of belief and/ or action largely deduced from the demand for approval of others."[10]

The case of Jessica Lessing discussed under Emotional Can'tstipation is instructive in this regard. Jessica's attempt to assert her individuality by refusing to go along with the prank calls to "that nerdy kid" resulted in her being ostracized by the group. For Jessica, this fall from grace among group members diminished her value as a human being. She was now a "loser." Indeed, if not the majority of humankind, a large percentage of it avoids such a fate by blindly conforming. It is therefore not surprising how mass genocides have been committed through robotic and inhumane conformity to the dictates of oppressive government regimes.

According to LBT, what drives the decision to conform is the demand for approval. One *must* have the approval of the group in order to maintain one's self-worth. From this popular phenomenological perspective, loss of group status is equivalent to loss of self-worth. I cannot tell you how many times I have been the odd man out in the course of my life. Growing up in a small middle and upper-middle class northeastern town (Fair Lawn) in the shadows of the Big Apple, I always seemed to be on the outside of the in-group—those popular kids who traveled in cliques. I never quite understood why I never quite fit in. Perhaps it was my tendency to be rebellious and not to accept things at face value; but, after systematically being rejected, I did come to think of myself as second-rate. It was not until I got out of Dodge and went off to college that it occurred to me that I was quite capable of amounting to something in this world even without the approval of the in-crowd. In fact, what I discovered was that many of these same popular kids established themselves after high school as "radical non-conformists." This was the 1970s and smoking pot, having free sex, long hair, and being antiwar were in fashion. Paradoxically, this in-group had found another bandwagon to jump on. And, as expected, I was still the odd man out. Yes, I had long hair and was antiwar; but I did not smoke pot or have free sex. Fast forward to the future and many in the group became staunch conservative Republicans, while I remained liberal in my views.

As I reflect on this journey through life, I can now see that my most valuable resource was thinking out of the box—that set of boundaries that demand social conformity. I discovered that many of the wisest choices I have made in my life have been against the grain. For example, when I decided to become a philosopher (I started out as an accounting major), my family did not quite know what to make of it since they were business people. However, in the annals of philosophical writings I came to understand many of my personal struggles, in particular, the quest for personal dignity and value. Through the writings of great thinkers from antiquity, I discovered that the creative spirit is deeply embedded in seeing the world from alternative perspectives rather than from the status quo. I suspect that this uniqueness in phenomenological perspective is what attracted me to philosophy in the first place.

But in my search for authenticity, I encountered a formidable bandwagon, even among philosophers. As a young philosopher just out of grad school, I found that the philosophical in-group was that of "purists" who believed that philosophy should investigate matters of concept and theory but should not set foot in the muck and mire of practical matters. So, while philosophers could wrestle with what makes right acts right, or whether moral judgments assert meaningful propositions, it was forbidden by this elite group to look into particular moral issues like whether abortion was right or whether it was ever permissible to pull the plug on a patient in a persistent vegetative state. Such questions, so the group claimed, were the province of politicians, medical practitioners, and lawyers, but not philosophers, whose job was primarily to clarify the concepts and language of ethics, not to examine substantive moral issues.

Again I found myself at odds with the in-crowd, for I wanted to apply my philosophical training to practical matters. In 1980, against the philosophical establishment (which included the American Philosophical Association), I established a journal called *Applied Philosophy* (later renamed the *International Journal of Applied Philosophy*), whose announced purpose was to apply philosophical theories and methods to the practical affairs of life. Here was the world's first comprehensive journal of applied philosophy. In the inaugural issue I published an article titled, "The Immorality of Applied Philosophy," which argued that applied philosophy was inferior because it diluted rigorous analysis with praxis and thereby shortchanged students of philosophy. I published it because I wanted to give the world the opportunity to see what was keeping applied philosophy off the radar of mainstream philosophy. Moreover, I thought it quite a hoot for the first comprehensive journal of applied philosophy to make its debut with an article that attacked its very foundation. In retrospect, I am glad I published it. Once again, I was the odd man out, even for an applied philosopher!

In the mid-eighties I took applied philosophy in a further direction. It had always seemed to me that people needlessly upset themselves by deducing irrational conclusions from fallacious premises. It was around this time that my wife, a budding mental health counselor, brought the work of psychologist Albert Ellis to my attention. Ellis was an avid reader of philosophy and sought to build the insights of Stoic philosopher Epictetus, among other thinkers, into the corpus of mainstream psychotherapy. According to this view, it is not the events in our lives that upset us. Instead, it is the way we think about these events that *cause* our mental disturbances. Put this insight together with my deductive approach and the result is a form of philosophical practice I called, "Logic-Based Therapy." Ellis's approach was called, "Rational-Emotive Therapy" (RET) at the time. He later changed the name to "Rational-Emotive Behavior Therapy" (REBT) to reflect the behavioral component of the theory. Here's the upshot: LBT got its start because I was not afraid to combine philosophy with psychotherapy and to think outside the box of mainstream philosophy of the time. This was the beginning of philosophical practice in the United States.

I have no doubt that I owe much of my productivity to having been the odd man out beginning in my formative years. I now wear my rejection as a badge of honor, and owe a special debt of gratitude to all those who have helped to make me the odd man out. The rejection freed me from the demand to get the approval of others, thereby liberating me to do things that I damn well knew would meet with the disapproval of the in-group. It worked for me, so, for all those who find themselves on the outside looking in: it could also work for you!

THE GUIDING VIRTUE OF
BANDWAGON REASONING: AUTHENTICITY

In his treatise, *On Liberty*, John Stuart Mill admonishes,

> He who lets the world, or his own portion of it, choose his plan of life for him, has no need of any other faculty than the ape-like one of imitation. He who chooses his plan for himself, employs all his faculties. He must use observation to see, reasoning and judgment to foresee, activity to gather materials for decision, discrimination to decide, and when he has decided, firmness and self-control to hold to his deliberate decision.

Here, Mill captures well the concept of rational autonomy, which aligns with several of LBT's Guiding Virtues, especially Objectivity, Scientificity, Foresightedness, and Temperance. As Mill explains, those who blindly conform to what others say or do (that is, without rational assessment) forfeit the opportunity to cultivate such human virtues. Inasmuch as the aforementioned virtues are intrinsic to human happiness, such a life of "ape-like imitation" fails to promote happiness. From a pragmatist's perspective the same result can also be inferred inasmuch as those who jump blindly onto the bandwagon tend to regret it.[11]

Authenticity involves rational autonomy in Mill's sense; but it also involves an element of spontaneity about the issues of life. Such spontaneity involves not only an intellectual investment in these issues by also an emotional one. Thus, an authentic person is not purely an automaton that logically decides and acts. An authentic person is also true to his emotional or affective side, which also gains expression in the decisions that he makes. Erich Fromm drives home the synergy that exists between the rational, conative, and emotive sides of human reality. "Spontaneous activity," he states, is "free activity of the self," wherein activity means "the quality of creative activity that can operate in one's emotional, intellectual, and sensuous experiences and in one's will as well." This integration involves "the acceptance of the total personality and the elimination of the split between 'reason' and 'nature;' for only if man does not repress essential parts of his self, only if he has become transparent to himself, and only if the different spheres of life have reached a fundamental integration, is spontaneous activity possible."[12]

As Sartre would express it, the authentic person does not live in "bad faith,"[13] that is, she does not lie to herself about her freedom to do otherwise. For example, the secretary who assists her employer in committing fraudulent actions because she "has no choice" is not being authentic. Nor is the person being authentic who (behaviorally) can'tstipates himself into refraining from doing something by saying "I can't" when he really means "I won't." As such, the authentic person cherishes a democratic lifestyle and its inherent personal freedoms, and does not hide her responsibility for life choices behind deterministic excuses.

Not only does the authentic person not live in "bad faith," by virtue of being "transparent to himself." Such a person is also *congruent*, so that his *external* self—how he acts and what he says—matches his *internal* self—what he truly thinks and how he really feels.[14] For example, a professor is not authentic if he does not allow his colleagues to know anything about his personal life. And a corporate officer lacks congruence who sells out his ethical principles for the sake of advancing the company's bottom line. Nor is a politician congruent who tows the party line even though he really does not believe in it.

An authentic person is therefore not a phony. He does not wear a mask or hide who he really is behind a social or professional façade. This does not mean that authenticity requires being self-disclosing about everything. Indeed, there is no inconsistency between authenticity and a protected sphere of privacy. For example, a professor can be quite authentic but that does not mean that she must disclose to her class whether she had a miscarriage. While what is perceived to be too personal to disclose can vary from one individual to another (for some, disclosing one's age is personal yet for others it is not), there is some information to which others, arguably, aren't entitled. Thus, there may be no good reason why students should know that their instructor had a miscarriage, and the professor need not be inauthentic in refusing to disclose such a personal fact. Congruence, as it relates to authenticity, is therefore not an all or nothing matter, but instead a matter of degree. There are thus limits to congruence that are quite compatible with being authentic.

Empathy is also linked to authenticity inasmuch as authentic (honest and open) relationships require mutual, reciprocal, empathetic understanding. Thus, a couple cannot speak openly and honestly to each other about their relationship problems unless they each can understand what is going on in each other's subjective worlds; and each cannot attain such an understanding unless each has the ability to get inside the other's subjective world, that is, to empathize with the other. As discussed later, in the case of LBT practice, the authentic practitioner cannot begin to gain suitable insight into the client's behavioral and emotional challenges unless she is able to resonate with the client's subjective world.[15]

An authentic person is no cog in the social establishment; however, she does not reject social norms just to be contrary. Rather, she is inclined to accept social norms that pass muster from a reflective perspective, and to reject them if they do not. This means that she has the capacity to reflect on her socialization and to critically assess, and even redefine, the social principles that may be impeding her happiness.[16]

Authenticity is also consistent with a communal ideology as well as individualism, and thus transcends cultural boundaries of East and West. In communal life, the authentic person is a cooperative member of groups consistent with what is reasonable. This proviso about rationality means that the authentic person does not participate blindly but instead discretely with an eye toward supporting worthwhile cooperative efforts. For example, he does not participate willingly in group activities that themselves thwart authenticity such as ones sponsored by oppressive government regimes that forbid freedom of thought and demand blind conformity. Similarly, authenticity is consistent with individualism in pursuit of interests or goals that promote personal happiness.[17]

Accordingly, authenticity implies negative freedom. That is, authentic persons tend to say no to activities that are contrary to their principles of right conduct, or at least recognize that they have the choice to say no. For example, Sartre states, "If I am mobilized in a war . . . I deserve it . . . because I could always get out of it by suicide or by desertion. . . . For lack of getting out of it, I have chosen it."[18] As such, the authentic person accepts the fact that he always has the choice to say no, even when the available options of refusing are as inherently unattractive as suicide or desertion.

MANIPULATION

By virtue of being congruent, authentic people tend to avoid deception, chicanery, and other forms of covert manipulation. In contrast, manipulative people tend to subscribe to the Machiavellian principle that the end justifies the means and will therefore resort to such tactics in order to attain their end. Manipulation can range from lies (misrepresenting one's credentials in order to get or keep a job) and half-truths (telling your date that you never had children while failing to mention that you have six adopted children), to intimidation ("Are you still going out with that loser?"), to outright threats to harm, injure, or even kill another ("Do what I say or I will destroy you!"). Some forms use emotional blackmail ("I won't love you anymore unless you do what I say"), while still others manipulate through appeals to pity ("You don't love me anymore!" said to get attention.

Generally, manipulative individuals (those who are habitually disposed toward manipulating others) also tend to suffer from Volitional Can'tstipation and find it difficult to wait patiently, accept challenges or responsibility, or put in due effort to get what they want. Such individuals often end up regretting their lack of diligence or patience but may nevertheless continue to engage in manipulation instead of learning from their mistakes. This does not mean that such individuals cannot change, however their tendency to be impatient often gets in the way of making a concerted effort to change. Thus, the key to constructive change often lies in dealing with Can'tstipation first. Once un-can'tstipated, a manipulative person may consider more respectful means of getting what he wants instead of resorting to Manipulation.

Manipulation is disrespectful because, in the words of Immanuel Kant, it treats others as "mere means" instead of "ends in themselves." That is, it objectifies others, treating them like objects or things, rather than as persons (autonomous beings having the capacity to make their own rational choices).[19] Philosophical antidotes to Manipulation therefore stress the use of rational argument to engage with others. Indeed, philosophy is itself such a rational activity.[20] Further, there is a difference between using language[21] to manipulate others into doing what you want and using it to justify or prove to another why they should listen to you. Authentic people tend to use language in the latter way, while manipulative people tend to use it in the former way. True, all or most of us do sometimes use language manipulatively ("Oh please, please help me," you say, while tears form in your eyes); however, language's primary purpose is to communicate ideas and emotions, not to frighten, intimidate, evoke pity, or otherwise manipulate others into doing things.[22]

Consider, in this regard, Leo Lenard, a twenty-seven-year-old con artist who has been in and out of prison since he was nineteen. The following discussion ensues between Leo and his therapist, Paul Stern, whom he is seeing as condition of his parole:

"Hi Leo, how are things?"

"Not very good, Doc."

"Tell me about it, Leo."

"It's my girlfriend, Mary. I really like her but she doesn't know that I'm an ex-con. I told her that I'm an attorney, a malpractice lawyer, and now she wants me to represent her in a legal case involving medical malpractice. I told her that it wouldn't be a good idea because we're involved. She is really angry that I don't want to represent her, and won't take no for an answer."

"Why did you tell her that you were a lawyer?"

"You think a classy woman like her would go out with a convict?"

"You could have waited to tell her that, but you didn't have to lie to her about being a lawyer."

"I messed up again, I know. But she really likes me a lot, so it worked!"

"Worked?"

"Right, I got her to go out with me and now she's hooked on me. We have been having sex two or three times a day, and believe me, she's really good in bed!"

"What if you told her the truth?"

"I couldn't stand to do that! It would be the end of our relationship!"

"And what if it were the end of your relationship? You could find someone else and, next time, start off on the right track."

"Not gonna happen! I couldn't stand to tell her the truth and let her go. This one's a keeper."

"Isn't this why you ended up in prison in the first place?"

"What do you mean by that?"

"You're a smart guy, but instead of finishing college, getting your degree in business, and getting a job, you chose the quick and easy route of conning people out of their money."

"What the hell does that have to do with Mary!?"

"You told me that you couldn't stand to wait to get your degree to start making 'real money.' Remember? Now you tell me you can't stand to let Mary know the truth. Isn't that the same thing?"

"I don't see your point."

"What I'm saying is that, when you face a challenge in your life, you look for the easy way out. And that's what gets you into trouble."

"Okay, I know I messed up before, but this is different! I really like her, and it was just a lie to prime the pump, get the relationship started. It's not like I did anything illegal again like embezzlement. I did my time for that! And don't worry; I'm not going to practice law without a license. I would get in trouble, right?"

"Right! Do you really want to be a lawyer?"

"I always did. Used to watch lawyer shows a lot and imagined myself one."

"What if you went back to school for a law degree? Then you wouldn't be lying if you told anyone you were a lawyer."

"Do you really think I'll get into law school with my criminal background, and how would I ever be able to practice? Anyway, it would take years going part time, and I just couldn't stand to put my life on hold for all those years. No, I just have to get out of this. I'll think of something to tell her!"

As is evident from the above dialogue, Leo is not likely to improve his life circumstances unless he gives up his habit of manipulating others through lies and deception. This was what had gotten him into trouble and it is what continues to get him into trouble. However, as the therapist correctly points out, the grounds of his manipulative ways is his refusal to "stand" life challenges, which requires patience and perseverance. Instead, Leo wants to get things without expending the effort. He suffers from "Low Frustration Tolerance" (LFT).[23] Instead of putting off short-term gratification for long-term satisfaction, one tells oneself that one can't stand to wait or accept a challenge. As a result, one pursues a short-term fix only to suffer long-term, regrettable consequences. Indeed, many of us suffer the same ill fate because we can'tstipate ourselves into making self-defeating mistakes. Many of those who end up in prison resort to hustling and other forms of manipulation to gain short-term, temporary, satisfaction instead of putting in the necessary effort to obtain long-term, lasting satisfaction. Leo is such a person. His behavioral and emotional reasoning proceeds along the following lines:

1. (Second Major Premise Rule) I must never have to deal with immediate challenges.

2. (Bridging Premise) If I must never have to deal with immediate challenges, then if Mary will leave me if she finds out the truth, then I can't stand to let her know the truth.

3. (First Major Premise Rule/Conclusion) So, if Mary will leave me if she finds out the truth, then I can't stand to let her know the truth.[24]

4. (Minor Premise Report) Mary will leave me if she finds out the truth.

5. (Primary Conclusion/Behavioral Justification) So, I can't stand to let her know the truth.

6. (Behavioral Rule) If I can't stand to let her know the truth, then I must continue to lie to her.

7. (Behavioral Conclusion) So, I must continue to lie to her.

As you can see, Leo's demand to avoid immediate challenges in his life (line 1) leads him to conclude that he can't stand to let Mary know the truth (line 5), which serves as his behavioral justification for continuing his charade (line 7). Unfortunately, unless Leo realizes the self-defeating nature of this syndrome, he will continue to make the same self-defeating mistake over and over again. The basis of his fallacy of Manipulation is clearly his LFT resulting from his perfectionistic demand that he not have to expend the effort to confront inevitable life challenges. So, as soon as he perceives that something will require effort, he resorts to Manipulation as a quick and easy fix. Unfortunately, there is often truth in the adage that one gets what one pays for; and the veneer of a quick fix is often a very thin one, indeed. Sooner or later it collapses under the weight of reality and one is left with a bigger mess to clean up than if one expended due effort, in the first place, to manage a difficult or challenging situation. So how can Leo begin to take rational control of his life?

A GUIDING VIRTUE FOR LEO: EMPOWERING OTHERS

LBT's answer to this question should be evident: Give up the demand that life consist of easy fixes. This means learning to accept the reality that life is not a series of quick fixes to the problems of living. The virtue here is thus that of Metaphysical Security, that is, accepting the challenges that responsible living entails. Yet, Metaphysical Security also keys into a further Guiding Virtue of LBT. This further virtue is Empowering Others: the Guiding Virtue of Manipulation. Indeed, the habit of manipulating others is a result of failure to accept the reality that human beings are self-determining beings, not mere objects to be manipulated. So, becoming more metaphysically secure about such human reality is a necessary condition of Empowering Others. That is, if one does not accept that human beings are self-determining, then one is not going to empower others to make their own decisions. Manipulative people do not recognize this human reality. They tend to be insecure about it, and accordingly treat others as though they were objects to be manipulated, used, or controlled.

Empowering Others militates against such manipulation by treating others as rational, self-determining agents instead of engaging in power plays, intimidation, and deceit. Such empowerment involves advising or recommending rather than manipulating; using rational argument rather than making threats; providing others with informed consent rather than deceiving them through factual omissions and/or lies; and treating others with dignity and respect, even amid adversarial conflicts or disagreements.[25]

Empowering Others also keys into the virtue of Authenticity because people who are themselves autonomous tend to value the same in others. Indeed, if I see autonomy as a human right to which I am entitled, then I am also (logically) committed to the same in other human beings. The value of autonomy is universalizable inasmuch as it cannot be a value for me unless I am prepared to recognize it as a value for others. Because authentic people value their autonomy and therefore want others to empower them, they are therefore (logically) committed to empowering others as well.

People who empower others are also congruent; they are not phony, because they cannot begin to empower others unless others can see into them and trust that they will not betray them. Carl Rogers has stressed this idea as a condition of successful therapy. Clients do not feel empowered and seek constructive change if they do not trust their therapists. Indeed, in any interpersonal relationship, open and free disclosure does not occur if one senses that the other is phony. Rational dialog cannot transpire if people do not feel comfortable in confiding with the other. So, congruence, which leads to trust, which leads to rational interpersonal exchanges, is a condition of Empowering Others.

Empowering Others occurs in democratic contexts where there is open sharing of ideas and respect for alternative ideas. Empowerment dies on the vine in oppressive, dictatorial contexts, which quash the opportunity to participate in a democratic forum where one's contrasting or opposing voice is heard. Empowering Others involves interpersonal partnerships and joint ventures where people are free to brainstorm and work cooperatively to solve problems of living. Workplaces that demand blind obedience to a supervisor generally lack creativity and spontaneity because workers are disempowered to engage in rational dialogue. Governments that are antidemocratic are likewise the enemies of empowerment, and typically breed contempt for the oppressors.

Empowerment of others is not the same as "anything goes," however. It is not the same as anarchy in which one is free to do whatever one wishes. There are natural boundaries here, namely those in which rational dialogue and mutual, respectful cooperation thrive. A lawless culture does not support rational dialogue any more than one in which people are oppressed. Freedom and Empowerment are mutually supportive concepts so long as the former does not mean freedom to do anything. Such an anarchical sense of freedom is one extreme to avoid; oppression is another. Freedom is then the Aristotelian mean in which there is freedom within reason. Such is the Culture of Empowerment. It is an ideal and it is never completely realized in any interpersonal relationship, family, community, state, nation, or world. Empowering Others means striving for such an ideal context of freedom and democratic relating.

Freedom of thought is another sense of freedom that is intimately tied to Empowering Others. People who demand blindly parroting back the "official" view, whether in a private or state context, subvert Empowerment. Rational argument is the enemy of blind adherence to doctrine; evidence is to dogmatic belief as garlic is to a vampire. Bullying, cajoling, deceiving, or other manner of manipulation supports dogmatic belief, while rational argument tends to expose it for what it is: groundless belief.

This does not mean that Empowering Others supports freedom to believe anything. Instead, it is evidence based, so, while those who believe dogmatically, or without adequate evidence, have a right to believe what they want, people who empower others do their best, within reason, to rationally expose the flaws in others' thinking. Socrates is a good example of someone who attempted to empower others in this way. Of course, Socrates died at the hands of those whom he attempted to empower or set free; and no one is expected to be a martyr as was he. But those in the virtuous habit of Empowering Others tend to stand firmly against dogmatic and irrational thinking.

People such as Leo, who are used to manipulating others—treating them as "mere means" or objects—are most likely to change if they themselves feel empowered. Then they can come to realize that such a value is a universal human one upon which one's own happiness as well as that of others depends. Such individuals who habitually manipulate others can liberate themselves and become more self-empowered by attempting to empower others through the use of rational argument instead of manipulation. Demanding the easy way out of the challenges of life tends to subvert Empowerment (of self or others) by supporting Manipulation instead. Pushing oneself to use reason instead of Manipulation can help one to overcome such a perfectionistic, self-defeating demand. This is a daunting challenge for those like Leo who have developed an entrenched habit of avoiding life challenges. Yet, paradoxically, it is only by accepting the challenge to overcome the demand *not* to accept challenges that one can hope to become self- and other-empowering.

NOTES

1. This is not the contrapositive of "Ought" implies "Can," which is "Not-Can'" implies "Not-Ought." "Not-Ought" is not the same as "Ought not." I am not therefore attempting to draw a valid deductive inference from Kant's doctrine.

2. Chapter 5.

3. Epictetus, *The Discourses of Epictetus*, tr. by P. E Matheson, Ch. 13. http://www.sacred-texts.com/cla/dep/dep045.htm

4. LBT does not deny that some emotional states, such as that of Major Depressive Disorder, may not always be under one's control. In cases where there is a physical problem, such as an unregulated thyroid gland, pharmacological interventions may be necessary.

5. Elliot D. Cohen, *What would Aristotle do? Self Control through the Power of Reason* (Amherst, NY: Prometheus Books, 2003).

6. According to Aristotle, most people identify happiness with pleasure. See Aristotle, *Ethics*, Book 1 Chs. 4–5.

7. Erich Fromm, *Escape from Freedom* (New York: Macmillan, 1994).

8. For a discussion of how this fallacy got its name, see Elliot D. Cohen, *Critical Thinking Unleashed*. (Lanham, MD: Rowman & Littlefield, 2009).

9. Elliot D. Cohen, *The Theory and Practice of Logic-Based Therapy*. (Newcastle upon Tyne: Cambridge Scholars Publishing, 2013).

10. Ibid.

11. Elliot D. Cohen, "Think for Yourself," *Psychology Today*, January 30, 2010. https://www.psychologytoday.com/blog/what-would-aristotle-do/201001/think-yourself

12. Erich Fromm, *Fear of Freedom* (New York: Farrar & Rinehart, 1942, p. 223 http://realsociology.edublogs.org/files/2013/09/erich-fromm-the-fear-of-freedom-escape-from-freedom-29wevxr.pdf.

13. Jean-Paul Sartre, *Being and Nothingness*, trans. Hazel E. Barnes (New York: Washington Square Press, 1993), Part 1, Ch. 2. http://www.dhspriory.org/kenny/PhilTexts/Sartre/BeingAndNothingness.pdf.

14. Carl Rogers, *On Becoming a Person (*Boston: Houghton Mifflin, 1961).

15. See Chapter 5.

16. Elliot D. Cohen, "The Philosopher as Counselor," in Elliot D. Cohen (Ed.), *Philosophers at Work: Issues and Practice of Philosophy* (Orlando: Harcourt, 2000), 457–67.

17. Here, "happiness" is intended in the Aristotelian sense, or in terms of LBT's Guiding Virtues.

18. Jean-Paul Sartre, *Being and Nothingness*, trans. Hazel E. Barnes (New York: Washington Square Press, 1993), p. 554.

19. Immanuel Kant, *Fundamental Principles of the Metaphysics of Morals*, Section 2. http://www.gutenberg.org/cache/epub/5682/pg5682.html.

20. Elliot D. Cohen, "The Activity of Philosophy," in Elliot D. Cohen (Ed.), *Philosophers at Work: Issues and Practice of Philosophy* (Orlando: Harcourt, 2000).

21. By "language" I mean strings of symbols used within a given culture to communication ideas and feelings according to a systematic set of conventions (syntactical rules that define grammar, and semantic rules that define sense and reference [meaning]).

22. The distinction I have in mind here is sometimes referred to as that between "illocutionary acts" versus "perlocutionary acts." The former is what one does *in* saying something. The latter is what one does *through* saying something. For example, in saying "Please help me," I have issued a plea for help. Through saying this I might have intimidated you into helping me. However, the primary purpose of language is to perform acts like asking, requesting things, not intimidating, frightening, evoking pity, etc. The latter are consequences of the use of language (things done *through* the use of language) and are parasitic of its primary uses. See, for example, J. L. Austin, *How to Do Things with Words* (Cambridge, MA: Harvard University Press, 1975); John R. Searle, *Speech Acts: An Essay in the Philosophy of Language* (Cambridge, UK: Cambridge University Press, 1970); P. H. Nowell-Smith, Ethics (Harmondsworth, UK: Penguin Books, 1964).

23. William J. Knaus, *How to Conquer Your Frustrations* (e-book) REBT Network. http://www.rebtnetwork.org/library/How_to_Conquer_Your_Frustrations.pdf.

24. In this premise, Volitional Can'tstipation is in the position of a Fallacy of Emotional Rules. While LBT classifies Volitional Can'tstipation as a Fallacy of Behavioral Rules, it is noteworthy that this fallacy can also occur within a major premise rule of emotional reasoning. This is because terms used to convey this Volitional Can'tstipation are typically not purely descriptive and imply the undesirability (badness, awfulness, etc.) of the situation thought to be beyond one's toleration. Thus, when Leo says that he couldn't stand to let Mary know the truth, he is implying that this situation is *so bad* that it would be beyond his ability to tolerate. Accordingly, such terms as "can't stand" and its synonyms can do double duty as both expressions of Volitional Can'tstipation and Awfulizing.

25. Elliot D. Cohen, *The New Rational Therapy*, (Lanham, MD: Rowman & Littlefield, 2007).

Part II

USING LBT TO COPE WITH STRESSFUL EMOTIONS

Chapter Five

Angry about a Girlfriend's Clutter

How to Apply the Six Steps of LBT

"The life which is unexamined is not worth living," stated Socrates, in defending himself against the Athenians at his trial. "[T]he greatest good of man," he admonished, "is daily to converse about virtue, and all that concerning which you hear me examining myself and others, and that the life which is unexamined is not worth living."[1] In these words, Socrates succinctly summed up one of the most powerful antidotes to blind conformity and dogmatic thinking: exposing the faulty thinking of oneself and others through "the examined life," that is, through the application of logic and philosophy. But read his words carefully, for he says "daily to converse about virtue," which is more, a lot more, than simply avoiding blind conformity and dogmatic thinking. Logic-Based Therapy proudly aligns itself with this venerable tradition; for it embraces Guiding Virtues to guide us out of a life mired in Cardinal Fallacies (Bandwagon Reasoning, Manipulation, Can'tstipation, Demanding Perfection, Awfulizing, The-World-Revolves-Around-Me Thinking, and the rest) to "the greatest good of man," a life according to virtue.

The six steps of LBT encapsulate this Socratic prescription, utilizing logic and the wisdom of the ages (philosophy), to ascend from a life steeped in irrational thinking to one of virtuous living—one enriched and enlivened by Authenticity, Empowerment, Temperance, Metaphysical Security, Courage, Empathy and the other Guiding Virtues. To use a famous Platonic metaphor, the six steps of LBT are designed to lead one up from the depths of the Cave (The Cardinal Fallacies) into the Daylight (Uplifting Philosophy), where one can finally look directly, with open eyes, at the Sun (the Guiding Virtues). These six steps, which were introduced in the introduction, are accordingly:

1. Identify the emotional reasoning
2. Check for Cardinal Fallacies in the premises

3. Refute any Cardinal Fallacy
4. Identify the Guiding Virtue for each fallacy
5. Find an Uplifting Philosophy that promotes the Guiding Virtue
6. Apply the philosophy by implementing a plan of action

One step moves logically to the next. Once you find the reasoning, you can find the fallacy, refute it, replace the fallacy with its Guiding Virtue, find a philosophy that maps a congenial pathway to the virtue, and, last but not least, set up a concrete plan of action that puts your philosophy into practice.

This sequence of steps is "logical" but this should not be confused with "mechanical." For the LBT steps do not merely provide a set of techniques. There is artfulness here, the humanities applied to life in the pursuit of happiness. I have always seen the theory as applied philosophy, which is not a social science.[2]

"Philosophy" in this context has come to life, instead of being chained to the academy as though it were the possession (and slave) of an elite group of academicians. In this context, philosophy is a public utility, free to anyone and everyone who seeks its guidance. Cicero gracefully expresses LBT's vision of philosophy in praise of it:

> O Philosophy, thou guide of life! thou discoverer of virtue and expeller of vices! what had not only I myself, but the whole life of man, been without you? To you it is that we owe the origin of cities; you it was who called together the dispersed race of men into social life; you united them together, first, by placing them near one another, then by marriages, and lastly, by the communication of speech and languages. You have been the inventress of laws; you have been our instructress in morals and discipline; to you we fly for refuge; from you we implore assistance; and as I formerly submitted to you in a great degree, so now I surrender up myself entirely to you. For one day spent well, and agreeably to your precepts, is preferable to an eternity of error.[3]

Philosophy in Cicero's praise is the artificer of life; it is what can deliver us from an "eternity of error," a life wrecked by self-defeating and regrettable emotions and actions due to twisted reasoning. It is "the guide of life" and "discoverer of virtue and expeller of vices!" Here, in Cicero's praise, we find an image of philosophy as uplifting, "an instructress in morals and discipline," as well as a provider of "assistance" and a "refuge." This idea of philosophy as uplifting, inspiring, and elevating us toward virtue is the idea that LBT seeks to convey in helping clients find philosophies congenial and to their liking.

As "the guide of life" and "discoverer of virtue and expeller of vices" philosophy shows us a myriad of ways to virtue and "expels" the vices of irrationality that hold us back. This is LBT in its essence—Uplifting Philosophy, lifting us up and away from the vices of Cardinal Fallacies, guided by the Guiding Virtues.

Cicero also calls philosophy "the culture of the mind." By which he means that which "plucks up vices by the roots; prepares the mind for the receiving of seeds; commits them to it, or, as I may say, sows them, in the hope that, when come to maturity, they may produce a plentiful harvest."[4] Here LBT's six steps find eloquent metaphorical expression. For LBT is itself such a "culture of the mind" that "plucks up vices by the roots"—it finds the Cardinal Fallacies hidden in the Major Premise Rules of one's emotional reasoning, and refutes them; thus preparing the mind to receive the "seeds" by identifying the Guiding Virtues; and "sows them" through the adoption of Uplifting Philosophies, which can, through their application, "produce a plentiful harvest," that is, happiness in terms of the Guiding Virtues.

Part of the beauty of this process is its congeniality and transparency. There is no hidden agenda that seeks to manipulate or control. Indeed, such would violate the very virtues that guide it. Accordingly, clients should be told, from the outset, what to expect. The case of twenty-five-year-old Fred Mallory, a nurse practitioner, provides an illustration:

"Hi Fred, I'm John Waddell, a Logic-Based Therapy Practitioner."

"Hi, I'm Fred Mallory, a nurse practitioner."

"It is nice to meet you, Fred. How much do you know about LBT practice?"

"I know that it's supposed to use philosophy to help you cope with problems."

"Yes. LBT is a form of philosophical practice. We LBT practitioners help people address their specific problems of living, while they learn some valuable reasoning skills that can be applied to other problems that might arise in their lives. We do not diagnose and look for causes of mental illness. So it is not a substitute for psychological practice."

"I like that. It's not like I am being psychoanalyzed or you are trying to find out if I am mentally ill."

"Correct! LBT is based on the idea that people upset themselves by deducing irrational conclusions from premises that contain faulty thinking errors called 'fallacies.' My job is to help you find and examine your reasoning, and to make constructive changes in your life through the use of philosophy. There are six steps to the process. I will guide you through each step. But it is your responsibility to choose your own philosophy and make your own choices."

"That's fine with me. I would prefer to make my own choices rather than having someone making them for me."

"Great! We handle specific problems of living, like dealing with a loss, midlife issues, or a moral problem. When the problem is adequately addressed through the six-step method, the assistance terminates. So it tends to be brief, often one to four, one-hour meetings. Is there anything else you might like to know about LBT at this point?"

"I know I'm making myself upset, but not sure how to go about changing. So, LBT will help me with this?"

"I hope so. While there are never any guaranties, that is one main goal. LBT looks at your reasoning with an eye toward helping you find more constructive philosophical perspectives about your presenting problem; and it aims at helping you to set more life-fulfilling goals. This brings us to why you came to see me. Tell me something about that."

Here, Fred seems to have grasped the essentials of LBT, which are:[5]

- examines one's reasoning
- holds that people upset themselves by deducing irrational conclusions from fallacious premises
- neither diagnoses nor looks for causes of mental illnesses
- addresses specific life problems as distinct from mental health problems, and is, therefore
- not a substitute for psychological counseling
- has six steps
- is relatively brief
- teaches valuable reasoning skills
- helps to set more fulfilling goals
- does not tell you what philosophy to embrace or what to do, although it
- corrects faulty thinking errors; and
- offers no guaranties that it will be successful

Of course, if Fred has further questions about LBT, at any time in the assistance process, then the practitioner should provide suitable responses; however, at inception, the practitioner should provide an overview of the LBT process rather than a detailed discussion of each step, inasmuch as the latter could confuse or overwhelm the client before he has had the opportunity to see the process at work in the context of addressing his life problem.

STEP 1: IDENTIFYING THE EMOTIONAL REASONING

The first step of LBT can be characterized as phenomenological, non-directive, and person-centered. The phenomenological character lies in the attempt to explore the clients' subjective world by understanding and clarifying it rather than by analyzing and critiquing it. This project of understanding and clarifying is the crux of the nondirective character of Step 1. It aims at helping the client to ascertain the elements of her emotional reasoning for the purpose of formulating it. This phase is also "person-centered" because it stresses "connecting" with the client by exhibiting person-centered personality traits such as Authenticity, Empathy, and Respect. At this juncture, LBT bears some resemblance to Carl Roger's "Person-Centered" counseling approach.

According to Rogers, there are three counselor "attitudes" that provide conditions of constructive client change, namely, empathy, unconditional positive regard, and congruence. As discussed in Chapter 2, Rogers defines empathy as a real-time, "here and now" sensing of the client's subjective world as if it were the counselor's own, but "without ever losing the 'as if' quality."[6] Counselors need to relate to clients on this "gut" level if their clients are to make progress in counseling, according to Rogers. This is because such an attitude makes it more likely that the client will trust, and therefore confide in, the counselor. If I believe that you understand what I am going through, I will be more likely to tell you things, and this will afford me an opportunity to get clearer on my feelings, and to work them through.

Further, empathy is related to what Rogers calls "reflection," which helps clients clarify their feelings. This involves the counselor's stating back to the client what she is feeling in a way that captures its essence.[7] Reflection works synergistically with empathy inasmuch as having access to the client's subjective world makes such clarification possible. It involves reformulating the client's description in a manner that *adds* to it. So reflection, as Rogers intended, is never merely a parroting back of what a client states. For example, the client might convey, "I don't know how I'm going to get through this!" And the counselor might reflect, "So, you are feeling very anxious about what might happen?"

Rogers also stresses active listening, which involves asking open-ended questions ("How do you feel about that?") instead of questions that could be answered with a yes or no ("Are you angry about that?"). Whereas the former permits one to describe one's feelings, hence to clarify them to oneself, the latter forecloses such an opportunity.

According to Rogers, *unconditional positive regard* is displayed when the counselor assumes a nonjudgmental attitude of acceptance of the client as a person. It involves the recognition of the client's right to be who she is, and can be, not what she is expected to be by others. It is therefore an attitude of unconditional acceptance of the client as a person, regardless of what she believes or does; or how she feels. As a result, the client is able to feel comfortable with self-exploration and gains trust in the counseling process. Unconditional positive regard should not, however, be confused with agreeing with everything the client says. It is rather an unconditional acceptance of the person. For example, a parent may have unconditional love of a child even when the child is acting inappropriately.[8]

As discussed in chapter 4, *congruence* involves being transparent, so that what you are on the inside, subjectively, matches what you are on the outside, objectively.[9] A congruent counselor is therefore genuine and honest, not a phony who acts or says one thing, and feels or thinks another. Consequently, the congruent counselor promotes the client's trust in the counselor so that the client is, again, disposed to open up in counseling.

According to Rogers, to the extent that the aforementioned attitudes (empathy, unconditional positive regard, and congruence) are practiced by the counselor, the client will predictably make progress in working through her issues for which she seeks counseling. On the other hand, when these conditions are lacking, the client is likely to be obstructed. Rogers, in fact, maintains that the lack of these three conditions in the client's life is what creates the need for counseling in the first place. Clients who have tended to be unloved, neglected, mocked, deceived, disempowered, disregarded, treated with indifference or unfeelingly, or in other related ways, are unlikely to thrive unless these deficits in the three said attitudinal conditions are addressed. According to Rogers, this is precisely the purpose of the "Person-Center" counseling approach.[10]

LBT largely accepts the Rogerian approach as described above as it applies to Step 1 of the LBT process. Indeed, the Guiding Virtues of Empathy, Authenticity, and Respect (for self and other) bear significant resemblance to the Rogerian attitudes of empathy, congruence, and unconditional positive regard, respectively. However, as will become clear, while Rogers' approach builds needed rapport between the client and counselor, it omits LBT's emphasis on reasoning, virtue, and philosophy.

The following continues the dialogue between Fred and his LBT practitioner, and illustrates how the LBT process unfolds in Step 1:

"I came to see you because I'm having a problem with my girlfriend."

"Tell me about that."

"Recently, we moved in together and it's not working out very well."

"How so?"

"Well, she goes shopping and buys a bunch of stuff. Then she puts it down on the living room couch or on the kitchen counters and just leaves it there. If I don't put it away it will just stay there. So I end up putting it away."

"Do you get upset about having to put it away for her?"

"No, it's that she just leaves it there cluttering up the house. I happen to be a very neat person. If I take something out, I put it away."

"So you are upset about your girlfriend buying stuff and leaving it on the living room couch or on the kitchen counters instead of putting it away."

"That sounds right."

"Okay, I think we have gotten some clarity about the object of your emotion. This is what you are upset about."

"Yes, I think so."

"So, imagine you come home one day and see this stuff cluttering up your house. There you are: a person who's neat and tidy. You walk into your house, which you have tried to keep neat and tidy, and there is that mess again!"

"Okay, I'm imagining it."

"On a 'badness scale' of one to ten where one is the least bad and ten is the worst, how bad are you now rating your girlfriends leaving this stuff around?"

"About a seven or eight."

"So, it sounds like you get quite angry."

"Yes, I do."

"Okay, I think we might now have clarified how you are rating the object of your emotion. In LBT we look for both the object and its rating—meaning how you are evaluating what you are upset about. Then, once we have the object and its rating, we can put together your emotional reasoning. So, is this what you are telling yourself? If your girlfriend buys stuff and leaves it on the couch or kitchen counters, instead of putting it away, then what she does is so bad that it measures seven to eight on the badness scale; and since this is exactly what she does, then she does something *that bad*."

"Yes, that's it!"

"Okay, so let's look at this rule of yours that says that, if your girlfriend buys stuff and leaves it around, then what she does is so bad that it measures seven to eight on the badness scale. Why do you believe that leaving the stuff around is *that bad*?"

"Because things need to be put away!"

"They 'need to be?' So this is a 'must,' not just something you prefer?"

"I think so. Things need to be put away, not just left cluttering up the place."

"Okay, so, since the world *must* be neat and tidy, when your girlfriend leaves stuff out without putting it away, it's so bad that it measures seven or eight on the badness scale. Is that what you are thinking when you see the stuff and get angry?"

"Yes it is."

As you can see, the LBT practitioner is nonjudgmental in this first step. He does not challenge Fred's beliefs or feelings but rather attempts to enter his subjective world in order to understand what he is thinking and feeling. Thus he is able to glean Fred's emotional object as well as the rating. And when Fred give the object a rating of seven or eight, the practitioner reflects back the emotion Fred is experiencing ("It sounds like you are quite angry"). This reflection follows the definition of anger, which LBT defines as an action (intentional object) with "a strong negative rating of the action or the person who performed it."[11]

The LBT practitioner resonates with the subjective world of the client in order to vividly describe what the client would be experiencing:

> So, imagine you come home one day and see this stuff cluttering up your house. There you are: a person who's neat and tidy. You walk into your house, which you have tried to keep neat and tidy, and there is that mess again!

The client, in turn, is able to use this imagery to replay the experience and, while replaying it, to assess it (as a seven or eight on the badness scale). This idea of allowing the client to replay the experience while going through the LBT process can be useful in clarifying the emotion; for while the client is replaying it, he can provide a more accurate picture (to both himself and the practitioner) of the emotion and its rating. This is because such imagery engages the part of the brain (the amygdala) that is responsible for emotional imagination. It is in the context of this experiential data that the client is best situated to relay the rating that he actually gives the emotional object in question when he confronts it in an actual life context. Thus, when Fred is imagining how he felt when he saw the clutter lining his kitchen counters yesterday, his rating of seven or eight is more reliable because he "feels" how bad it felt when he experienced it yesterday.

Here lies the phenomenological nature of Step 1. The LBT practitioner helps the client to key into his subjective world by asking open-ended questions, reflecting back what the client is experiencing, empathizing, and providing the client an opportunity to replay, in his imagination, the experience of the emotion, its object, and rating. As a result, the LBT practitioner can help the client to articulate the emotional object, its rating, and, finally, the client's emotional reasoning. Indeed, once the practitioner has the intentional object (O) and its rating (R), he is able to "reflect back" the emotional reasoning itself:

> So, is this what you are telling yourself? If your girlfriend buys stuff and leaves it on the couch or kitchen counters, instead of putting it away, then what she does is so bad that it measures seven to eight on the badness scale; and since this is exactly what she does, then she does something *that bad*.

Here, the LBT practitioner receives confirmation from Fred that this is, in fact, his reasoning. Of course, if Fred had disconfirmed that this was his reasoning, then the process of clarification would have continued until a more accurate formulation could be attained. I have come to think of the formulation of clients' emotional reasoning on the analogy of an optometrist who asks the patient "Which slide is clearer, one or two?" Eventually the LBT practitioner finds the closest fit!

Notice also that the client looked deeper into the premise driving Fred's first major premise rule:

> Okay, so let's look at this rule of yours that says that, if your girlfriend buys stuff and leaves it around, then what she does is so bad that it measures seven to eight on the badness scale. Why do you believe that leaving the stuff around is *that bad*?

This query enables the practitioner to find a "higher-level" major premise rule upon which the above rule rests, namely, that the world *must* be neat and tidy. Once this second syllogism is formulated (and confirmed), Step 1 of LBT is complete;[12] and the next step, that of identifying the Cardinal Fallacies, begins.

STEP 2: IDENTIFYING THE CARDINAL FALLACIES

It is here that the Rogerian approach embedded in Step 1 receives an infusion of philosophy. This does not mean that the LBT practitioner ceases to be empathetic, authentic, and respectful. Indeed, these virtues are inherent parts of the LBT process from start to finish. The client continues to be guided through a human relationship with the practitioner. LBT does not change its stripes when it becomes philosophical. But it does add on a further, analytic dimension. Let's see how Fred and his LBT practitioner proceed in Step 2:

> "So, Fred, now that we have an idea about the reasoning that is promoting your anger, let's take a look at some of the assumptions you are making. The one that seems to be the wind behind the sail is your assumption that the world must be neat and tidy. From this you deduce that it's seven or eight on the bad scale when your girlfriend doesn't put away the stuff she bought. So, let's look at this 'must' first. LBT calls this Demanding Perfection since you are demanding that the world be neat and tidy, which is what the world might be if it were perfect."

> "Yes, I see that."

> "Now LBT would refer to your second belief as Awfulizing because it seems to be assuming that what your girlfriend is doing is awful—or at least pretty awful."

"Okay. That sounds right to me. I think it is pretty awful."

"I know. But according to LBT both of these beliefs are fallacies. A fallacy is a way of thinking that is irrational and self-defeating. LBT recognizes eleven Cardinal Fallacies. These are the biggest offenders, the ones that create the most problems for people's personal and interpersonal lives. Demanding Perfection and Awfulizing are two of these fallacies."

"So why are they fallacies? I'm not getting it."

As you can see, Step 2 involves introducing the idea of a fallacy, and identifying the fallacies in the given reasoning. It also involves pointing out how the identified fallacies relate to one another, that is, how one follows from the other. This concept of a series of fallacies in a hierarchical chain of syllogisms is what LBT calls a fallacy syndrome. The present syndrome consists of the Demand for Perfection deducing Awfulizing ("Since the world is not the way it must be, therefore, it's awful"). LBT distinguishes between a number of different fallacy syndromes, of which the Demanding Perfection—Awfulizing Syndrome is one.[13]

However, it is not enough simply to tell a client that one or more of his beliefs are fallacious. As in the case of Fred, this does not go very far because the client often believes that there is nothing wrong with his beliefs. In fact, according to LBT, the difference between a repressed belief (a belief that is held on a subconscious level) and a suppressed premise (a belief in emotional reasoning that is merely assumed) is that the former is too threatening to be accepted on a conscious level and is therefore typically rejected by a client if called to his attention ("My father a good man; he would never do anything to hurt me!"). In contrast, an assumed premise in a client's emotional reasoning[14] is typically met with emphatic agreement when called to his attention ("The world must be neat and tidy; that's the way the world must be!").[15] So, the challenge is to convince the client that these seductive premises are fallacies. This requires that they be refuted, which is the purpose of Step 3.

STEP 3: REFUTING THE CARDINAL FALLACIES

Indeed, Fred has some sense that the two beliefs in question are related to his anger but he does not understand why they should, therefore, be called fallacies. In fact, in such cases, clients tend to have mixed opinions about their emotions. On the one hand, the emotion is unwanted ("I wish I didn't get so angry at her"); on the other, the emotion seems "appropriate" under the circumstances ("She's messing up my house and making me live like this! Why shouldn't I be pissed!"). So Fred is caught in an emotional tug of war—not yet willing to condemn the emotion as irrational, yet feeling unduly "stressed out" by it. The key to relieving this stress lies in LBT's Step 3 refutation. To see this, let's continue with Fred's LBT session:

"Fair question, Fred. Take your premise that the world must be neat and tidy. Can you prove that the world *must* be neat and tidy?"

"Yes, this is the way it must be."

"What evidence do you have to *prove* this? You just repeated your belief. You need independent evidence."

"I don't have any, I suppose."

"But you do have a lot of evidence to prove it false."

"What do you mean?"

"If the world really must be neat and tidy, then the world would always be that way. Isn't that what *must* means here? When we say that the earth must have water to support life, doesn't that mean that we won't find any life without water?"

"Yes, I think so."

"But there are lots of cases in which the world is not neat and tidy. Can you think of any examples?"

"Yes, there are messy places, like the garbage on the side of the parkway. And a lot of things get messed up when there are natural disasters."

"Very good examples! The world is not always neat and tidy, so it makes no sense to say that it *must* be neat and tidy. That is refuted by the facts."

"I see what you mean, but it still should be neat and tidy even when it's not."

"Why *should* it be neat and tidy? Does it make sense to demand that something should be what it cannot be? Doesn't 'should' imply 'can?' So if the world, as you admit, is not always neat and tidy, then how can you say that it should be?"

"Well maybe it should be when it comes to my house."

"So why should it be neat and tidy when it comes to your house?"

"That's the way I want it to be. I feel good when it's neat and tidy."

"Okay, so what you are saying is this is the way you *prefer* your house to be."

"Yes, that's right!"

"But notice that there is a big difference between preferring something and demanding that it must be a certain way. In this world we can prefer things but that doesn't mean we must have them."

"Yes, I see your point."

"You are entitled to your preferences, Fred, but that's all it is, a preference, not a must."

"Okay, so what difference does that make?"

"Let's try something. Imagine again that you are coming home and as you step into your house, you see your girlfriend's stuff cluttering up not only your couch and counters. This is the worst you have ever seen it. Stuff all over the place! Are you there now?"

"Yes I am imagining it."

"How are you feeling?"

"Pissed; very, very pissed!"

"Now change your 'must' to a preference. The world does not have to be neat and tidy. You prefer it this way; but it doesn't have to be. Let me know when you are there."

"Yes I prefer it, but it doesn't have to be the way I prefer it."

"How are you feeling now?"

"I am feeling displeased because I didn't get what I wanted, but I am not really pissed anymore. I could always clean it up. It really isn't the worst thing in the world either. I can deal with it."

"Okay, fantastic. Did you come to any new conclusions?"

"Yes, I am really stressing myself out by demanding that things must be the way I prefer them to be. It's really incredible how I didn't realize this before when it was staring me right in the face. I see what you mean now about this being a fallacy."

Clearly, refutation can be very powerful in helping clients see the fallacious character of their fallacies. Refutation can proceed in different ways.[16] There were at least three ways illustrated above. First the LBT practitioner showed Fred that he had no evidence to support that the world must be neat and tidy. Second, he challenged Fred to show that there are counterexamples to his belief that the world must be neat and tidy. Helpfully, the practitioner in this case engaged the client in the refutation by challenging Fred to come up with his own counterexamples, that is, cases that contradict his belief. For example, the existence of turmoil produced by natural disasters is such a counterexample because it shows that the world is not always neat and tidy; and therefore that it doesn't *have* to be. Then when Fred said the world should always be neat and tidy, the LBT practitioner helped Fred to see that, if this were true then it would be possible for this to be true. Keying into the Kantian concept that "ought" (or "should") implies "can," the practitioner helped Fred to see that his belief—that the world should always be neat and tidy—implied a false statement, namely that it *can* always be neat and tidy.

Finally, the practitioner helped Fred to see the logical difference between preferring and demanding that something be a certain way. Here, the LBT practitioner used an analytic technique to refute Fred's belief that the world must (or should) be neat and tidy. In effect, he helped the client to see that he is deducing a "must" from a want or preference. This is a fallacy in itself, the so-called naturalistic fallacy,[17] which says that you cannot deduce a normative claim from one that is purely factual. Thus, just because, as a matter of fact, I want something, does not mean that I must have it.[18] This profoundly important insight was first made by David Hume, who eloquently stated the point:

> In every system of morality, which I have hitherto met with, I have always remark'd, that the author proceeds for some time in the ordinary way of reasoning, and establishes the being of a God, or makes observations concerning human affairs; when of a sudden I am surpriz'd to find, that instead of the usual copulations of propositions, is, and is not, I meet with no proposition that is not connected with an ought, or an ought not. This change is imperceptible; but is, however, of the last consequence. For as this ought, or ought not, expresses some new relation or affirmation, 'tis necessary that it shou'd be observ'd and explain'd; and at the same time that a reason should be given, for what seems altogether inconceivable, how this new relation can be a deduction from others, which are entirely different from it.[19]

Hume did not apply this point to philosophical practice, but he very well might have; for almost like clockwork, clients infer shoulds, musts, and oughts from factual claims about their wants, desires, and preferences. The inference or "change" of vocabulary is, indeed, "imperceptible" to the client who draws the inference, and it is up to the LBT practitioner to call it to his attention. This is a very powerful refutation; for once the client sees the difference between what one wills and what must be, he can also see that it is silly to upset himself over such an inference. Accordingly, when Fred became aware of the distinction, he was able to return to the visualization of his experience, imagining his home in utter disarray, and nevertheless realizing that, although he preferred that his home not be so messy, he was no longer so stressed about it.

With the "must" deflated like a hot air balloon, the Awfulizing deduced from it is also deflated, for no longer does Fred rate his girlfriend's failure to put things away as a seven or eight. Instead it is reduced to a degree that is perhaps annoying but not evocative of anger. Generally speaking, when one fallacy is deduced from another, if it can be shown that the first is truly a fallacy, then the second also tends to lose its sting. Of course, it is also possible to refute the second fallacy independently of the first. For example, the practitioner could ask Fred to imagine something much worse than the messy house, say a tsunami in which hundreds of thousands lose their life (a much bigger, incomparably more tragic mess), then the rating of the messy house is easily seen to have been overrated when given a seven or eight relative to the mass devastation of the tsunami.[20] Indeed, once armed with such a heightened awareness of the fallacies inherent in his premises, Fred is ready to move to Step 4 of LBT, which is to identify the pertinent Guiding Virtues.

STEP 4: IDENTIFYING THE GUIDING VIRTUES

LBT matches each Cardinal Fallacy to a Guiding Virtue that has the potential to "guide" one away from the commission of the life-debilitating fallacy and toward a life affirming and enhancing ideal. As ideals, these virtues are never entirely realizable and there is always room for growth. Indeed, this is what makes these ends so invigorating. They are life pursuits that keep one moving to higher and higher levels of aspiration without any diminishing returns. For example, Authenticity is always a challenge no matter how authentic one becomes en route. So, you may, at different stages of your life, encounter different contexts that present challenges to your authenticity. As a youth, in your formative years, you may wrestle with peer pressures to conform to often dangerous and unproductive activities, from taking designer drugs to treacherous and mindless hazing activities. As you grow older, there are other packs open to membership that can have dangerous side effects, such as becoming a drone for a corporation that engages in socially irresponsible and dangerous business practices. At every turn in life there are temptations to jump on a bandwagon either for monetary gain or for acceptance. Politicians can sell out their moral integrity to get and stay in power; doctors can prescribe drugs because they are given perks by big pharma; corporate attorneys on retainer for corporate clients can help these clients to manufacture dangerous products or to pollute the atmosphere with lethal chemicals; teachers can sell out their academic standards by giving grades away in order to gain high success rates. Virtually any walk of life has its temptations, succumbing to which can compromise one's authenticity. Sometimes we backslide, and sometimes we make forward progress; but we are never fully actualized. All of the Guiding Virtues follow suit. As Aristotle rightly surmised, it is a matter of practice and cultivation of rational habits over time, with the constancy of working to improve one's skills. You make a mistake at work and try to lie yourself out of it, and end up losing your job. Is it a bad thing? Yes, if you continue to do the same thing next time. Otherwise you learn from the experience and the knowledge informs your judgment next time. This is how one builds strong virtuous habits. Experience can either build character or it can be wasted.

Perfection is not an option but ameliorating one's situation is. Being comfortable enough with oneself to admit one's weaknesses can help to set one on the road toward greater happiness. This is the case with Fred. Once he realizes his fallacies, he can treat them with some ancient wisdom and strive not only to overcome these fallacies but to aspire to human excellence or virtue. Fred's fallacies are Demanding Perfection and Awfulizing wherein the former feeds on the latter. Working on both of these fallacies simultaneously can have a synergistic effect. So by striving toward Courage, the Guiding Virtue of Awfulizing, Fred can aspire to Metaphysical Security, the Guiding Virtue of Demanding Perfection. This is because Courage implies the ability to accept a reasonable degree of risk, and Metaphysical Security is about being comfortable with reality, part of which is the inescapable existence of risk. So the Guiding Virtues tend to form an interlocking, mutually supportive system of aspirations. When one works on one Guiding Virtue, one can make strides toward another virtue. Let's see how Fred's session plays out during Step 4:

> "It is really great, Fred, to see that you have such a clear working understanding of the refutations of your fallacies. This is because the refutation provides a gateway toward conquering it and moving beyond it."

> "What do you mean?"

> "According to LBT, each Cardinal Fallacy—which includes Demanding Perfection and Awfulizing—has a corresponding Guiding Virtue that offsets it and helps you to move in a much healthier, life-affirming direction. When you see what the refutation of a fallacy is, you can clearly appreciate what the fix is for it."

> "Can you explain this?"

> "Yes, take Demanding Perfection, which we have just refuted. You nicely saw that the world is not capable of being perfect. That is indeed why there is no evidence to show that the world must always be neat and tidy. If this *must* were true then the world would always be neat and tidy, period. But the world isn't always neat and tidy, so this *must* is false to fact, so we might as well face it: the world is not a perfect place."

> "I get that. What does this have to do with virtues?"

> "Well, once we see, through the refutation of your fallacy, that the world is inherently imperfect, we can either protest this fact or learn to live rationally with

it. The former amounts to a refusal to live comfortably in the imperfect world along with its burdens and benefits. People who take this route resign from life; they become recluses, drug addicts, suicides, or look for other self-defeating, regrettable escape routes. Unless they succeed in killing themselves, these people still must inevitably live in the world, even as they retreat from it; so they only serve to defeat their own purposes. The only reasonable approach is, therefore, to take the rational route. This is where the Guiding Virtue of Demanding Perfection comes into play."

"What is it?"

"LBT refers to it as Metaphysical Security. Metaphysics is the branch of philosophy that deals with the nature of reality itself. Metaphysical Security is the virtue or habit of being secure about reality itself. The metaphysically secure person is philosophically enlightened and has a rational grasp of reality. This person is at home in the world, even though it is imperfect. He welcomes imperfection as a chance to learn and grow; the uncertainty of the future as an exciting opportunity to take reasonable chances and see where they lead; the existence of evil in the world as an opportunity to make the world better. This person doesn't demand perfection but instead strives to make the world—his life as well as others—a better place."

"That really sounds like an interesting virtue. I never thought about a virtue about reality before. It sounds like something I'd like to work on."

"Excellent! You can also work on the Guiding Virtue of Awfulizing too."

"What's that virtue?"

"Well, Awfulizing involves exaggerating the badness of things, which leads people to have anxiety about bad things happening in the future; or to worry about the bad things that have already happened. So the Guiding Virtue of Awfulizing would have to do with rationally confronting this anxiety or worry. So what virtue do you think this might be?"

"Sounds like it might be not being afraid of things."

"Right! And what do we call a person who's not afraid of things they shouldn't be?"

"Maybe, brave or courageous?"

"Right again! The Guiding Virtue of Awfulizing is Courage! Aristotle said that courage is the middle ground between being foolhardy and being a coward. It's when you take rational risks and aren't afraid to do so, but you also know when you would be foolish to take risks, say ones that are unnecessary or unlikely to bear fruit."

"I like that idea. Instead of Awfulizing about things like my house becoming a disaster area, I can be courageous and not worry about it."

"Good! Notice too that the courageous person, like the metaphysically secure person, is not afraid to take reasonable risks; so you can work on being courageous at the same time you work on being metaphysically secure."

"So how do I do that?"

In this dialogue you can glean how the Guiding Virtue is related to the refutation. The refutation of a fallacy points to the Guiding Virtue. For example, showing that the world is not perfect and that, therefore, it is futile to demand perfection, points to the idea of living, rationally, within the world despite its imperfections (= Metaphysical Security). Similarly, showing that one is exaggerating just how bad something is, and that, therefore, it is unreasonable to worry or be anxious about it, points to the idea of rationally accepting the risks and dangers inherent in the world (= Courage). And, as you can see, these virtues work synergistically with one another. Courage supports Metaphysical Security, and vice versa; and likewise for the rest of the Guiding Virtues in relation to one another.

It is, therefore, a rather seamless move from Step 3 to Step 4, so much so that, as you have seen in the above dialogue, Fred is able to gain insight into the relationship between these concepts through the use of Socratic dialogue, as when, for example, Fred is able to adduce what the Guiding Virtue of Awfulizing is. This symmetry and seamlessness is emblematic of LBT, and is, as such, inherent in the subsequent steps, Steps 5 and 6, of the LBT Process.

STEP 5: FINDING AN UPLIFTING PHILOSOPHY

The Guiding Virtues lead the way for the adoption of an Uplifting Philosophy, which is a philosophy that "lifts us up" toward the Guiding Virtue. This should be a congenial philosophy, which means that, not only does it promote the Guiding Virtue, it is at peace with the client. That is, it fits in with the world view of the client. For example, some clients are nonbelievers in God. It would be inappropriate to prescribe to such an individual that she embrace a God-centered philosophy, say like Aquinas'. On the other hand, one would not want to prescribe an atheistic philosophy to a believer, for example, telling the client to accept that "God is dead" (Nietzsche's declaration) in order to take responsibility for her life in aspiring to be authentic.

In fact, it would be inappropriate in LBT to *prescribe* any philosophy because the client is better served by choosing her own philosophy. This is because a philosophy forced on a client is not likely to be very uplifting. Rather, it is more likely to be accepted in a mechanical and lifeless manner. The client should resonate with the philosophy. It should touch her soul (if there is one!). It is should be "second nature" to the client.

Of course, most clients are not experts in philosophy and do not have philosophies up their sleeves. Nevertheless, they do have beliefs and attitudes about the world, whether or not they agree they are philosophical. They have preferences for ideas just as they have preferences for food. This is not to say that there aren't any bad ideas just as there are bad foods (foods not good for you). Indeed, LBT identifies such bad food for thought using its eleven Cardinal Fallacies. Any philosophy worth its salt does not commit any of these fallacies, according to LBT. So, within these broad parameters, there is truly a wide array of philosophical ideas to choose from. I have attempted to advance some of these ideas as they relate to specific Guiding Virtues in my book, *The New Rational Therapy*.[21] But those who practice LBT are constantly adding to these philosophical "antidotes."

Indeed, LBT practitioners should feel clients out (get an idea of the look and feel of the client's belief system) before suggesting (not prescribing) a philosophy. Let's return to the case of Fred to see how this works:

"LBT teaches people to work on attaining their Guiding Virtues by adopting philosophies that promote these virtues. These philosophies can be ancient insights of great philosophers, but sometimes clients have their own ideas about life that they may not have ascribed to any great thinker, but these ideas really seem to resonate with them and make sense. The point is to choose a philosophy that you feel comfortable with and which can work for you."

"Okay, so give me an example."

"Sure, suppose you were trying to become more self-controlled. Aristotle admonished that one doesn't achieve such virtues by simply reading a book on virtues. You have to practice them in order to cultivate a habit of self-control. So, for the person who says that he will control himself next time, the million dollar question would be 'How are you going to do it if you haven't practiced self-control?'

"I think I see. It's practical advice about how to work on your virtues."

"Yes, that's right. According to LBT, philosophy is a rich treasure trove of such practical advice, if only we can put it to work in our everyday lives to address our problems of living."

"Okay, I think I have it. So the question is what sort of practical advice can I give myself to help me work on becoming Metaphysically Secure and Courageous?"

"That's right. They should be ideas that you think can really help you."

"So when my girlfriend leaves stuff hanging around I suppose I can look at it as something that's not so bad. We said that, right?"

"Very good! This is called reframing, and LBT teaches you how to use philosophical ideas to reframe a situation so it is no longer as stressful."

"So I can just tell myself that it isn't really so bad?"

"You could, but we could develop that idea a bit further. What you are saying sounds very much like the advice Buddha might have given you."

"Tell me about that. I was always interested in learning more about Buddhism."

"Well, the First Noble Truth of Buddhism, which is one of its bases, says that life is painful. Death, aging, illness, separation, not getting what you want are among other things, inevitable parts of life, and these things are painful. You can run but you can't hide. The problem arises when you try to cling to these things with demands or cravings that these things not happen. However, according to Buddhism, life itself, and all the things in our sensible world are fleeting and impermanent, so you can't demand that they stay as they are. It is when people make such demands that they suffer. So pain is inevitable but suffering is not. You only suffer when you demand, crave, or cling to things. So the Uplifting Philosophy here is to let these things go. It isn't pleasant but you don't have to suffer, which mean stress out over it."

"That makes a lot of sense to me. I can see how that could help. So when my girlfriend leaves things around I don't have to like it but I don't need to suffer either. I can let it go because that's the way things are—they are not permanent and I shouldn't demand that they be what they aren't. Some day that house won't even be standing, and I will probably rot away before it will anyway! No more clinging! That's what causes the suffering. I can really see how this can be 'uplifting,' as you say. I am really excited about this!"

As you can see, the LBT practitioner in this case looks for a lead-in to a philosophy before suggesting it. He gives Fred an opportunity to point in a given direction. The practitioner then makes a connection between what Fred is saying (that he shouldn't think that leaving things around is so bad) and what a given philosophy says, namely Buddhism. Undoubted, this could have dead-ended because Fred may have not liked what Buddha had to say. In that case, the practitioner could have tried a different philosophy—listened more to Fred's own ideas first and then taken them in a different philosophical direction. For example, Heraclitus and Plato also had the idea of the impermanence of the material world; and Epictetus admonished us not to try to demand control of what's not in our power to control, including what others do. Schopenhauer would admonish one to stand up to the blind chaotic force that is leading one to make self-destructive demands on the world. He would tell you to recognize your blind chaotic drive for perfection for what it is—a manifestation of an evil will operative in nature—and to detach yourself from it intellectually. He would tell Fred to take an aesthetic perspective viewing his girlfriend's messiness from the disinterested perspective of "a pure subject of will-less knowledge."[22] In this way, he could get over his stress over his girlfriend's actions by seeing it from this disinterested, artistic vantage point. Like watching a blizzard from within a warm house, the snow blowing and the wind howling cannot harm you. It takes on an air of a work of art. It can be liberating!

Indeed, we could amplify on the bountiful philosophical routes to Metaphysical Security.

Notice too that these philosophies could also support Courage. Whether it's Buddha, Epictetus, Schopenhauer, some combination thereof, or other philosophical theories that resonate with the client, a philosophy can sometimes work synergistically to simultaneously support two or more Guiding Virtues. For example, the Buddhistic idea of accepting that life is painful can help build courage by encouraging one to (courageously) confront the pains of life and avoid the suffering that comes with craving and clinging. The possibilities of working with a client to develop and unleash the uplifting power of a philosophy or set of philosophies is one of the most rewarding aspects of LBT practice. The excitement evinced by Fred in the above case is true to life. Clients often do get such inspiration from an interesting philosophy that is well adapted and congenial to their manner of thinking. And so do philosophers who have sometimes, in their darker moments, wondered whether their tools of the trade (philosophical theories) can indeed bake any bread.

Once the client has adopted a congenial philosophy, then the next and final step is to apply the philosophy. Here is where the rubber meets the road!

STEP 6: APPLYING THE UPLIFTING PHILOSOPHY

The solidarity between the client and a congenial, uplifting philosophy is the cement that binds LBT to praxis. This last step in the process is where the client has the opportunity to express himself authentically through the application of this philosophy. This is why it is of the utmost importance that the adopted philosophy is close to the client's heart. Indeed, he is expected to live this philosophy, in a quite literal sense. Fred's session comes to a close with the following dialogue:

> "Great job, Fred! You really seem to feel comfortable with the Buddhist philosophy."
>
> "Yes, very much so."
>
> "This is good because your commitment to it has practical implications."
>
> "I would imagine so; but what do you mean?"
>
> "To truly embrace Buddhism means to live according to its tenets. Are you prepared to embrace the Buddhist idea of letting go of your perfectionistic demand for permanence?"
>
> "Yes, I believe so."

"You mentioned that you usually put the things away that your girlfriend leaves out."

"Yes, I do."

"And you do this because?"

"I do it so that things are back in order, as I think they must be."

"But now that you are embracing Buddhism, are you still going to do the same thing?"

"I see what you mean. If I really accept this idea of giving up clinging to things, I would have to let this go, leave the stuff out."

"Very good! So, let's suppose that you have this strong desire to put the things away. Imagine how you feel when you are about to put the things away. Can you imagine this?"

"Yes, I am feeling it now."

"What are you telling yourself?"

"That I have to get rid of this damn mess, right now!"

"It's an eyesore?"

"Yes, it's almost like my girlfriend just puked all over the place and she's just leaving it there, stinking up the place!"

"So how do you feel about just leaving it there and walking away?"

"It's difficult."

"Right! You are experiencing what we call 'cognitive dissonance.' This is when you intellectually appreciate that what you are thinking is irrational but you still feel attached to it, nonetheless."

"Yes, that's exactly right. I know it's irrational to cling to this idea that things have to be put away, but it really does feel like they must be. What can I do about it?"

"Do you have any suggestions?"

"I could force myself to just leave the stuff there, just walk away and let it stay there."

"Yes, you could. And how do you think you would feel if you did?"

"I would really be uncomfortable about leaving it there."

"Right, but this would give you an opportunity to apply your philosophy."

"I see that. I could think about what Buddha would do."

"And what do you think Buddha would do?"

"I think he would let it go even if he wanted it put away because he knows not to cling to things. I think he would accept it. But does that mean that I have to be passive and just let everything go?"

"No, I don't think so. When you put the things away because you think you must, is that what you mean about not being passive?"

"I thought so but I can see that I am almost like a slave to my craving."

"Good point! If you are truly free, then you have the freedom to do or forebear from doing something."

"So, if I can choose to let go of putting the things away, then I am free; but if I tell myself that I *must* put them away, then I am not giving myself a choice, and so I am not free."

"That's right. So you could still choose to put things away if you did it without this sense of compulsion about what *must* be."

"But then in putting stuff away am I just caving to my craving?"

"Yes, but only at first. What if you practiced not putting things away even though you felt compelled to put them away?"

"I could do that, and then when I stopped demanding that things be put away, I would be free to put them away or not."

"Excellent! So are you prepared to practice leaving the stuff out when your girlfriend doesn't put it away?"

"Yes, I am."

"Are there any other situations you might practice the same skill of letting go?"

"Yes, I think so. I have often told myself that I am not a materialistic person; so I don't buy many things for myself. But sometimes I want things and don't buy them because I think that I won't have a place for them and things will be messy around the house."

"Good. So what do you suggest?"

"I think I am going to buy some things I have wanted for quite some time. A riding lawn mower is one of them. I thought it would clutter up the garage so I refused to get one, but I always wanted one, and it would be nice to get outside more rather than hire someone to do something I really would enjoy doing myself."

"Okay. Great! Anything else?"

"Yes, sometimes I'm also kind of anal about putting some of my own stuff away. For example, I tell myself that I can't work at my desk unless my desk is completely cleaned off and all papers are filed away. Maybe I can try working at my desk even when it's a bit messy."

"Good idea! That would, indeed, give you more practice in standing up to your demand that things always be neat and tidy."

"I think it would."

"So it appears that we have a plan! You will practice not putting your girlfriend's stuff away; you will go out and buy a riding lawn mower; you will work at your desk without completely cleaning it off first. Is this okay?"

"Yes it is!"

In this last step, the LBT practitioner and client put together a plan of action to implement the Buddhist philosophy that the client embraced. To truly embrace this philosophy, however, means living according to it, which is what the action plan is intended to accomplish.

Notice that, at first, the practitioner gets clear on what the client usually does when his girlfriend does not put thing away, namely, that he puts them away for her. This is an important aspect of Step 6. This is because Fred's action of putting things away is the behavioral conclusion he is currently deducing from his demand that things be neat and tidy. The plan of action, therefore, needs to address this behavior by deducing an opposing set of behavior from the Uplifting Philosophy adopted by the client. Effectively, there are two opposing practical syllogisms:

Syllogism A

(Demanding Perfection) Things must always be neat and tidy.

If things must always be neat and tidy, then I must always put away my girlfriend's things.

So, I must always put away my girlfriend's things.

Syllogism B

(Uplifting Philosophy) I should not cling to ideas, but should instead let them go.

If I should not cling to ideas but should instead let them go, then I should not demand that I put my girlfriend's things away but instead let it go.

So, I should not demand that I put my girlfriend's things away but instead let it go.

As you can see, Syllogism A prescribes Fred's putting away his girlfriend's things; whereas Syllogism B prescribes Fred's letting go of this prescription. Syllogisms A is a deduction from Fred's Demand for Perfection; whereas

Syllogism B is a deduction from Fred's Uplifting Philosophy (Buddhism). The two syllogisms thus pull Fred in opposing directions, one that is based on a Cardinal Fallacy, the other that is rational. This tension between what Fred knows to be rational and his irrational disposition to demand perfection is known as "cognitive dissonance." According to LBT such cognitive dissonance amounts to progress in making constructive change. This is true because someone who knows he is behaving irrationally, or is inclined to behave irrationally, is in a reasonable position to make constructive changes based on this knowledge. In contrast, one who feels inclined to act irrationally and lacks awareness of the irrationality of the inclination, as well as what to do to overcome it, is not likely to make any constructive changes.[23]

As Aristotle admonishes, the way to make constructive change is by cultivating a rational habit through practice. The plan of action established in Step 6 is intended to be the blueprint for such practical change. In Fred's case, it amounts to working cognitively, emotively, and behaviorally to resist his irrational craving to make the world perfectly neat and tidy—a demand that is both unrealistic and stressful. This plan of action is challenging, indeed; it portends that Fred confront his disposition to demand perfection head-on by pushing himself to oppose it. It means speaking to himself in the new language of his Uplifting Buddhist Philosophy, underscoring the reality of change and the unreality of permanence; and the difference between pain and suffering—that not getting everything one wants is in the nature of reality, and that suffering resides in clinging to such an unrealistic idea. As such, Fred's goal is to *pull himself away* from Demanding Perfection, and *push himself toward* its Guiding Virtue, Metaphysical Security, through practical application of an Uplifting Philosophy based on key Buddhist tenets. In the end, the success of Fred's project will depend on his tenacity in applying his new philosophical lights. Like all endeavors in this imperfect world, this success cannot be measured in absolutistic terms but rather in terms of relative improvement. Can Fred or anyone else hope to attain an entirely stress-free existence? LBT makes no such unrealistic promise; but it does provide the framework for making one's life considerably less stressful, and, indeed, happier. The subsequent three chapters of this book are dedicated to illustrating this thesis through further case presentations of the six-step method of LBT as applied to guilt, anxiety, and sadness.

NOTES

1. Plato, *Apology*, trans. Benjamin Jowett. http://classics.mit.edu/Plato/apology.html.

2. See introduction to this book.

3. Marcus Tullius Cicero, *Cicero's Tusculan Disputations*, trans. C. D. Yonge (New York: Harper & Brothers Publishers, 1877), Book 5, p. 164. http://www.guten berg.org/files/14988/14988-h/14988-h.htm.

4. Ibid., Book 2, p. 69.

5. Other aspects of informed consent such as confidentiality, exceptions to confidentiality, fees, meeting times and places, etc. are not broached here. For a comprehensive discussion of informed consent in counseling, see Elliot D. and Gale S. Cohen, *The Virtuous Therapist: Issues and Practice of Counseling and Psychotherapy* (Belmont, CA: Brooks/Cole, 1999), Chapter 4.

6. Carl Rogers, *Dialogues*, ed. Kirschenbaum and Henderson (London: Constable, 1990) p. 15.

7. Elliot D. and Gale S. Cohen, *The Virtuous Therapist*, p. 61.

8. Ibid.

9. Carl Rogers, *On Becoming a Person* (Boston: Houghton Mifflin, 1961).

10. Ibid.

11. See definition of anger in Chapter 1.

12. Typically, in conducting LBT sessions, the LBT practitioner does not include "Bridging Premises." However, formally stated, Fred's emotional reasoning is as follows:

1. (Second Major Premise Rule) The world must be neat and tidy.

2. (Bridging Premise) If the world must be neat and tidy, then if your girlfriend leaves stuff out without putting it away, it's so bad that it is a seven or eight on the badness scale.

3. (Conclusion/First Major Premise Rule) So, if your girlfriend leaves stuff out without putting it away, it's so bad that it is a seven or eight on the badness scale.

4. (Minor Premise Report) My girlfriend leaves stuff out without putting it away

5. (Primary Conclusion) So, it's so bad that it is a seven or eight on the badness scale.

13. Elliot D. Cohen, *What would Aristotle do? Self-Control through the Power of Reason* (Amherst, NY: Prometheus Books, 2003); Elliot D. Cohen, *The Theory and Practice of Logic-Based Therapy*. (Newcastle upon Tyne: Cambridge Scholars Publishing, 2013).

14. The two fallacious premises in Fred's reasoning are both assumed premises. The client never stated them explicitly; instead the practitioner had to add them to the emotional reasoning in order to validate it. In the present case both of the assumed premises in question are major premise rules. See premises 1 and 3 in note 12. It is very commonplace for major premise rules to be suppressed premises of a person's emotional reasoning.

15. Elliot D. Cohen, "Critical Thinking, Not Head Shrinking," in Peter Raabe, Ed., *Philosophical Counseling and the Unconscious* (Amherst, NY: Trivium Publications, 2005).

16. See Cohen, *Critical Thinking Unleashed*, (Lanham, MD: Rowman & Littlefield, 2009). Ch. 15 on "Refutations in Practical Reasoning."

17. G. E. Moore, *Principia Ethica* (Amherst, NY: Prometheus Books, 1903). http://fair-use.org/g-e-moore/principia-ethica

18. Elliot D. Cohen, "'I Want, Therefore It Must Be': Treating Fascistic Inferences in Logic-Based Therapy," *Journal of Humanities Therapy*, Summer 2015, Seoul Korea.

19. David Hume, *A Treatise of Human Nature*, Guttenberg e-book, 2012, Book 3, Part I, Sect. I. http://www.gutenberg.org/files/4705/4705-h/4705-h.htm.

20. This is a version of the "double standards" refutation in which one shows that one is being inconsistent in one's rating of relevantly similar or relevantly different things. For example, in rating the messy house as seven or eight, one is being inconsistent in rating something else that is much worse as the same, for example, also rating the death of someone as a seven or eight.

21. Cohen, *The New Rational Therapy: Thinking Your Way to Serenity, Success, and Profound Happiness* (Lanham, MD: Rowman & Littlefield, 2006).

22. Ibid., p. 58.

23. Cohen, *What would Aristotle do?*

Chapter Six

Mom Keeps Son from Seeing Manic Dad

Confronting the Guilt

In the last chapter, a case of anger was presented, and each of the six steps of the LBT process was examined in the light of the case example. Therefore, it should now be clear how the process of LBT unfolds. It should also be evident that the method of LBT approaches problems of living by looking at the emotional stress that arises in the context of problems of living. Indeed, a core idea behind a *problem* of living is its stressful nature. For example, what makes problematic such things as midlife crises, moral dilemmas, divorce, family feuds, job losses, and deaths in the family is the emotional stress associated with them. True, these problems often call for strategizing; for example, how to find a new job or start a rewarding new career. But how to deal rationally with the emotions associated with such issues appears to be the most basic challenge. For example, if one can get past the dysphoria associated with the loss of one's job, then one can then more effectively deal with logistics of finding a new job. The emotional stress tends to be a major impediment to such strategizing because emotional stress thwarts the ability to think clearly, impairs the memory and powers of concentration, and, in general, obstructs one's ability to deal rationally and effectively with the inevitable challenges of living. So LBT's *modus operandi* is to help one develop a systematic way to deal with the stresses of everyday life as a means to helping one deal effectively with such problems. LBT also offers a proactive model of decision making, especially as it applies in contexts involving chronic problems of worry.[1] Thus, LBT is a comprehensive framework that offers both standards of rational decision making as well as a methodological approach to stress management. Even more, it offers a framework for striving for a fulfilling life as measured in terms of one's progress toward its Guiding Virtues. Not exactly "good for what ails you," but clearly a step toward ameliorating one's quality of living.

This chapter presents a narrative of an LBT session that concerns a problem of living associated with guilt. Guilt can be a powerfully debilitating emotion, especially when it is of a depressive nature.[2] It can also be a constructive emotion when it leads one to regret one's past mistakes for the sake of not repeating them in the future. "Repentance is good for the soul," it is sometimes said. This has a note of truth; but much depends on the style of penitence. If one damns oneself and condemns oneself to a life of hell on earth, it does no one much, if any, good. "Evil and totally worthless monsters" can do no good, now or in the future. Guilt of this condemnatory nature tends to be worse than useless since it needlessly thwarts the possibility for productive living.

The case of guilt presented in this chapter is a rather subtle brew, one that is insidious and quite commonplace in the everyday lives of many of us. Presented here is the case of Martina Cornelius, a professor of English literature, and wife to Nelsen Cornelius, a very talented, manic, impressionistic artist with an IQ of about 180.[3] Martina and Nelsen married and lived together for five years before they separated. Still married but living apart, they have one child, a four-year-old boy, Max, who lives with his mother.[4]

"Good afternoon, Dr. Cohen."

"Good afternoon, Dr. Cornelius."

"Oh please, do call me Martina. I am the client, after all."

"Okay, sure. So tell me something about yourself, Martina, and why you are seeking philosophical assistance."

"That's a good question. I suppose that I was attracted to it because you stick to helping people address their problems without diagnosing mental illnesses. I also heard of you through someone at my university and she said you helped her. I was a philosophy major in undergraduate school and philosophy has given me some great insights for literary analysis, so I get the idea that it may somehow work as a helping profession, but I am not exactly sure how."

"I think this should become clear to you as we proceed. The approach I use is called Logic-Based Therapy or LBT for short."

"Oh yes, I read about it online. I do understand the basis of it. You look for faulty thinking in people's reasoning. You use logic to set up syllogisms as I understand it. I generally do not like to put things into syllogisms. Anything that resembles math gets me nervous. That's why I went into English lit!" [She declared this with a note of sarcasm in her voice.]

"Okay, that's good to know. LBT in practice does not wear itself out with formal logic, but employs just enough to help the client see her reasoning. Aristotle, as you know, said that human beings were rational animals, and "rationality" for him was largely a function of the ability to draw logical conclusions; yet I do not think he was reserving the term "human being" just for logicians; so I suspect that, like most people, you won't have a problem with the formal logic involved in LBT."

"That's reassuring, Dr. Cohen."

"So tell me about the problem you want to discuss with me."

"As I mentioned to you on the phone, I am presently separated from my husband, Nelsen. We were together for eight years, and it's been almost one year since we separated. I have custody of our son, Max."

"Tell me more about your situation."

"It was my idea to separate."

"Tell me more about that."

"Do you know what it's like to live with a manic? Nelsen is extremely intelligent. He is a genius, has an IQ of about 180. And he's really creative when he's manic. He's an artist, does impressionistic art. He is very well known and he is incredible! I was really blown away by his talent when we first met, and it seemed really romantic at first—you know, the wild-eyed artist and his literary, bohemian wife. We always had fun at parties with colleagues, mostly professors and artists. But things change when you have a child and the reality of parental responsibility sets in."

"Tell me more about that."

"Nelsen is a nice guy but when he is manic, he doesn't know how to take care of a child. He is amazing on the canvas, but away from the canvas he is a disaster waiting to happen."

"So did he ever consider getting medicated?"

"Oh yes, and he said he felt 'dull.' He claimed that he couldn't work and he was absolutely miserable. He said he felt soulless and dead inside. So he refused to take his lithium, even though we had arguments about it on a regular basis before we split."

"So you were upset that he refused to take his meds?"

"Yes, I was, because he could never be a father to our son when he was a wild man. He had also gotten worse and I was afraid he might also do something to harm himself. But he just wouldn't listen, and I blame a lot of this on his mother."

"His mother?"

"Oh yes, she is a manic too! And she is also not medicated. In fact, she's constantly preaching the evils of medication, as though she was trying to save his soul from the devil; and he listens to her and not me. It's like the blind leading the blind, and there's nothing I have been able to say to convince him to go back on the medication. I had him committed twice, and then when he was released, he went off the meds and I had to try to get him back on them and to stay on them. It was a constant struggle."

"So last year I made the decision to separate from Nelsen. It's been very hard. I have custody of Max, and he rarely sees his father. This is really the hardest part!"

"Tell me about this. What exactly is the hardest part?"

"Nelsen loves Max. There's no question about that; but he is not willing to give up his manic highs, not for me, not for Max. He listens to Momma. So I really had no choice. I just don't trust him around Max. No telling what he's capable of doing. I have to protect Max."

"What do you think he might do?"

"He could do something crazy, like go to the top of a building with him and lead him out on a ledge. Who knows!"

"So, despite that you think it would be too risky to allow Max to be with his father, you are still upset about not allowing this to happen?"

"I allow him to see him sometimes but only when I am there and it's for very brief periods of time, and not very often. Max keeps asking about his father and I try to avoid talking about him."

"So you are upset about Max's asking questions about his father?"

"Oh yes, I feel so guilty when he brings him up!"

"Guilty?"

"Yes. He is still his father!"

"So you feel guilty about keeping Max from getting to know his father and having a relationship with him?"

"Yes, that's right!"

"I can understand how you feel. You feel like you are doing something wrong in keeping Max from his father, even though you are just trying to protect him."

"That's true."

"Are you rating yourself too?"

"What do you mean?"

"Are you saying anything negative about yourself?"

"Yes, I think so. I am a bad person because what kind of mother does this to her son?"

"So you are telling yourself that if you keep Max from getting to know and having a relationship with his father, that makes you a bad mother. So, since this is what you are doing, you are a bad mother. Is this your reasoning?"

"That sounds about right. Sometimes I hate myself so much."

"When is that?"

"When Max starts asking me questions about his dad and I change the subject or give him a vague answer."

"So, imagine yourself in this situation. Max is asking you questions about his dad; and you are changing the subject and giving him evasive answers. Are you imagining this?"

"Yes, I am."

"What questions is he asking?"

"He wants to know why his dad is not here with us."

"And what are you telling him?"

"I am telling him that his dad is very far away and that it's bedtime."

"How are you feeling?"

"Very guilty; like I am betraying my own son."

"And are you judging yourself negatively?"

"Yes."

"What are you saying about yourself?"

"That I am a fraud; I am a despicable excuse for a mother. He trusts me and I am betraying him about his father and keeping him from knowing him."

"Okay, so you are telling yourself that if you betray Max's trust about his father, then you are a fraud and a despicable excuse for a mother. And since you are not telling Max the truth about his father and keeping him from getting to know his father, then you are such a fraud and despicable excuse for a mother. Is this your reasoning?"

"Yes, that really hits the nail on the head. That's exactly what I am telling myself."

"Okay, so let's look at your premises. Why do you think that you are betraying Max?"

"I am not telling him the truth and he trusts me to tell him the truth."

"Do you think that it's your duty to tell him the truth about his father?"

"Yes, what kind of parent does such a thing! I know I am trying to protect him, but still!"

"Okay, so you are thinking that you have a moral duty to tell Max the truth about his father and to not to keep him from getting to know him. So, since you have this duty and have not abided by it, you are betraying Max. As such you are a fraud and a despicable excuse for a mother."

"That's right!"

"Okay, let's look at this moral principle of yours that you have a duty to tell Max the truth about his father and to not keep him from getting to know him. If you were Max and your mother did the same thing to you, under the same circumstances, would you think that she betrayed you and was a fraud and despicable excuse for a mother?"

"No I think I would understand when I got older. It's a difficult situation. It's not easy being a parent."

"Okay, so it appears that your moral principle is rather absolutistic. You seem to be demanding that there not be any exceptions to this rule when you are applying it to your own situation; yet you would be willing to make an exception if your own mother were in your situation."

"Yes I think that's accurate."

"So your moral principle really does have exceptions and your situation is one such exception?"

"Yes, that's true."

"Okay, what we have done so far is to identify your emotional reasoning—the reasoning that makes you feel guilty. We have identified a basic rule underlying your guilt, the demand that you tell your son the truth about his father and not keep him from getting to know his father; and we have refuted it by showing that it is not without exceptions. This rule, however, leads you to damn yourself—telling yourself that you're a fraud and a despicable excuse for a mother."

"I see that. But what am I supposed to do about it?"

"In LBT we identify the Cardinal Fallacy and refute it. In your case, you appear to be *demanding perfection* about telling Max the truth about his father and fostering a father-son relationship between them. But a five-year-old is not likely to understand that his father has a mental illness, and that he is too unstable at this point to be a responsible parent. These are adult issues. In a perfect world, perhaps we would not be in such a position as parents; but this is not a perfect world and there are exceptional situations such as yours."

"Alright, so I am demanding perfection. I see that."

"And you are also self-damning. You demand perfection of yourself and when you do not deliver on it, you damn yourself."

"Now that you put it that way, I can see where you are going with this."

"Okay, great! So let's take this a step further. According to LBT, for every Cardinal Fallacy, including Demanding Perfection and Self-Damnation, there is a Guiding Virtue that counteracts it. According to Buddhist philosophy, one can convert negative energy into positive energy by focusing on the positive instead of the negative. LBT is similar in that we replace the irrational, self-disturbing thinking with the positive virtue."

"Okay, so what are my Guiding Virtues?"

"The Guiding Virtue that replaces Demanding Perfection is called Metaphysical Security. The virtue for Self-Damnation is Self-Respect. Metaphysical Security is about being secure in a world that is imperfect, where you can't always have it the way you want it to be; where you have lots of possibilities but not certainty; where even moral rules do not always get to be satisfied perfectly; where ideals such as Truth and Justice are never completely satisfied on earth; where human beings are not perfect creatures and make mistakes."

"I get the idea. What about Self-Respect?"

"This Guiding Virtue is about accepting yourself as a fallible, imperfect person. It is about giving yourself permission to be imperfect without degrading and demeaning yourself. It is about recognizing your worth and dignity instead of seeing yourself as an object that has only value so long as it is useful. For example, you are Max's mother, but you are not just his mother. You are a person in your own right too. It is about recognizing that you can make mistakes or be less than perfect but still be a worthy person."

"This is so much like literary analysis. I feel like my life is a novel and you are providing the principles for literary analysis and evaluation."

"That's a good point! LBT is about looking at life narratives and changing them for the better."

"So how do I use these virtues to improve my narrative?"

"These Guiding Virtues can help you to change your outlook on life, give you a fresh ideal at which to aim, with the understanding that there is always room for improvement in this imperfect world."

"But, of course! I'm not supposed to be demanding perfection. But how can I make such changes when I keep getting bogged down in feeling like such a heel."

"At this juncture, LBT helps you to find suitable philosophies that can help you to move toward your virtues. It calls these philosophies "Uplifting Philosophies" because they provide ways to aim at the Guiding Virtues. They are philosophies that you accept and feel comfortable with. They fit in with your ways of thinking. They are spiritually uplifting, and can help you to feel better about yourself and your life. You are a literature professor, so you might tap into your own literary toolbox to find some philosophies that work for you."

"As you speak, I keep thinking about postmodernists like Foucault and Derrida who talk about constructing and deconstructing reality."

"That's excellent. Tell me more about this."

"I am telling myself that I have to be perfect in order to be a good person but maybe I can change the rules of life, so to speak, 'deconstruct' them to form a different sort of life script."

"Go on!"

"My world is different than one where the father is a responsible parent. My life narrative needs to be changed to depict a reality that allows parents to depart from everyday conventions that most people subscribe to. In my world, a responsible parent can protect her child from a manic dad who may unwittingly kill him and not understand how it happened. I have to, so to speak, invent the rules of the 'truth game,' to use Foucault's term. How am I doing?"

"You are doing great! If this works for you then you should go with it!"

"Okay, and so I shall. It does feel uplifting to think outside the box like this. That is what literary analysis is supposed to do and it seems to be working here. But in the back of mind there is still that sinking sense that I am a treasonous wretch."

"That's quite normal to have such a conflict going on. It's called 'cognitive dissonance.'"

"Oh yes, when you think one way and feel another. So how do I bring my new way of thinking in line with the way I feel?"

"Let me give you an analogy. I see you are wearing your watch on your left hand."

"Yes, you discovered that I am a lefty!"

"I see that. So suppose you were to put your watch on your other hand. Go ahead and do it."

"Okay. Just a second, it's been on here for a while."

"Take your time."

[She removes the watch from her left wrist and slips in onto the right one.] "Okay, so now what?"

"How does your watch feel on your other hand?"

"It feels really strange. Somewhat uncomfortable!"

"Just keep it there for now and we'll return to the question about how it feels later. For now, let's talk about your Uplifting Philosophy. The final step of LBT involves applying your philosophy. This involves creating a plan of action for putting your philosophy into practice. What do you do now when you feel guilty?"

"Sometimes I punish myself."

"How so?"

"I avoid going to socials with colleagues; I sometimes don't prepare for lectures and then tell myself that I'm a poor lecturer. I caught myself doing this yesterday when I totally trashed T.S. Eliot's *Waste Land*. I sometimes cancel office hours and go home early. I have been curt to students, even to some of my very bright students who enjoy literature."

"Okay, that's helpful. Clearly, if you tell yourself that you have breached a moral principle and are therefore a bad person—a 'fraud,' 'treasonous wretch,' 'despicable excuse for a mother'—then we might expect you to 'punish' yourself by acting in these ways. So we can work on turning this behavior around by rewriting your narrative to accommodate the new reality where you are no longer subject to the ordinary moral standards of people who have mentally competent spouses. According to your new narrative, what sort of things would you do instead?"

"Well, I wouldn't punish myself. I would basically do the opposite of the things I'm doing now. I would function as a responsible parent, professor, and colleague. I would take care of my child as always, teach my lessons to the best of my ability, treat my students as they deserve, keep my office hours, socialize with colleagues, and so on. How's that?"

"Excellent! So now you have a plan of action that aligns with your Foucaultean philosophy. Give yourself some time to start feeling comfortable with this new way of interpreting reality. At first you will still have cognitive dissonance; but as you continue to apply your philosophy you are likely to start feeling less dissonance and more comfortable living in your new reality. This means working cognitively, behaviorally, and emotionally on your new philosophy. So when you put your action plan into operation you should keep that new reality before you, reminding yourself that your narrative is different than that of other parents who have competent husbands to father their children. You should get used to living according to the new narrative as time goes on."

"I really hope so."

"By the way, how does the watch feel now?"

"Actually, it's starting to feel a lot more comfortable, much better than it did when I first changed hands. Still a little strange though, especially when I focus on it."

"You'll get increasingly used to it, and eventually you will feel more comfortable with it on your left hand instead of on your right!"

"Got it!"

Martina's guilt is illustrative of many cases in which people suffer needlessly from misconceptions about the nature of moral commitment. LBT is critical of moral absolutism as it is of any form of demanding perfection. In Martina's case, there were special circumstances that militated against being completely honest with Max about his father. Ideally, Max and his father would be permitted to cultivate a father-son relationship without the supervision and constraints that Martina applied. However, the circumstances were not ideal and, in Martina's considered judgment, there were significant risks to her child in applying standards intended to suit circumstances in which the father in question was mentally competent. In this world of impermanent and changeable realities, there is not a one-size-fits-all model that works in every context. To those who read morality as an unconditional imperative that does not admit of extenuating conditions, this position is likely to be disquieting. But LBT is tolerant up until the point that a Cardinal Fallacy is breached. To the extent that absolutism in morality (wherein moral principles with action-guiding potential are taken to be exception free) makes a demand for perfection, LBT rejects it. It does so because such a view militates against living successfully in a less than perfect universe. Thus the problem in Martina's case was not her response to her difficult circumstances, but rather the perfectionistic, absolutistic moral standard upon which she judged herself and her actions. Becoming metaphysically secure in her particular circumstances permitted a reinterpretation of traditional moral expectations. It allowed a different "truth game" in which children of incompetent fathers could justifiably be treated differently than children with responsible fathers.

Effectively, such an alternative "truth game"[5] required that Martina examine her own socialization. She was raised to believe that parents do not deceive their children or place obstacles between a father and his child. Yet this socialization, as an absolute, was out of alignment with her parental reality.

Could Martina overcome the pain associated with excluding Max's father from Max's life? As the Buddhist would admonish, life is not without pain, so the parental exclusion would always be a sore point; but Martina need not suffer guilt over it. This potential to avoid such suffering regarding a less than perfect (external) reality is that over which human beings can have considerable power. LBT lights the path to unleashing this potential. It is not a pain-free approach devoid of any regrets—this would be to demand perfection; but it can alleviate agonizing, debilitating, and unnecessary guilt.

NOTES

1. See Elliot D. Cohen, *The Dutiful Worrier: How to Stop Compulsive Worry without Feeling Guilty* (Oakland, CA: New Harbinger, 2011).

2. See discussion in chapter 1 about the relationship between guilt and depression.

3. People with IQs of 140+ are generally considered to be geniuses.

4. This case is a fictionalized version of a case that I worked on, so I serve as the practitioner in the narrative.

5. Elliot D. Cohen, *The New Rational Therapy: Thinking Your Way to Serenity, Success, and Profound Happiness* (Lanham, MD: Rowman & Littlefield, 2006), p. 68.

Chapter Seven

He Loves Me, He Loves Me Not

Dealing with Anxiety about a Prospective Engagement

The last chapter looked at guilt in the context of an LBT session. This chapter explores anxiety. As you have seen (chapter 1), anxiety is a future oriented, intrinsically iffy emotion. The intentional object of anxiety is always conditional. More exactly, it forecasts certain consequences *if* certain conditions are fulfilled ("If I don't get the job then I will end up homeless") and it rates this conditional state of affairs negatively. The degree of anxiety may also be proportional to the rating. Thus mild anxiety might attend an intentional object that is rated undesirable but not awful ("If I don't get the job then I will have wasted my time preparing for that interview").

In effect, anxiety is about possibilities, not actualities. Its rating is about how bad certain possibilities are if they are actualized ("If it actually happens that I don't get the job then I will end up homeless"). Therefore, the emotion stems from the uncertainty of the future, which is an unavoidable feature of the future.

Anxiety is not necessarily a bad emotion if it is mild and undemanding. So I might be anxious about doing well on my oral presentation when I am up for a promotion. Here, the anxiety can be debilitating if I demand that I do well; for in such a case I will invariably perceive the possibility of not doing well as devastating or catastrophic. On the other hand, if I do not demand, or "cling" to the idea, that I do well, but am open to accept whatever comes to pass, then I may experience anxiety nonetheless, but not intense anxiety; for I will not, in such a case, perceive my conditional emotional object in catastrophic terms although I may still think it undesirable.

Focusing on the here and now is the strongest antidote for avoidance of anxiety because anxiety is essentially future-oriented and cannot exist when one lives in the here and now. This is why Buddhist philosophies are such potent antidotes to anxiety. "Let go of the past, let go of the future," Buddha advises, "let go of the present, and cross over to the farther shore of existence. With mind wholly liberated, you shall come no more to birth and death."[1] Through such mindfulness (as attained through meditation) one is released from the clutches of time and the demands or "cravings" that attend it. Unfortunately, most of the human population is not so liberated and many live in the future even when the present can be enjoyed. I have seen some plan a vacation while on vacation, thereby missing the opportunity to be on vacation. These people often live in fear of the future and never seem to realize that time is made up of moment to moment, that there is no intrinsic difference between the present moment and the future moment, and that living for the future moment without enjoying the present moment is a vicious cycle whereby one reaps no moments of enjoyment.

As such, anxiety can be existentially challenging. It is part of the human condition. As creatures with one foot in the now and the other in the future, we feel the tension between our legs. Indeed, part of our evolutionary claim to fame is our ability to adjust our behavior to future possibilities. We see the sky turning gray and we head for shelter. It is not possible not to live (or to live very long) without exercising our rational predictive powers. But "rational" is a key word here. This is where LBT can help moderate between living needlessly, excessively, and self-defeatingly in the future, and attaining the "golden mean" or balance between past, present, and future living. The case presentation in this chapter is intended to help light the way toward the latter balance.

This case regards a twenty-six-year-old, single woman, Stacey Montego, who is in an uncommitted relationship. I am the philosophical practitioner of record.

"Hello Stacey. It is good to meet you."

"Hello Dr. Cohen, thanks for meeting with me so quickly. I know this wasn't a convenient time for you but it was really very kind of you, and I greatly appreciate it."

"I know you appeared to be very upset when we chatted briefly over the phone, so I do hope I can be of assistance."

"I hope so too."

"We chatted about LBT on the phone. Do you have any more questions about how LBT works?"

"No, not at the moment. I am very excited about our session and very eager to get started."

"Okay, then, let's begin with your telling me more about your issue."

"As I told you on the phone, I have been going out with my boyfriend for two years now. We were supposed to get engaged after he graduated law school. Now that he has graduated, he says that he just doesn't have the time right now to get the ring and 'do it right.' He says that he still wants to get engaged but that he wants to do it after he gets settled at his new job. He was offered this great job in Chicago at a top notch law firm. He wants me to come to Chicago to get engaged after he gets settled there. I am a nurse so it wouldn't be too hard for me to get a job in Chicago after we got engaged, but that's really not the problem."

"So what do you think the problem is?"

"What if he doesn't go through with it again? Then he would have wasted more of my time."

"You say that he would have wasted more of your time. Do you think that he is taking you for granted, treating you like your time doesn't matter? Is this the gist of what you mean by 'wasting more of your time?'"

"Yes, it really is. It would mean that he really didn't think I mattered enough to him to commit to me."

"So you appear to be anxious about the possibility of his not committing to you again, because that will mean you don't matter enough to him."

"Yes, that's right."

"So let's suppose that he doesn't commit to you again because you don't matter enough to him. Imagine that this actually happened. Let me know when you are imagining this as actually having happened."

[A moment's pause] "Okay, I am imagining it."

"What are you telling yourself about what happened?"

"That I can't believe he would do such a thing to me, like I wasn't good enough for him."

"Are you questioning your self-worth?"

"Yes, I am."

"Okay, so is this your reasoning? If he doesn't commit to you again then you don't matter enough to him to commit to you; and if that's the case, then there must be something wrong with you. So, you are inferring that, if he doesn't commit to you again, then there must be something wrong with you?"

"Yes, that is what I am telling myself; that it would be me."

"Okay, so let's look at your premise that if you don't matter enough to him to commit to you then there's something wrong with you. Are you, then, basing your self-worth on whether or not he approves of you?"

"I think so."

"So are you saying that you *must* have the approval of your boyfriend and if you don't then there's something wrong with you?"

"I am."

"Okay, so I think we have gotten clear on the reasoning behind your anxiety. You are demanding the approval of your boyfriend, so, if you don't get it, then you think there's something wrong with you. Your anxiety then seems to stem from this self-doubt about whether your boyfriend will finally approve of you by committing to you. Is this accurate?"

"That is it, exactly!"

"Okay, but do you really *need* your boyfriend's approval? Will you turn into a pumpkin if he doesn't?"

"No, I will still be me" [she states with a chuckle].

"What evidence do you have that you *must* have the approval of your boyfriend? Is there a law of nature that says he must approve of you?"

"No."

"It might be preferable, but just because something is desirable, or you want it to be true, does that mean that it *has* to be?"

"No. There are lots of things that I want but don't get. Yes I want him to approve of me, but I realize that doesn't mean he must."

"And if he doesn't give you his approval by committing to you, does that mean that there's something wrong with you? What about the possibility that he's simply afraid of commitment?"

"Yes! That would then be his problem, not a reflection on me."

"And do you know anyone else whom you respect who was not approved of by others?"

"Lot's of people in history. Look at Galileo or Copernicus, or Martin Luther King."

"Excellent! They were persecuted or killed; but that doesn't mean there was something wrong with them. Instead, the problem was with their persecutors and assassins, not them."

"So I am telling myself things that don't make sense, like I have to have the approval of my boyfriend and that there's something wrong with me if I don't get it."

"Right! People often upset themselves needless by telling themselves such things that don't make sense. Your demand for approval is a form of Demanding Perfection, which is one of the main offenders. LBT calls it a 'Cardinal Fallacy.'

And your idea that there's something wrong with you if you don't get your boyfriend's approval is another Cardinal Fallacy, known as 'Self-Damnation.'"

"Okay, I am starting to see where this is going. If I can get rid of these fallacies then I can feel better. So, how do I get rid of them? I see now that they are stupid, but I still feel anxious."

"I understand where you're coming from. You can appreciate that these beliefs—your demand for approval and your self-damning judgment—are irrational on an intellectual level, but still you feel attached to them emotionally."

"Yes, that's exactly how I feel."

"This tension you are feeling between intellect and emotion is called 'cognitive dissonance.' Our goal now is to bring the two into alignment so that you are no longer emotionally attached to these irrational beliefs."

"So how do I do that?"

"We can begin by replacing each of your beliefs with a more positive, constructive idea. LBT calls these ideas Guiding Virtues. In particular, instead of demanding the approval of others, you can strive to be more accepting of the imperfections in the world so that it's okay even if you don't get the approval of others such as your boyfriend. LBT calls this virtue 'Metaphysical Security.' It's about feeling comfortable with reality even though there's often a gap between what *is* and what you think *should* be."

"So, I would work on this idea that it's unrealistic to demand that my boyfriend accept me."

"Right, and if he does, that's well and good; but if he doesn't, then that's just the way it is."

"That makes sense."

"And LBT also offers a Guiding Virtue for your tendency to negatively judge yourself when you think your boyfriend might not accept you. This is the virtue of Self-Respect."

"That makes sense too. So I work on being more secure and more self-respecting?"

"Exactly! Do you have any suggestions about how to do this? Let's take being more secure about things like not always getting someone's approval."

"I suppose I can just not give a damn!"

"Actually, there are seeds of a philosophical outlook in your suggestion. Buddha said that one who wants nothing, who is desire-free, is himself free.[2] From this perspective you can liberate yourself when you stop seeking your boyfriend's approval. Buddha also said that from craving or demanding comes fear; and that when you stop demanding, you stop fearing.[3] So, your anxiety is due to your demanding things like the approval of your boyfriend. Anxiety is also future-oriented, but Buddhism focuses on the here and now, not on what might or might not be down the road. Buddhism says to let go of the future in order to find peace of mind."

"I am starting to figure this out. People are their own worst enemies. It's not what happens in the world that creates the anxiety. It's the way we think about it. This is Buddhism?"

"Yes, it is, and it is also the basis of LBT, which is derived from a theory of psychotherapy known as Rational-Emotive Behavior Therapy, which started with the same basic idea. In fact, REBT was also influenced by Stoic philosophers like Epictetus, who said that it isn't the events in the world that disturb us, but instead our perception of these events. And Epictetus also admonished us not to try to control the events in the external world. This includes getting the approval of others."

"Why did he say not to try to control these things?"

"He said this because it's self-defeating to try to control things that are not in our control to begin with. This is how we make ourselves upset—we try to control what is not in our power to control. But we can control things like whether we demand things, what we wish for, and so on. Buddhism is based on the same idea. The external world is beyond our control. We should stop trying to control it and control what we can control, namely our own minds. This is the basis of meditation, which aims at calming the mind and releasing it of its demands and cravings."[4]

"I can really see how these philosophies support each other. That's really cool. I think I can get into this!"

"Excellent! So, you can use both Stoic ideas and Buddhist ones together to help you to strive for greater Metaphysical Security about things not in your control, like the approval of others. These philosophies can also help you in your striving for Self-Respect too because, in giving up your demand for approval you can stop judging yourself negatively when you don't get that approval. But we can also add some philosophies that directly address your tendency to negatively rate yourself. Do you have any philosophical insights about Self-Respect?"

"'Charity begins at home.' You have to take care of yourself before you can help others."

"Great insight! Aristotle also said that a person should be her own best friend. At the very least, this implies that a person should speak rationally about oneself, just as she does about others. Berating yourself, because someone doesn't accept you, is a good example of speaking irrationally about yourself, and definitely not the way to be your own best friend."

"I like that. Be my own best friend, not my own worst enemy. That doesn't mean putting myself down."

"These philosophies—Buddhism, Stoicism, Aristotle's idea of self-friendship—are reasonable philosophies for you to embrace. But to do so they need to be applied to your life. It is one thing to pay lip service to these ideas and another to actually *live* them. LBT emphasizes living philosophy, not just preaching it."

"I'm not sure I can be a Buddhist monk or a Socrates." [spoken with a hint of sarcasm].

"And you shouldn't expect to be. That would be putting another demand on your plate."

"I think I understand. I can do my best."

"Right, which means imperfectly, just like the rest of the human race!"

"I can do that!"

"Okay, so let's talk about putting these philosophies into action."

"Okay."

"How did you respond to your boyfriend when he said that he wanted to postpone your engagement until he got settled in Chicago?"

"I was very upset. I told him that I was disappointed and asked him if he was sure? I suppose I acted very insecure. To be honest, I was thinking that he was never going to commit to me and I guess I seemed desperate. How long are you going to wait, I asked him; but he was very vague about it, and I was really saddened; and I am sure I showed it."

"How are you handling it now?"

"I try not to show how I feel but I am not very good at hiding my true feelings, so I am sure he knows I am still feeling insecure. I am also sort of putting my life on hold."

"What do you mean?"

"When he is out, I wait for him to come home instead of going out. I make a special effort to be with him. I guess I have been a bit clingy."

"This information is helpful. Do you think the philosophies you have just decided to adopt would tell you to do the same sorts of things you are now doing? Let's take Buddhism first."

"No, definitely not. If I am to live in the here and now, I need to stop dwelling on the future, stop putting things off, waiting for that magical moment when I am engaged; stop living like my life depends on this guy to make me whole; stop waiting around like a puppy dog, and go on with my life. I am not going to run after him. If he goes through with the engagement, well and good; but I am going to free myself of these invisible chains I have put on myself."

"Excellent! Another thing Buddha would recommend as part of your action plan to help you let go of the future and stop your demanding is meditation. Buddha taught many types of meditation, but there is one that I think might be especially useful for dealing with anxiety. It is called "Mindfulness of Breathing," which uses your breathing as a focal point. Here are some directions for how to do this sort of meditating.[5] Would you like to add meditation to your action plan?"

"Yes, I really would like to try it. I have always wanted to try it anyway!

"Great! And what advice do you think you might get from Epictetus?"

"He says not to try to control what's not in your power to control. So I am not going to try to control my boyfriend. He will do what he wants anyway, but I *can* control how I react to what he does, so no more puppy dog! I will stop living for the future and enjoy the here and now; stop trying to control what my boyfriend does by doting over him and acting dependent and desperate."

"Very good! And it sounds like you are also going to be your own best friend, as Aristotle would advise."

"Yes, I am going to stop degrading myself, telling myself I need my boyfriend's approval in order to be worthy. No more worst enemy!"

"This is a very promising plan of action."

"Yes, I think so. I am very excited about it!"

The line of emotional reasoning that drives Stacey's anxiety is a syndrome I have witnessed countless times in my many years of philosophical practice. Indeed, this syndrome was addressed earlier in this book under Bandwagon Reasoning in chapter 4. As mentioned, it is rampant in the human population and can often lead to blind conformity and the loss of autonomy. Moreover, those who are rejected by the person or persons from whom approval is sought can experience intense sadness, forlornness, or depression.[6]

What is important to emphasize here, however, is that this I-must-have-approval-else-I-am-unworthy deduction can also be a progenitor of intense anxiety. "What if I don't get approval?" This question dangles in thin air as one waits upon the future, as though one's life depends on the answer. "Will I be a worthy person or will I be demoted to a reject, a loser, a piece of garbage that nobody wants?" This is a daunting question when one perceives the stakes to be so high. It is, therefore, not surprising that this syndrome generates intense anxiety. For anxiety of any stripe lives in the future; its emotional object is a prediction about what will or might happen if . . .

As you can see, Stacey's anxiety about whether or not her boyfriend would finally commit to her kept her in limbo, preventing her from moving forward with her life. Like the proverbial watched phone that doesn't ring, she put her life on hold in anticipation of that (diamond) ring. Ironically, what mattered most was how she coped with the precariousness of the future; for the future is always ahead of us, and the same scenario of waiting can become a vicious cycle that can eventually, moment by moment, consume one's life.

Stacey enlisted a blend of Stoic, Buddhist, and Aristotelian ideas to gain greater security about the uncertainty of the future, and greater self-respect in confronting it. I think these combined philosophies resonated well with her. Indeed, there were other candidate philosophies that also could have spoken relevantly to the uncertainty of the future, notably existential philosophies. Thus, Sartre would have admonished Stacey to live her life, not to put it on hold; for, according to this reasonable perspective, it is only through doing things, not sitting around and waiting, that one can be fulfilled. Of course, there is always the danger of taking a philosophy, indeed any philosophy, to the extreme, wherein one short-circuits future possibilities by acting precipitously in the interest of not waiting for Godot.[7] Subscribing to Buddhism can suffer a similar fate when its emphasis on the here and now is taken to the extreme.

Still, we can glean some sobering advice from Aristotle about just how realistic the dangers are of clients actually going to extremes in applying a sober philosophy. Aristotle instructed that, when one has a tendency to go to one extreme, trying to go to the opposite extreme will not necessarily *lead* one to go to the opposite extreme. Instead, one will, more likely, end up somewhere closer to the middle.[8] I believe this is a good rule of thumb in creating a client plan for implementing an Uplifting Philosophy, whatever that philosophy may be. Such plans typically involve acting against the tide of clients' current inclinations. In Stacey's case, she had built a robust plan to live squarely in the here and now and to give up her demands about the future. Applying a bit of Aristotelian wisdom, I was reasonably confident that Stacey would more rationally manage her future while not neglecting her present. Balance is important here; sitting and meditating from dawn to dusk would not be very practical. On the other hand, using every waking moment of one's existence to plan for the future would be self-defeating. However, dipping into the moment for a while, resurfacing to navigate the future, and dipping back down into the moment, if coordinated like a finely conducted orchestra, can provide the "golden mean" between these extremes. Such a life calls forth the Guiding Virtues in concert with one another: Foresightedness to make reasonable predictions; Courage to confront the uncertainty of the future; Metaphysical Security to relinquish unrealistic, perfectionistic cravings; and Self-Respect to maintain personal dignity through the trials and inescapable tribulations of life.

In the end, Stacey's boyfriend did propose to her. What is heartening is that, in the interim period prior to the proposal, she did not continue to suffer the intense anxiety she had previously suffered. In working to overcome her demand to control what was not in her power to control, in not clinging to what she wished for (namely a future commitment from her boyfriend), in being her own best friend, she truly changed her life.

It is a small wonder why we humans universally suffer from anxiety in pandemic proportions. We are fragile and vulnerable to the damage done by our tendencies to unrealistically and counterproductively confront the future. As illustrated in this chapter, LBT has the philosophical resources to help guide us out of these quagmires of our own devices. The next chapter will focus on a further universal mode of human suffering, sadness due to loss.

NOTES

1. Buddha, *The Dhammapada: The Buddha's Path of Wisdom*, trans. Acharya Buddharakkhita, Buddha Dharma Education Association, 1985, v. 348. http://www.buddhanet.net/pdf_file/scrndhamma.pdf.

2. Buddha, *The Dhammapada,* v. 410.

3. Ibid., v. 216.

4. Ibid., v. 362.

5. "Mindful Awareness of Breathing," Dharma Realm Buddhist Young Adults, 2009. http://www.drby.net/attachments/041_Meditation%20Instructions.pdf

6. See, for example, the case of Jessica Lessing discussed in chapter 4 under both Can'tstipation and Bandwagon Reasoning.

7. Sartre, an atheistic existentialist, would not be very congenial for a religious client.

8. Aristotle, *Nicomachean Ethics*, Book 2, Ch. 9. See also Elliot D. Cohen, *New Rational Therapy: Thinking Your Way to Serenity, Success, and Profound Happiness* (Lanham, MD: Rowman & Littlefield, 2006), pp. 25–26.

Chapter Eight

The Loss of a Beloved Dog

Addressing Bereavement Complicated by Guilt

Sadness, as such, is not a mental illness else we'd all be mentally ill. The fact is that there are painful experiences that we all go through in life. Feeling sad about the loss of a near and dear friend is as universal as life itself. For in life there is birth and death, joy at the beginning of life and grief at the end. Grief itself is not the same as depression in a clinical, diagnostic sense (Major Depressive Disorder), which is considered a mental illness. In grief there is pain but also pleasant memories attached to the deceased. In clinical depression there is constant or almost constant painful moods and ideation without positive ideation. In clinical depression there tends to be a sense that one's own life, or self, is worthless. In grief there are moments when one sees oneself, or one's life, as having worth. Philosophical practitioners without mental health qualifications typically refer clients who are suffering from clinical depression; however, grief, as a problem of living, is appropriate for philosophical practitioners who have their degrees exclusively in philosophy. Indeed, armed with Uplifting Philosophies and Guiding Virtues, LBT philosophical practitioners can be most qualified to assist clients in working through their grief.

There is, however, a normal working-through process—a point made explicitly in the preface of this book in connection with the death of my father. Like the Platonic metaphor of coming out of one's dark cave into the light of day, there is a time of habituation before one's eyes are adjusted and ready to see the light of day. When a person is ready to talk about the loss with an eye toward working through it, it is appropriate for a philosophical practitioner to assist; otherwise, it is best to wait until the person is ready.

This working-through process can be significantly thwarted by residual feelings of guilt related to the death of the deceased: "Did I do the best I could for him when he was alive?" "Why didn't I tell her I loved her when I could!?" "How could I have done such an awful thing to him?" "What kind of person am I?" This chapter presents such a case of loss and unresolved guilt. I am, again, the LBT practitioner of record. The case involves a philosopher, Dr. Edward Davidson, who grieved the loss of a near and dear friend, his dog, a West Highland terrier named Bartholomew. Bartholomew was thirteen when he died. He had oral melanoma, which had metastasized throughout his body, including his lungs. A strong willed and somewhat stubborn soul, Bartholomew fought for his life valiantly. He had undergone rounds of surgery, chemotherapy, radiation therapy, and a melanoma vaccine.

"Dr. Cohen, it has been four years, and I still have unresolved feelings about Bartholomew's death. I think about him often and thought that maybe LBT could help me sort things out."

"I do hope LBT can help you. You are a philosopher by training, so we may be calling on your own expertise to help the process along."

"Do you think that my being a philosopher will help?"

"I don't know yet. I have known some philosophers who have been rather poor clients, inclined to lecture their way through a session, or look for some flaw in the process, rather than to acquiesce in it as a partner. On the other hand, many philosophers whom I have trained in LBT have been excellent clients. So we will see."

"Okay, so I am eager to find out. Shall we?"

"Okay, then. Tell me more about your issue."

"It was not just that Bartholomew died; it was the way he died."

"Tell me about that."

"We did everything we could for him. I had to decide whether to remove his lower jawbone. The vet said that dogs can do alright without a jawbone, but he was such a handsome dog and the thought of deforming him like that was abhorrent to me; so I chose surgery to remove the tumor from his mouth without removing his jawbone. Maybe this was a mistake because the cancer later metastasized throughout his body. Maybe removing his lower jaw would have saved his life, but I don't know because the cancer could have already begun to spread by the time we discovered it. It is a very aggressive form of cancer."

"So, are you upset that you didn't perform the surgery to remove his jawbone?"

"I have mixed feelings about that. But that isn't what I am really upset about."

"Tell me more about what you're really upset about."

"I had him euthanized. The cancer had spread to his lungs and he was having labored breathing. He was not able to hold any food down and then he was unable to drink either. I tried forcing water down him and he struggled. The vet said he had at most a week to live. As a last resort, I took him to the emergency center to get an injection of cortisone to help relieve his strained breathing, but it didn't appear to work."

"Okay, it sounds like you were concerned about Bartholomew's suffering."

"I was. I loved him so much. He was always by my side when I worked. He seemed to like it when I played guitar and sang. I played and sang to him right before I took him to be euthanized, and he seemed to perk up for a bit. It was very difficult seeing him incontinent and as weak as he was. He was always such a strong dog."

"It sounds like you had a difficult time letting go."

"I did. I was very conflicted about taking him to the vet to be euthanized. He was my baby and he always relied on me for nurture, and now I was taking him to be put to death."

"Yes, but he was suffering."

"I wouldn't have killed him if he was a human child. Why then was it okay because he was a canine who depended on me just like a child?"

"It sounds like you think you might have done something morally wrong by having him euthanized."

"If I had to make the decision again, I would not have done it."

"Tell me about that."

"It was about midweek when I took him to be euthanized. The upcoming weekend I had plans to attend a philosophy conference. I was scheduled to read a paper. I didn't want to cancel it. It was expedient to euthanize him rather than to prolong the inevitable. I think I was influenced by the conference. I feel like I might have killed my dog prematurely in order to attend a conference; and now I don't even remember what the paper was on that I presented. But the thought still haunts me. When I took Bartholomew to the vet, he was too weak to get out of the car. I was upset and I spoke firmly to him, and I have no idea why, since these were going to be his last minutes on earth. It wasn't like this was a routine office visit! When he was on the vet's examining table, before the vet came into the examining room, I hugged Bartholomew and he let out this load whine. I could not determine whether it was a result of the pain he was in from the cancer or if he knew that this was the end. The vet entered, examined him, and concluded that it was best to euthanize him. I thought about not going through with it but I stayed. I watched the vet give Bartholomew an injection, which rendered him unconscious. He seemed to be breathing peacefully, not labored at all. Then the vet asked me if I wanted to witness the lethal injection; he was not very encouraging and I declined. He took Bartholomew out of the examining room and closed the door. That was the last time I ever saw him."

"You said you would have done it differently if you had to do it again. What would you have done?"

"I would have cancelled my conference and stayed home with Bartholomew, where he could have died with his family in the comfort of his own bed, in a familiar environment. He was my baby and I feel like I betrayed him."

"So you are upset because you think you betrayed him by euthanizing him instead of cancelling your trip and staying home with him during his last days."

"Yes, that is accurate, I believe."

"It sounds like you think that what you did was morally wrong."

"That's right. I betrayed my dear friend in his time of emotional and physical need."

"Are you just negatively rating your action or are you also negatively rating *yourself* for having done what you did?"

"I think I am negatively rating myself too."

"What are you telling yourself about yourself?"

"That I am a bad person for having betrayed my dear friend. He was a baby who depended on me and I betrayed him. Instead of cancelling my trip and comforting him, I took him to the vet to be killed."

"Okay, so it sounds like your reasoning is this: you are telling yourself that, if you did not cancel your trip, and had your dog euthanized instead of staying home with him and comforting him in his last days, then you betrayed him; and since you did not cancel your trip and had him euthanized instead of staying home with him, you betrayed him. And, if you betrayed Bartholomew, then you are a bad person. So, you are a bad person."

"Yes, I think that is my reasoning."

"It sounds like you are feeling guilty because you think you betrayed Bartholomew. Is this true?"

"Yes, I think so."

"Guilt is a moral emotion and there is always a perceived violation of one of your moral principles when you feel guilty about something. This perception can be rational or not. In either case, a person can still feel guilty."

"I know that."

"Okay, so let's take a look at your premise that, if you did not cancel your trip and had Bartholomew euthanized instead of staying home to comfort him in his last days, then you betrayed him. Why do you think you betrayed Bartholomew by going to your conference and having him euthanized?"

"Because he depended on me and I placed my interest in going to a conference above his life."

"So do you believe that you had a duty to sacrifice your interests for Bartholomew's well-being?"

"Yes, especially something like reading a paper at a conference."

"And you violated this moral duty of yours."

"Yes."

"So, if you had this duty and violated it, then you are a bad person."

"Yes."

"Okay, so let's look at your moral principle. Are you saying that you have a duty to sacrifice any interests of yours for Bartholomew's well-being?"

"No, not any interests, but reading a paper at a conference is not compelling enough to override Bartholomew's well-being."

"Okay so let's look at your judgment that you betrayed this duty. This would mean that you put your interest above that of Bartholomew's well-being in going to your conference; but is this true? Would it have been in Bartholomew's well-being for you to have cancelled your conference and stayed home with him, or would it have been for *your* emotional well-being, since you would have felt better about having stayed home with Bartholomew? Would Bartholomew have really benefitted by prolonging his suffering so that you could feel better about staying home with him?"

"I honestly never thought about it this way, and I have been over this again and again in my mind. I am not looking for a rationalization to make myself feel better now, though. I want to believe what's true. I am a philosopher, after all."

"But are you rationalizing anything? Would it truly have benefitted Bartholomew or would it have benefitted you, emotionally?"

"It definitely would have benefitted me emotionally, especially looking at it in retrospect; but I am not really sure whether this would have been best for Bartholomew. Yes, he would have been in a familiar environment when he finally succumbed to the cancer; but then, again, he would have also suffered longer. He could no longer eat or drink. I think maybe I would have been doing it more for myself than for Bartholomew."

"Okay, so we refuted your judgment that you betrayed Bartholomew's wellbeing because it rests on a moral principle that you do not appear to have violated."

"That sounds reasonable."

"And you have told yourself that you are a bad person because you betrayed Bartholomew. However, your Self-Damnation depends on your perception of having violated a moral principle, which you did not really violate."

"Okay, but what if I did really betray him? I keep thinking that maybe I am just rationalizing."

"That is an important question. Even if it were true that you did violate your moral principle, does that really make you a bad person? Indeed, if everyone who, in his own eyes, did something morally wrong was a bad person, then we'd all be bad persons, which is absurd."

"I see that, but I still feel conflicted."

"That is understandable. After all, you have been hanging on to this perception for four years. But we can work on breaking the emotional hold it has had on your perception of yourself."

"I don't always think of myself as a bad person. It's just when I think about Bartholomew's death."

"I understand. But you said you think about him often, right?"

"Yes, quite often."

"How often?"

"I'd say every week, at least once. I have a picture of him in my living room and another in my bedroom that sits on a shelf on the headboard above my head. When I see these pictures, which is inevitable, I think about how he died and that's when I feel guilty."

"Of course you could take the pictures down, but I do not think that this would solve your problem."

"I think I would feel guilty about doing that too!"

"That's because you would still be harboring your irrational belief that you betrayed Bartholomew. Taking down the picture might then be perceived as another betrayal of Bartholomew in order to conceal the original betrayal. So it makes sense to work on getting rid of your perception of having betrayed him in the first place."

"I agree. How do I do that?"

"According to LBT every Cardinal Fallacy has a Guiding Virtue, which can replace it. The Guiding Virtue for Self-Damnation, as you might suspect, is Self-Respect."

"Yes, I can see that it would be the appropriate virtue. I would aim at being more self-respecting rather than putting myself down."

"That's right. At this point, LBT introduces an Uplifting Philosophy to help you work towards the Guiding Virtue."

"So I would use philosophical ideas to help me to become more self-respecting?"

"Yes, do you have any in mind? You're a philosopher."

"I have always been interested in applying philosophy to everyday life problems. Let me give this some thought. [There is a period of silence.] I like Nietzsche's take on suffering. He says that suffering makes you stronger. I really suffered a great deal over the way Bartholomew died. The entire ordeal I went through was humbling, though. There was the brief remission and a sense that the cancer was being defeated; and then there was the reemergence of the tumor with greater force and resolution to destroy this wonderfully spirited dog. I suffered so much along with Bartholomew. I have no doubt about that. I also think I learned something from it. I know what it feels like to see cancer take its toll on someone you love regardless of what you do to try to stop it—the sense of helplessness, the realization that medicine itself is impotent against this powerful, malignant adversary. I also used to think that people who were against euthanasia were narrow-minded. I think I have a better appreciation of the other side now. When I teach my applied ethics class, I usually cover a section on euthanasia. I actually find myself being more empathetic toward those students who are opposed to euthanasia than I did before, because I now understand better what people go through. We learn from experience. Those who have not had the experience, and have not suffered along with the patient, do not really know what it's like. Of course, this was my dog, not my birth child, but I loved him with all my heart and soul."

"So you think you are, in a sense, better for having suffered as you have?"

"Yes, I feel like that, now that I think about it. I have become a better person, not a worse one. I should at least respect myself for having learned such an important life lesson. Can I add any other philosophies?"

"Yes, sure!"

"I understand that LBT stresses virtue, and I think of Aristotle."

"Right, LBT's theory of virtue is based on Aristotle's theory of virtue."

"I have always liked Aristotle's theory of pride. As you know, according to Aristotle, pride is the mean between the extremes of vanity or conceit, on the one hand, and humility or not giving oneself due credit, on the other. I think I would be a better person, I mean a prouder person, by confronting the death of Bartholomew without degrading myself."

"That's a great philosophical antidote to Self-Damnation!"

"True, the cancer was not my fault; I did my best to try to save him, and the cancer won. I deserve some credit for trying as hard as I did."

"That's right, which means your global damnation of yourself as a bad person is irrational. Someone who tends to be as compassionate as you cannot reasonably called a 'bad' person. Indeed, people who feel guilt are actually people who *have* a moral conscience."

"That's true, and regardless of whether or not I attended the conference or had Bartholomew euthanized, that doesn't make me a bad person. So, I think I would not be giving myself due credit by degrading myself by calling myself 'bad.'"

"Great! Now, the last step in LBT is to apply your philosophies, that is, put them into practice. For this, we need to build a plan of action. To do this, it is helpful to identify the things you now do that you would do differently in applying your Uplifting Philosophies. So, what do you do now when you blame yourself and feel guilty about Bartholomew?"

"A lot of times when others in the family talk about Bartholomew, I try to avoid talking about him. I still keep a lot of his medicines on top of the refrigerator. I know I should throw them out, but it almost feels like I would be throwing him out if I did it. I think I would feel guilty about throwing them out. I also find myself becoming somewhat withdrawn when I have thoughts about being responsible for euthanizing him. I might avoid family members, or relive the experience in my mind, and then feel guilty about it."

"This information is very helpful. So your plan of action can consist of joining family members in talking about Bartholomew; discarding the old medicines; not withdrawing after having thoughts about Bartholomew—not avoiding family members, and not setting yourself up by reliving the experience in order to blame yourself. These are great ways to apply your philosophy that your suffering can make you stronger; and to apply your philosophy about being proud. Is there anything else?"

"Well yes. I also do not ever talk to anyone about my decision to go to the conference rather than to stay home with Bartholomew. I am afraid people will think me a bad person."

"This information is also helpful. LBT sometimes suggests 'shame attacking' exercises as part of an action plan. Maybe you could deliberately bring up this aspect of Bartholomew's death, and then work on it cognitively and emotionally by refuting your perception that you violated your moral principle, and thinking about your Uplifting Philosophies—how you are or can be stronger for having suffered the experience; and how you can make yourself prouder by being honest about this situation, rather than concealing it because you are afraid people will think you a bad person."

"This last thing might be the hardest."

"I can understand that. You are so used to negatively judging yourself about this, so you expect others to do the same thing. But I suspect that, with knowing the circumstances, most people will not negatively judge you. But even if some do, this is your opportunity to work this through rationally, instead of hiding it from others as well as yourself."

"I agree. I need to confront it in order to work it through. Thank you!"

This case of a philosopher as client shows how bereavement and guilt can be intimately connected. LBT casts its net wide enough to key into the guilty intentional object of the sadness, in this case, that of having Bartholomew euthanized instead of cancelling the conference presentation. The rating of this object is in terms of rating the person performing the act, not just the act itself. This is important because there is a difference between guilt that negatively rates the guilty act and guilt that negatively rates the person performing the act. In the latter case, the guilt is irrational and tends to thwart constructive action. In the former case, the guilt can sometimes serve as a spur for making constructive changes in the future. So, even if the client perceived himself to have violated his moral principle, his guilt could still possibly serve a useful purpose. However, in the present case, the guilt in question is laden with Self-Damnation, which leads this client to act in self-defeating ways.

The plan of action, in turn, used two Uplifting Philosophies concomitantly to promote the Guiding Virtue of Self-Respect, namely, Nietzsche's theory of suffering and Aristotle's theory of pride. Both of these theories worked synergistically to help support the client's perception of himself as growing stronger through his suffering and moving toward greater self-respect through taking greater pride in himself. These theories, in turn, guided a new action plan for the client consisting of participating in discussions with family members about Bartholomew; discarding his medicines on the top of the refrigerator; not withdrawing after having thoughts about Bartholomew—not avoiding family members, and not setting himself up by reliving the experience in order to blame himself; and speaking openly about the last days of Bartholomew's life, including his decision to attend the conference.

The last component of this action plan—speaking openly— did, indeed, take the most willpower as I learned from Dr. Davidson in a follow-up session. While he still could not honestly say that he fully emotionally appreciated that what he had done in not cancelling his presentation and having Bartholomew euthanized was not a violation of his moral principle (although he thought that it might not have been), he was less prone to judge himself for it. Moreover, prior to the first session, he really did not think about the possibility that he would have been cancelling his conference presentation in order to appease himself rather than to help Bartholomew. This companion and close friend had already lost the fight with cancer and his death was imminent, regardless of what my client did.

As you can see, human emotions can be complex and intertwined. In the present case, guilt had kept Dr. Davidson from sufficiently working through the death of his dog. Overcoming the guilt thus had the potential to liberate him from his unresolved bereavement. Of course, such working through does not mean that his sadness about Bartholomew's death would go away; nor did he want it to. It is the way we humans pay tribute and honor to the departed whom we adored. LBT does not attempt to help us to overcome such healthy emotions. But not all emotions are equal. Guilt that is self-damning, and therefore self-defeating, does not promote happiness. On the other hand, aspiring to Self-Respect does, indeed, promote happiness. LBT can help here, as I hope the present case illustrates.

This case also invites one to engage one's own powers of Empathy in appreciating what Dr. Davidson was going through in dealing with the complexities of Bartholomew's death. As Buddhists have emphasized, death is universal and inescapable. "Neither in the sky nor in mid-ocean," said Buddha, "nor by entering into mountain clefts, nowhere in the world is there a place where one will not be overcome by death."[1] Yet, only the living inevitably bear witness to death; not one's own, but that of others. These personal encounters with death, from the perspective of the living, are as universal as death itself. They hone our empathetic powers and prepare us to feel the suffering of others who have lost loved ones. Can you recall how you felt when someone you loved or deeply cared about died? Now imagine that you *believe* that you acted against your own moral principles in helping to bring about that death. Never mind that this individual would have soon died anyway; and never mind that you may not have truly violated your moral principle. How do you *feel*? It is quite normal to feel guilty in such a situation, and quite abnormal not to. This is the power of Empathy I am describing, gleaned from the human experiences of death from the perspective of the living; permitting one to experience the suffering of others without having been in precisely the same situation. For you can imagine because you know what it is like to experience the death of a dear one. And in this empathetic experience, you can see how one emotion such as sadness can give rise to another such as guilt. In this way, too, the case of Bartholomew can teach us a good deal about some of the challenges of death for the living.

Such is the power of Empathy, one of the Guiding Virtues of LBT. As an LBT practitioner, I have deeply resonated with the plight of Dr. Davidson; for I know what it is like to lose a loved one, including one's dog. Seeing inside the subjective world of clients through a honed ability to empathize is not just a good idea in LBT practice, it is essential. The next and final chapter will accordingly address the virtues of LBT practitioners.

NOTE

1. Buddha, *The Dhammapada: The Buddha's path of Wisdom*, trans. Acharya Buddharakkhita, Buddha Dharma Education Association, 1985, v. 128. http://www.buddhanet.net/pdf_file/scrndhamma.pdf.

Chapter Nine

The Emotional Temperament of
LBT Practitioners

This book has used case illustrations to build an understanding of the practice of LBT, particularly in approaching human emotions arising in the context of problems of living. Indeed, as should be clear from these cases, the myriad of problems that people confront in the course of everyday life cannot be separated from their emotional responses to such everyday issues. Clearly, calling them "problems" takes on meaning insofar as these issues (anything from having a problem with a roommate to losing a loved one) impact us emotionally.

The focus of this study has been primarily on emotion as it relates to the clients seen by LBT practitioners. In this final chapter, I turn to the emotional temperament of LBT practitioners themselves; for, as I hope is evident from the diverse case presentations, practitioners' affective characteristics, as well as their intellectual or philosophical abilities, figure essentially in helping clients to address their problems of living. Thus, an adequate understanding of LBT practice also engenders an understanding of the emotional temperament of practitioners.

The process of LBT is not merely a set of techniques to be applied by a technician. Indeed, effective LBT counselors or consultants exemplify this process *in their own lives.* This is because people often learn best by example and a consistent practitioner is more likely to encourage such an "examined life" than one who does not practice what he preaches. Importantly, because LBT features the cultivation of virtue, applying the LBT process to one's own life means that LBT practitioners must commit to virtuous living as an end. This portends cultivation of virtuous "personality traits," that is, formed habits to think, act, and feel in virtuous ways. For example, being courageous amounts to a habit of rationally coping with perceived threats, avoiding the extremes, neither overreacting nor underreacting (cognitively, behaviorally, and emotionally).

This does not mean that the LBT practitioner must be perfect. Clearly, as I have emphasized repeatedly, human reality is imperfect and virtues are ideals that are never completely attained in this material world of ours. Nevertheless, a practitioner who genuinely aspires to be metaphysically secure, respectful, courageous, temperate, authentic, empathetic, prudent, empowering, foresighted, objective, and scientific is more likely to inspire these same ends in others. In addition, when modeled by practitioners, virtues such as Empathy and Authenticity help to facilitate identification of clients' emotional reasoning.[1]

Consequently, in the National Philosophical Counseling Association's LBT Certificate Training Programs, the importance of the Guiding Virtues is emphasized, not only as aspects of the LBT process, but also as character traits of practitioners themselves. LBT practitioners' commitment to the practice of LBT is also a commitment to a way of life that fosters these virtues as well as the other critical thinking skill applied in the LBT process.

THE COMMITTED LBT PRACTITIONER:
THE CASE OF DR. SAMUEL ZINAICH

A good example of such a life commitment is that of my friend and colleague, Dr. Samuel Zinaich, a professor of philosophy at Purdue University-Northwest. Dr. Zinaich and I first met when he was a student in one of my philosophy courses about thirty years ago. He immediately took an interest in LBT, which befit his personality. LBT is logic-oriented, of course, but it is also focused on human emotion. Dr. Zinaich is and has always been an authentic and empathetic person. His disposition to listen reflectively to others and to connect both cognitively and emotionally with the plights of others made him, from the start, a very suitable candidate for work in LBT.

A case in point is the LBT program he created and conducted at the Jerome Combs Detention Center (JCDC) in Kankakee, Illinois. Indeed, anyone who has worked in a prison can attest to the stresses inmates confront as a result of living conditions and the manner in which they are treated. Autonomy is greatly restricted and failure to cooperate with correctional officers is often visited with punitive measures that may not be proportional to the misdeed. Dr. Zinaich relates: "Although not all of the correctional officers acted in inappropriate ways, many of them were drunk with the power they had over the inmates and used that, in ways that were detrimental to the emotional and psychological stability of the inmates."[2] For example, he states, "Although using the taser is permissible only as a last resort for noncompliance, it is often used as an effective first-response tactic to defuse the problem that the inmate is causing. In either case, whether the taser is used or not, the inmate will be locked down in solitary confinement."[3]

Now, imagine yourself being placed in solitary confinement for long periods of time (days, weeks, months, or years) without any contact with the outside world. While some may dismiss such harsh measures with clichés like, "Do the crime, do the time," Dr. Zinaich could not begin to conduct LBT with the inmates without understanding the despair of being treated in such an inhumane manner. True, some so treated have themselves perpetrated inhumane acts; however, appreciating the plight of these inmates is not merely a matter of seeing such punitive measures as just deserts or retributive justice served; it is a matter of relating on a much deeper emotional level, feeling the sense of forlornness, the destitution that accompanies being degraded to a status of less than human. Appropriately, Zinach zeroed in on the premium these individuals placed on being respected:

> Everyone I spoke with demanded respect, at least for themselves. In fact, I spoke with one inmate who looked at me, and with a Stoic, cold face said to me, "If we were in a neighborhood and you didn't show me the proper respect I deserve, I would beat you until you gave me the respect I deserve." The problem was to convince them to show respect to other inmates.[4]

As an LBT practitioner, Zinaich could not even begin to help the inmates address their Cardinal Fallacies (according to him, the Perfectionistic Demand for Control, Awfulizing, and Can'tstipation) without a deep appreciation for the emotional side of being in such a dehumanizing situation. Zinaich's approach was to apply Kant's famous Categorical Imperative in the form of the Golden Rule: "Treat others like you would like to be treated (Positive Formulation) and do not treat others the way you would not like to be treated (Negative Formulation)."[5] By presenting philosophy at this human level, he believed he could help the inmates relate to other inmates in a way that they themselves could understand. With candor, Zinaich concluded, "Although I don't know if anyone came to fully accept such a viewpoint, nevertheless, for some inmates, their behavior changed and the opportunities for conflict dissipated."[6]

In this way, Dr. Zinaich opened up his practice, and his heart, to disenfranchised members of society. He did not have any preconceived notions that the project would bear fruit, but he was willing to take the risk for the sake of helping others. Indeed, the success of the JCDC LBT program (having supervised the program, I can attest that there were some clear success stories) was largely the result of Zinaich's ability to not only apply the process of LBT, but also to exemplify it in his own life, especially in his commitment to the Guiding Virtues as intrinsic goals in the attainment of human happiness.

THE PLACE OF EMOTIONS IN
LBT AND ITS PRACTICE

This idea of a committed LBT practitioner should not be confused with the stereotypical image of a committed philosopher as a purely rational individual who is devoid of emotional temperament. Indeed, one criticism of LBT (and other so-called cognitive-behavioral approaches to the human services) has been that it emphasizes the cognitive side to the exclusion of the affective side.[7] This criticism, however, is far afield from the truth, as I hope this book has shown. Indeed, the first step of the LBT process is primarily about the phenomenological and affective. It is about getting inside the subjective world of the client for purposes of identifying the client's emotion. True, in LBT, emotions are identified by particular cognitions, namely their intentional objects (O) and their ratings (R). However, this does not mean that it neglects the noncognitive aspects—visceral, perceptual, and sensory.

As discussed in chapter 1, LBT distinguishes between primary and secondary emotions. The former are the "gut" responses to external environmental stimuli or to recollection of them. These responses are handled primarily by the limbic system and are automatic responses. In contrast, secondary emotions integrate cognitive (cerebrocortical) "thought" content into emotional responses by interpreting primary emotional responses. LBT's (O + R) analysis is thus aimed at secondary emotions because these are the set of emotional responses that include such a cognitive component. Primary emotions are comprised of recalled images of prior emotionally charged experiences along with replaying of prior visceral responses (stored in the amygdala), sensory perceptions (visual, auditory, etc.), physiological changes (for example, increased heart rate and respiration), and sensations of these physiological changes (for example, a lump in one's throat, trembling). LBT does not neglect such emotional responses inasmuch as it can include philosophical activities such as meditation and the use of advance imagery (imagining oneself in a situation) as enshrined in Buddhist practice;[8] and the Aristotelian-based adjustment of one's "conditioned" behavioral responses to external stimuli (for example, panicking when giving a public speech) through reframing the situation in alignment with Uplifting Philosophies and Guiding Virtues. Indeed, LBT maintains that primary emotions are sustained by emotional reasoning, which, when fallacious, can permit such primary emotions to fester unless adequately addressed by LBT's six-step method. So LBT's net is cast wide enough to include activities that can both directly and indirectly help to modify primary emotional responses that may be interfering with a client's satisfactorily addressing a problem of living. And, LBT's framework is definitely flexible enough to add to the manners in which it can address primary emotions.

So LBT practitioners who appropriately represent the practice of LBT need to recognize that the emotional life of their clients (and themselves) cannot, without gross oversimplification, be reduced to cognition rooted in the "higher" brain functions. Indeed, the traditional training of philosophers has primarily stressed abstract conceptual analysis and theorizing as the way to approach their discipline. But this does not work when philosophy is injected into the context of addressing life problems, which are deeply embedded in the emotional, including that which gets processed at the "gut" level (that is, at the level of primary emotions). Thus, committed LBT practitioners should resonate with their clients as passionate, full-blooded human beings who are not immune to noncognitive, nonrational emotional responses to threatening aspects of their external environment; the "hard-wired" drive for survival; material desires; the physical needs for food, water, clothing, shelter, and sex; other human (animal) inclinations. Aristotle long ago realized this when he recognized that human beings are not entirely self-sufficient for the life of contemplation but instead require a certain measure of material goods (including money) in order to be happy. In the light of what is now known about the emotional and intellectual capacities of human beings, this insight needs to be extended to include an understanding of the brain processes involved in "gut-level" primary emotional responses as well as the more cerebrocortical, secondary, cognitive ones.[9]

THE EMOTIONALITY OF LBT PRACTITIONERS

Part of this nonrational (noncognitive), emotional endowment of human beings, no less than that of LBT practitioners, appears to be one's emotionality, that is, the distinct manner and tone of an individual's affect. For example, some people present as "warm" or "affectionate," while others as "cold" or "unaffectionate"; some as "dispirited," while others as "lively" or "bubbly." Such characterizations of one's emotional personality can most realistically be understood in terms of tendencies since a rather "dull" person can sometimes be "lively" (for example, after a few cold ones). Such emotional personalities are probably not rooted primarily in cognitive brain functions (the cerebral cortex), but instead in the brain's limbic system.[10] As such, we cannot expect a person who tends to present in monotone with relatively low emotionality to become a warm, compassionate LBT practitioner. This suggests the possibility that some emotional personality types might not be right for the job, regardless of how much training they receive. This should not come as a surprise, any more than it would be surprising that some people are less musically inclined than are others, or are better at math than at the humanities. The upshot is that LBT practice invites individuals who tend to be reasonably sociable with a reasonable degree of emotional energy. In keeping with the Aristotelian mean of "reasonability," this is to emphasize not going to the extremes. Thus being warm and sociable does not mean being obsequious or fawning.

LBT AND MENTALLY ILL PRACTITIONERS

In some cases a diminished affect can itself be the result of an underlying mental illness such as depression. LBT practitioners with unaddressed, serious psychological problems (that is, ones that cause them substantial distress in their own lives) are not ordinarily good candidates for LBT practice. If they try to hide how they feel inside behind a professional façade, then they are not being congruent or authentic; on the other hand, if they present as themselves, then they will probably not model the rational, emotional, and/or behavioral tenets they profess. Moreover, it is unethical for philosophical practitioners to use their practice as a forum for addressing their own problems rather than that of the client. Such individuals have an ethical responsibility to address their own psychological problems (or any other issues) that might impair their ability to practice competently.[11]

LBT'S THEORY OF HAPPINESS

LBT is an inherently ethical practice. This clearly follows from the fact that LBT practitioners are expected to practice what they preach, which is aspiration toward the Guiding Virtues. A commitment of this magnitude means that one aspires to be prudent, secure about reality (including their own imperfections as well as those of others), respectful, courageous, empathetic, objective, foresighted, scientific, temperate, authentic, and empowering (of others). These virtues comprise LBT's idea of what it means to be a happy person. So the theory aligns with the tradition of self-actualization theories, the oldest and most developed of which is that of Aristotle, as contained in his *Ethics*.[12] Indeed, these virtues provide a common intersection of goals that all human beings can reasonably accept, regardless of what concrete objectives they might have. For example, some people want to be rich and famous; others are content to have moderate means and to have a small number of close friends; still others prefer to devote themselves to their work and find intrinsic value in the activity itself. None of these people, however, could rationally claim that it was a bad thing to be prudent, or secure, or respectful. The hater who pledges to hate others (and/or himself) clearly does not value Respect. Such an individual damns others (and/or himself), and experiences much stress in interpersonal relationships. Clearly, such a life is inconsistent with most rational life plans inasmuch as they require getting along with others. The upshot is that the Guiding Virtues are not optional. They are the core of what ultimately brings happiness.

Notice that this is not a hedonistic theory of happiness wherein the goal is to amass the most pleasure. LBT realizes that not all pleasures are conducive to happiness (in its Aristotelian, virtue-based sense). For example, people who seek short-term pleasures (such as through the use of addictive, recreational drugs) end up having long-term pains that outweigh their pleasures (from getting high). While other pleasures have long-term potential to promote further pleasures without counterbalancing pains (such as pleasures connected with providing useful goods or services), the pleasure itself is not likely to be the motivating goal. Thus, a great artist paints, not because he enjoys the activity, although that is a good thing. Rather, he does so because it expresses something deeply ingrained in his person: the drive for authentic self-expression, or the attempt to gain insight into the nature of reality, or the expression of a message about humanity, and so forth. Similarly, I enjoy writing. Each sentence as it develops across my monitor screen has a certain aesthetic character that I enjoy in a perceptual, aesthetic sense. But what motivates me to write is the goal of helping others; making contributions to the human fund of knowledge. I seek to empower others, to express my authentic self, sometimes (especially in my political writings) to say what I think needs to be said even if it will be negatively received, or worse, fall on deaf ears. This is what I mean by saying that the Guiding Virtues define human happiness, and that pleasure, while serving as the proverbial icing on the cake, is not itself the cake. That is where the virtues come in.

LBT's concept of happiness does not discriminate. Those who are devoutly religious or theistic as well as those who are nonreligious, atheistic, or agnostic can find it suitable. According to the NPCA Standards of Ethical Practice, "Philosophical practitioners should be sensitive to alternative 'world views'and philosophical perspectives including those based upon cultural or gender distinctions among diverse client populations."[13] Indeed, LBT is true to this standard of practice.

Further, as you have seen in the many case illustrations presented in this book, LBT constructs its Uplifting Philosophies according to the "world view" of the client, so that effective practitioners do not attempt to proselytize, impose their own philosophies, or otherwise circumscribe the range of philosophical perspectives that can be brought to bear on aspiring toward the Guiding Virtues. Whether it is St. Augustine or Nietzsche, Maimonides or Buddha, LBT practitioners should not tell clients what world view to embrace—although they may nonimposingly suggest ideas for their consideration. There are three primary requisites for selection of an Uplifting Philosophy, namely that (1) it is *relevant* (that is, can be keyed in to the Guiding Virtue sought); (2) it is *congenial* (comfortably fits in with the client's own beliefs); and (3) it does not commit any of the Cardinal Fallacies. This opens the door to a myriad of diverse philosophical perspectives that can be harnessed to provide uplifting philosophical antidotes to the Cardinal Fallacies. Indeed, LBT is constantly adding to this repertoire of useful philosophies. For example, there is currently much activity in the East (notably, Taiwan, Korea, and China) in applying the teachings of Buddha to LBT.[14]

One criticism of LBT's theory of happiness is that the set of philosophies that LBT embraces are inconsistent.[15] For example, Nietzsche proclaims that "God is dead," while Augustine emphasizes salvation in the *The City of God*. However, this criticism is not a criticism of LBT, any more than it is a criticism of democracy, claiming that it allows alternative social and political perspectives. Indeed, LBT, like democracy, permits many different voices within its conceptual scope. The theory is itself internally consistent. The fact that it accepts a lot of different philosophies as possible Uplifting Philosophies is consistent with its pluralistic nature.

What binds these diverse philosophies together under one consistent roof is that they can serve to help people to move from the commission of Cardinal Fallacies in their emotional reasoning, which are antipathetic to their happiness, toward the Guiding Virtues. In this sense, LBT is pragmatic at its core. Insofar as these philosophies "work" to help clients overcome their self-defeating emotions and behavior and to set them on the track toward happiness, they are acceptable. That is, they are acceptable within the three parameters mentioned above, which are themselves pragmatic considerations.

THE VIRTUOUS LBT PRACTITIONER

Accordingly, we are left with a theory of human assistance that encourages compassion as well as reason, is democratic, and very practical. LBT practitioners who practice in a manner consistent with LBT's tenets are therefore likely to be open-minded and socially liberal. As empathetic people, they have the ability to key into the suffering of others. As authentic people, they are willing to openly and honestly represent their own perspectives instead of blindly conforming to the dictates of others. As empowering people, they seek to inspire others rather than to manipulate and use them for their own devices. As metaphysically secure people, they are willing to accept their own limitations as well as those of others, and do not set unrealistic goals, either for themselves or for others. As respectful individuals, they do not damn people (neither themselves nor others) even though they may disagree with what they are saying or doing. As temperate individuals, they are passionate but not prone to outbursts, tirades, and other similar manner of emotional response. As foresighted people, they do not magnify risks about future endeavors. As objective people, they tend to judge others fairly, without preconceptions or stereotypes; and, as scientific individuals, they base their factual claims on adequate empirical evidence and avoid magical thinking, "coulda-woulda shoulda thinking," and other manners of being unscientific.

Of course, these virtues are ideals and we are all, as Plato would say, in a state of becoming without ever realizing our full potential. This is what makes LBT so exciting, however. It is a lifelong pursuit. Still, it does not have diminishing returns. The more I have attempted to build the process of LBT into my personal life choices and activities, the more often I have felt and done better. It has become easy to see where and when I go astray, and invariably LBT points the way. When I fall off the wagon, I do what I can to get back on. I am fond of saying that, like drug and alcohol addiction, we are, all of us, at best, in recovery—but never fully recovered—when it comes to commission of fallacies. So there is always going to be behavioral and emotional backsliding; but there can also be genuine progress with each incremental constructive change made in one's life. I have been evolving for three decades now, along with the theory. Neither of us are "there" as of yet; nor will we ever be. Such is the nature of the imperfect world inhabited by us imperfect human beings.

NOTES

1. As discussed under Step 1.
2. Samuel Zinaich, unpublished manuscript.
3. Ibid.
4. Ibid.
5. Ibid.
6. Ibid.
7. "Logic-Based Therapy," Wikipedia. https://en.wikipedia.org/wiki/Logic Based_Therapy.
8. Buddha Dharma Education Association, "Guided Meditation for Primary Students," Buddhanet. http://www.buddhanet.net/pdf_file/med-guided2.pdf.
9. This, however, still does not speak to the question of whether human beings are a deterministic set of biological processes or instead possess free will. Indeed, LBT

maintains that people have the capacity to exercise willpower in order to make constructive changes in their lives. See, for example, Elliot D. Cohen, *The New Rational Therapy: Thinking Your Way to Serenity, Success, and Profound Happiness* (Lanham, MD: Rowman & Littlefield, 2007). This includes, within limits, the ability to overcome tendencies to overreact behaviorally and emotionally to external events; as well as the ability to suspend, or change primary emotional responses to situations that may be creating problems for clients (for example, traumatic events). Whether there are underlying causal explanations for such exercise of will in overcoming such problems is an open question according to LBT. As was emphasized in the introduction to this book, LBT is a humanities approach to addressing problems of living and, as such, does not look for underlying causal etiologies of maladaptive behavior (mental disorders) in the first place. So it need not be committed to an affirmative response to this question. Further, philosophical practitioners who do not have degrees in mental health (philosophical consultants) do not address problems of living involving mental disorders. See also Table I.3 on referral indicators in the introduction to this book.

10. Julio Rocha do Amaral and Jorge Martins de Oliviera, "Limbic System: The Center of Emotions," The Healing Center Online. http://www.healing-arts.org/n-r-limbic.htm.

11. American Counseling Association, *Code of Ethics*, 2014, C2g http://www.counseling.org/resources/aca-code-of-ethics.pdf National Philosophical Counseling Association, *Standards of Ethical Practice,* Standard 1. http://npcassoc.org/wp-content/uploads/2014/08/NCPA_-Standards-of-Ethical-Practice-_-2014.pdf.

12. Aristotle, *Nicomachean Ethics*, trans. W. D. Ross, http://classics.mit.edu/Aristotle/nicomachean.html.

13. National Philosophical Counseling Association, Standards of Ethical Practice, Standard 3.

14. Ho-Ling HSU, "Interpretation of the Movie 'Peaceful Warrior'–From the Views of Ch'an Philosophy and Logic-based Therapy (LBT), *International Journal of Philosophical Practice*, Vol. 3, No. 4, Fall 2015.

15. Mike Martin, "Happiness, Virtue, and Truth in Cohen's Logic-Based Therapy," *International Journal of Applied Philosophy* 21 (1):129–33 (2007).

Bibliography

Achenbach, Gerd B. "Philosophy, Philosophical Practice, and Psychotherapy." In Lahav, R. and M.D. Tillmanns, (Eds.), *Essays on Philosophical Counseling* (pp. 61–74). Lanham, MD: University Press of America, 1995.

American Counseling Association. *Code of Ethics.* Alexandria, VA: ACA, 2014. Retrieved at http://www.counseling.org/resources/aca-code-of-ethics.pdf

American Psychiatric Association, *Diagnostic and Statistical Manual of Mental Disorders,* 5th Ed. Arlington, VA: American Psychiatric Publishing, 2013.

Aristotle, Metaphysics. In McKeon, R. (Ed.), *The Basic Works of Aristotle* (pp. 681–926). New York: Random House, 1941.

Aristotle. *Nicomachean Ethics.* In McKeon, R. (Ed.), *The Basic Works of Aristotle* (pp. 928–1112). New York: Random House, 1941.

Aristotle, *On the Generation of Animals.* In McKeon, R. (Ed.), *The Basic Works of Aristotle* (pp. 663–80). New York: Random House, 1941.

Austin, J. L. *How to Do Things with Words.* Cambridge, MA: Harvard University Press, 1975.

Beck, Aaron T. *Cognitive Therapy and the Emotional Disorders.* New York: Penguin Books, 1979.

Bergland, Christopher. "Two New PTSD Treatments Offer Hope for Veterans," *Psychology Today*, November 23, 2013.

Buber, Martin. *I and Thou.* Walter Kaufmann (Trans.). New York: Simon and Schuster, 1971.

Buddha, *The Dhammapada: The Buddha's Path of Wisdom* trans. Acharya Buddharakkhita, Buddha Dharma Education Association, 1985. Retrieved at http://www.buddhanet.net/pdf_file/scrndhamma.pdf.

———. *The Teachings of the Compassionate Buddha: Early Discourses, The Dhammapada, and Later Basic Writings.* E. A. Burtt (Tr.) New York: Penguin, 1991.

Burns, David D. *Feeling Good: The New Mood Therapy.* New York: Penguin, 1980.

Carlson, Jon and William Knaus (Eds.). *Albert Ellis Revisited.* New York: Routledge, 2013.

Cicero, Marcus Tullius. *Cicero's Tusculan Disputations.* C. D. Yonge (Tr.) New York: Harper & Brothers Publishers, 1877.

Clifford, William K. "The Ethics of Belief," *Contemporary Review*, 1877. Retrieved at http://myweb.lmu.edu/tshanahan/Clifford-Ethics_of_Belief.html

Cohen, Elliot D. *Making Value Judgments: Principles of Sound Reasoning.* Malabar, FL: Robert E. Krieger, Inc., 1985.

———. "Use of Syllogism in Rational Emotive Therapy," *Journal of Counseling & Development,* Vol. 66, No. 1, 1987.

———. "Philosophical Counseling: A Computer-Assisted, Logic-Based Approach," *Inquiry: Critical Thinking Across the Disciplines*, Vol.15, No.2, Winter 1995.

———. Philosophical Counseling: Some Roles of Critical Thinking." In Ran Lahav and Maria da Venza Tillmanns (Eds.), *Essays in Philosophical Counseling.* Lanham, MD: University Press of America, 1995.

———. and Gale S. Cohen, *The Virtuous Therapist: Ethical Practice in Counseling and Psychotherapy.* Belmont CA: Brooks Cole/Wadsworth, 1999.

———. (Ed.). *Philosophers at Work: An Introduction to the Issues and Practical Uses of Philosophy.* 2nd Ed. Orlando, FL: Harcourt Brace, 2000.

———. "The Activity of Philosophy." In Elliot D. Cohen (Ed.), *Philosophers at Work: Issues and Practice of Philosophy.* Orlando, FL: Harcourt Brace, 2000.

———. "The Philosopher as Counselor." In Elliot D. Cohen (Ed.), *Philosophers at Work: Issues and Practice of Philosophy.* Orlando, FL: Harcourt Brace, 2000, 457–67.

———. "Critical Thinking Beyond the Academy: Using Interactive Software to Help Students Cope with Problems of Living," *The Successful Professor*, Spring 2002.

———. "Philosophical Principles of Logic-Based Therapy," *Practical Philosophy* Vol. 6, No.1, 2003.

———. "The Process of Logic-Based Therapy," *Pratiche Filosofiche*, Vol. 2, Fall 2003.

———. *What Would Aristotle Do? Self-Control Through the Power of Reason.* Amherst, NY: Prometheus Books, 2003.

———. "Absolute Nonsense: The Irrationality of Perfectionistic Thinking," *International Journal of Philosophical Practice*, Vol. 2, No. 4, Spring 2005.

———. "Critical Thinking, Not Head Shrinking." In Raabe, P. (Ed.), *Philosophical Counseling and the Unconscious* (pp. 156–66). Amherst, NY: Trivium Publications, 2005.

———. "The Metaphysics of Logic-Based Therapy," *International Journal of Philosophical Practice,* Vol. 3, No. 1, Summer 2005.

———. "Logic-Based Therapy: The New Philosophical Frontier for REBT," REBT Network, 2006. Retrieved at http://www.rebtnetwork.org/essays/logic.html.

———. *The New Rational Therapy: Thinking Your Way to Serenity, Success, and Profound Happiness.* Lanham, MD: Rowman & Littlefield, 2007.

———. "Albert Ellis' Philosophical Revolution: A Memoriam Address Presented to the American Psychological Association" (San Francisco, August 17, 2007), *International Journal of Applied Philosophy,* Vol. 21, No. 2, Fall 2007.

———. "The New Rational Therapy: A Response to Martin," *International Journal of Applied Philosophy*, Vol. 21, No. 1, Spring 2007.

———. "Metaphysical Insecurity," *Practical Philosophy*, Vol. p, No. 1, January, 2008.

———. "Relieving your Can't-stipation: Some Potent Philosophical Enemas," *Practical Philosophy*, Vol. 9, No. 2, July 2008.

———. *Critical Thinking Unleashed*. Lanham, MD: Rowman & Littlefield, 2009.

———. "Think for Yourself," *Psychology Today*, January 30, 2010.

———. *The Dutiful Worrier: How to Stop Compulsive Worry without Feeling Guilty*, Oakland, CA: New Harbinger, 2011.

———. "How Good are You at Loving?" *Psychology Today*, January 25, 2012.

———. "Is Perfectionism a Mental Disorder," *International Journal of Applied Philosophy*, Vol. 26, No. 2, Fall 2012.

———. "Stop Playing the Blame Game," *Psychology Today*, July 29, 2012.

———. *Caution: Faulty Thinking Can Be Harmful to Your Happiness, Logic for Everyday Living*, 2nd Ed. Fort Pierce, IL: Trace-WilCo, 2013, Kindle Edition.

———. "Logic-Based Therapy and its Virtues." In Elliot D. Cohen and Samuel Zinaich (Eds.), *Philosophy, Counseling, and Psychotherapy*. Newcastle upon Tyne, UK: Cambridge Scholars Publishing, 2013.

Cohen, Elliot and Zinaich, Samuel (Eds.). *Philosophy, Counseling, and Psychotherapy*. Newcastle upon Tyne, UK: Cambridge Scholars Publishing, 2013.

Cohen, Elliot D. "The New Rational Therapy for the 21st Century: Putting Philosophy to Work in Psychology," *Journal of Nanjing University* (Philosophy, Humanities and Social Sciences) No. 4, 2013 (China).

Cohen, Elliot D. "The Future of CBT/REBT." In Carlson, Jon and William Knaus (Eds.). *Albert Ellis Revisited*. New York: Routledge, 2013.

Cohen, Elliot D. *Theory and Practice of Logic-Based Therapy: Integrating Critical Thinking and Philosophy into Psychotherapy*. London: Cambridge Scholars Publishers, 2013.

Cohen, Elliot D. "Logic-Based Therapy to Go: A Step-By-Step Primer On How LBT Can Work For You," *Psychology Today*, March 19, 2014.

Cohen, Elliot D. "Counseling Hume: Using Logic-Based Therapy to Address Generalized Anxiety Disorder," *International Journal of Philosophical Practice*, Vol. 3, No. 4, Fall 2015.

Cohen, Elliot D. "How to be Empathetic," *Psychology Today*, May 17, 2015.

Cohen, Elliot D. "I Want Therefore It Must Be: Treating Fascistic Inferences in Logic-Based Therapy," *Journal of Humanities Therapy*, Vol. 6, No.1, June 2015. Kangwon National University, Korea.

Cohen, Elliot D. "What Else Can you Do with Philosophy Besides Teach?" *International Journal of Philosophical Practice*, Vol. 3, No. 3, Spring 2015.

Cohen, Gale S. "Theories of Counseling and the Free Will–Determinism Issue." In Elliot D. Cohen (Ed.), *Philosophers at Work: Issues and Practice of Philosophy*. 2nd Ed. Orlando, FL: Harcourt Brace, 2000.

Damasio, Antonio. *Descartes' Error: Emotion, Reason, and the Human Brain*. New York: Penguin Books, 2005.

Defife, Jared. "New Treatments to Combat PTSD," *Psychology Today*, January 27, 2012.

DeGeorge, Richard T. "The Origins of Applied Philosophy." In Elliott D. Cohen (Ed.), *Philosophers At Work: Issues and Practice of Philosophy* (pp. 9–14). Orlando, FL: Harcourt Brace, 2000.

Einstein, Albert. "Science, Philosophy and Religion, A Symposium," Conference on Science, Philosophy and Religion in Their Relation to the Democratic Way of Life, New York, 1941.

Epictetus. *The Discourses and Manual, Together With Fragments of His Writings.* P. E Matheson (Tr.) Oxford, UK: Clarendon Press, 1916.

Ellis, Albert. *Reason and Emotion in Psychotherapy.* Seacaucus, NJ: Citadel Press, 1962.

———. and Robert Harper. *A New Guide to Rational Living.* N. Hollywood, CA: Wilshire Book Co., 1975.

———. and Russell Grieger. *Handbook of Rational-Emotive Therapy.* Vol. 2. New York: Springer Publishing Co., 1986.

———. "The Philosophical Basis of Rational-Emotive Therapy (RET)." *International Journal of Applied Philosophy*, Vol. 5, No. 2, Fall 1990.

———. *Feeling Better, Getting Better, Staying Better.* Atascadero, CA: Impact Publishers, 2001.

———. *Overcoming Destructive Beliefs, Feelings, and Behaviors.* Amherst, NY: Prometheus Books, 2001.

Epictetus. *Encheiridion.* In Baird, Forrest E. and Walter Kaufmann (Eds.), *From Plato to Derrida*, 4th ed. Upper Saddle River, N.J.: Prentice Hall, 2003.

Fromm, Erich. *Escape from Freedom* New York: Macmillan, 1994.

Gilligan, Carol. *In a Different Voice: Psychological Theory and Women's Development.* Cambridge, MA: Harvard University Press, 1982.

Gladding, Samuel. *Counseling: A Comprehensive Profession.* 3rd Ed. Englewood Cliffs, NJ: Simon and Schuster, 1996.

Goleman, Daniel. *Emotional Intelligence.* New York: Doubleday Dell, 1997.

Hanh, Thich Nhat. *The Art of Communicating.* New York: Harper Collins, 2014.

Hara Estroff Marano, "Anxiety and Depression Together," *Psychology Today*, January 20, 2011. Retrieved at http://www.psychologytoday.com/articles/200310/anxiety-and-depression-together.

HSU, Ho-Ling. "Interpretation of the Movie 'Peaceful Warrior': From the Views of Ch'an Philosophy and Logic-Based Therapy (LBT)," *International Journal of Philosophical Practice*, Vol. 3, No. 4, Fall 2015.

Hume, David. *An Inquiry Concerning Human Understanding.* New York: Oxford University Press, 2007.

———. *Treatise of Human Nature.* New York: Oxford University Press, 2000.

Husserl, Edmund. *The Paris Lectures.* 2nd ed. P. Koestenbaum (Trans.) The Hague, Netherlands: Martinus Nijohoff Publisher, 1967.

James, William. *Pragmatism.* New York: Dover, 1995.

———. *The Principles of Psychology.* Vols. 1–2. Cambridge, MA: Harvard University Press, 1981.

Kant, Immanuel. *Groundwork of the Metaphysics of Morals.* New York: Harper & Row, 1964.

Knaus, William J. *How to Conquer Your Frustrations* (e-book) REBT Network. Retrieved at http://www.rebtnetwork.org/library/How_to_Conquer_Your_Frustra tions.pdf

———. *The Cognitive Behavioral Workbook for Anxiety.* 2nd Ed. Oakland, CA: New Harbinger, 2014.

Lahav, R. and M. D. Tillmanns, (Eds.). *Essays on Philosophical Counseling.* Lanham, MD: University Press of America, 1995.

Lippmann, Walter. *Public Opinion.* New York: Penguin Books, 1946.

Lovgren, Stefan. "Evolution and Religion Can Coexist, Scientists Say," *National Geographic News*, October 18, 2004.

Martin, Mike W. "Happiness, Virtue, And Truth in Cohen's Logic-Based Therapy," *International Journal of Applied Philosophy*, Vol. 21, No. 1, 2007.

Mill, John Stuart. *On Liberty.* Mineola, NY: Dover, 2002.

———. The "Subjection of Women." In Elliot D. Cohen, (Ed.), *Philosophers at Work: Issues and Practice of Philosophy.* Orlando, FL: Harcourt Brace, 2000.

Moore, G. E. *Principia Ethica* (Amherst, NY: Prometheus Books, 1903).

National Philosophical Counseling Association. "Philosophical Counselors versus Philosophical Consultants," NPCA website. Retrieved at http://npcassoc.org/practice-areas-boundaries/.

———. "Philosophical Practice," NPCA website. Retrieved at http://npcassoc.org/philosophical-practice/.

———. "Standards of Ethical Practice." Retrieved at http://npcassoc.org/wp-content/uploads/2014/08/NCPA_-Standards-of-Ethical-Practice-_-2014.pdf.

Newton, Phil. "Traumatic Brain Injury Leads to Problems with Emotional Processing," *Psychology Today*, January 3, 2010.

Nietzsche, Friedrich. *The Philosophy of Nietzsche.* New York: Random House, 1954.

Nowell-Smith, P. H. *Ethics.* New York: Penguin Books, 1964.

Nowinkski, Joseph. "When Does Grief Become Depression?" *Psychology Today*, March 21, 2012.

Patteson, James D. "Rational Buddhism: Antidotes to the Eleven Cardinal Fallacies Presented in Elliot D. Cohen's *The New Rational Therapy* from Buddha and Some of His Greatest Disciples," *International Journal of Philosophical Practice.* Vol. 3, No. 3, Spring 2015.

Plato, *Apology*. Benjamin Jowett (Trans.). University of Adelaide, 2014. Retrieved at https://ebooks.adelaide.edu.au/p/plato/p71ap/.

Reuther, Bryan T. "The Elucidation of Emotional Life: A Philosophical, Eclectic Approach to Psychotherapy." In Elliot D. Cohen and Samuel Zinaich (Eds.), *Philosophy, Counseling, and Psychotherapy.* Newcastle upon Tyne, UK: Cambridge Scholars Publishing, 2013.

Rogers, Carl. *Dialogues.* Howard Kirschenbaum and Valerie Land Henderson (Eds.). Edinburgh, UK: Constable, 1990.

———. *On Becoming A Person: A Therapist's View of Psychotherapy.* New York: Mariner Books, 1995.

Russell, Bertrand. *The Problems of Philosophy.* New York: Oxford University Press, 1972.

Sartre, Jean-Paul. "Existentialism is a Humanism." In Walter Kaufman (Ed.), *Existentialism from Dostoyevsky to Sartre*. Oklahoma City: Meridian Publishing Company, 1989.

Searle, John R. *Speech Acts: An Essay in the Philosophy of Language*. Cambridge, UK: Cambridge University Press, 1970.

Solomon, Robert C. *The Passions: The Myth and Nature of Human Emotions*. Garden City, NY: Anchor Books, 1977.

Stevenson, Charles L. *Ethics and Language*. New Haven, CT: Yale University Press, 1964.

Zinaich, Samuel. "Elliot D. Cohen on the Metaphysics of Logic-Based Therapy," *International Journal of Philosophical Practice*, Vol. 3, No. 1, Summer 2005.

Index